The Ecclesiology of Donald Robinson and D. Broughton Knox

The Ecclesiology of
Donald Robinson and
D. Broughton Knox

Exposition, Analysis, and Theological Evaluation

CHASE R. KUHN

WIPF & STOCK · Eugene, Oregon

THE ECCLESIOLOGY OF DONALD ROBINSON AND D. BROUGHTON KNOX
Exposition, Analysis, and Theological Evaluation

Copyright © 2017 Chase R. Kuhn. All rights reserved. Except for brief quotations in critical publications or reviews, no part of this book may be reproduced in any manner without prior written permission from the publisher. Write: Permissions, Wipf and Stock Publishers, 199 W. 8th Ave., Suite 3, Eugene, OR 97401.

Wipf & Stock
An Imprint of Wipf and Stock Publishers
199 W. 8th Ave., Suite 3
Eugene, OR 97401

www.wipfandstock.com

PAPERBACK ISBN: 978-1-4982-9814-8
HARDCOVER ISBN: 978-1-4982-9816-2
EBOOK ISBN: 978-1-4982-9815-5

Manufactured in the U.S.A.   APRIL 11, 2017

Scripture quotations are from the ESV® Bible (The Holy Bible, English Standard Version®), copyright © 2001 by Crossway, a publishing ministry of Good News Publishers. Used by permission. All rights reserved.

When Scripture is quoted within a quote, the version is either KJV or RSV, as noted in the copyright of the authors.

The chapter on the Ecclesiological Influence of T. C. Hammond was previously printed in a similar form in Churchman 127/4, 2013. Used by permission.

There are many long quotes included from Donald Robinson in order to present his ecclesiology in his own words. These are used by the permission of the Australian Church Record.

There are many long quotes included from D. Broughton Knox in order to present his ecclesiology in his own words. These are used by the permission of Matthias Media.

For Amy

Contents

List of Tables | *viii*
Acknowledgments | *ix*
Abbreviations | *xi*
Introduction | *xiii*

Section I: Historical and Theological Milieu

1 The Ecclesiological Influence of Nathaniel Jones | 3
2 The Ecclesiological Influence of T. C. Hammond | 14
3 Ecumenism and the World Council of Churches | 30
4 The Australian Church Constitution | 41

Section II: Donald William Bradley Robinson

5 The Ecclesiology of Donald Robinson | 49
6 Evaluation of Robinson's Ecclesiology | 97

Section III: David Broughton Knox

7 The Ecclesiology of D. Broughton Knox | 131
8 Evaluation of Knox's Ecclesiology | 182

Section IV: Conclusion

9 Conclusion | 207

Bibliography | *215*
Names Index | *223*
Subject Index | *225*
Scripture Index | *231*

List of Tables

Place, Form, and Continuity in the Ecclesiology of Donald Robinson | 73
Presence in the Ecclesiology of D. Broughton Knox | 160

Acknowledgments

THERE ARE MANY PEOPLE who deserve credit in seeing this work to completion. This book is an adaptation of my PhD thesis, completed through the University of Western Sydney and Moore Theological College. I am indebted to Dr. Mark Thompson who served as a supervisor. He patiently helped to develop my writing skills and offered great expertise in my research area. In addition to supervision, he has served as a mentor and has shaped me greatly as a Christian. Perhaps most significant has been his encouragement to do theology for the church. Dr. Chris Fleming also supervised this project. He taught me a great deal about writing, particularly syntax. His perspective as a scholar outside of my discipline has been invaluable, challenging me to think carefully about what I say and how I say it. I have also benefited from his sense of humor and refined taste in music.

I am grateful for Susanna Baldwin's careful editing, formatting, and indexing of the book. She has a keen eye and has offered many useful corrections. Dr. Peter Bolt also read through an earlier draft and offered helpful comments. The Wipf & Stock team have been very kind, helpful and punctual in the editing and publishing process. In the end, any remaining errors are my own.

The people of St. Thomas' Anglican Church North Sydney have demonstrated incredible kindness, hospitality, and generosity towards our family. I truly would not have been able to complete this project without their prayers and the provision the Lord supplied through them. Being a part of the fellowship at St. Thomas' has shown me more than ever the significance and wonder of gathering together with God's people. I am especially grateful for Simon Manchester who has been a faithful pastor and kind friend. He and his wife Kathy have been like family to us in Australia.

Dr. Paul House has been a friend and mentor for many years now. He first introduced me to the work of Robinson and Knox, and it was because of his encouragement that I undertook this research. His correspondence with me—always timely and rich with wisdom and comforting words—often kept me going.

Finally, my family have loved me and supported me through this work. My wife, Amy, has prayed for me faithfully, cared for our home wonderfully, and demonstrated patience when the working hours have been long. My kids Olive and Ezra have kept life exciting. I love you all very much.

Abbreviations

ABR	*Australian Biblical Review*
ACR	*Australian Church Record*
BDAG	*A Greek-English Lexicon of the New Testament and Other Early Christian Literature*
BECNT	Baker Exegetical Commentary on the New Testament
NICNT	New International Commentary on the New Testament
PNTC	Pillar New Testament Commentary
RTR	*Reformed Theological Review*
TDNT	*Theological Dictionary of the New Testament*
WBC	Word Biblical Commentary

[Authorship cited in brackets indicates the author(s) attributed to articles in D. B. Knox's personal annotated copies of the ACR. Knox served as editor of the journal and therefore was aware of authorship of articles printed anonymously]

*There are many quotes from different authors in which the diacritical marks are incorrect or not present. Rather than indicating these errors with SIC I have left the transliterations as they are in the originals. I have aimed to present the correct diacritical marks in my own use of foreign languages.

Introduction

THE QUESTION/PROBLEM

THE TWENTIETH CENTURY HAS often been called the "century of the church."[1] Veli-Matti Kärkäinen has correctly acknowledged that "the main catalyst for the rapidly growing ecclesiological interest has been the ecumenical movement. No other movement in the history of the Christian church, perhaps with the exception of Reformation, has shaped the thinking and practice of Christendom as much as the modern movement for Christian unity."[2] He states, "Any talk about the unity of the church presupposes some tentative understanding of what the church is. One cannot unite entities without knowing what kind of organisms one is trying to put together. The ecumenical movement has helped open up a fruitful dialogue about the church and related issues."[3] It was in the midst of this century of the church and its ecumenical dialogues that Donald Robinson and D. Broughton Knox developed their ecclesiologies. As the Church of England in Australia reconsidered its constitution, and as many denominations were taking part in the World Council of Churches, it was important for Sydney Anglicans to identify what they believed about the nature of the church.

The fruit of Knox and Robinson's ecclesiological inquiry has been appraised by historians Stephen Judd and Kenneth Cable as the most

---

1. This title was first given, almost prophetically, by Otto Dibelius, *Das Jahrhundert der Kirche*. This title was later used, among others, by Avery Dulles, "A Half Century of Ecclesiology," 419. Stephen Neill changed the title to be "the century of the *churches*" (emphasis mine); see *Men of Unity*, 12.

2. Kärkäinen, *Introduction to Ecclesiology*, 7–8.

3. Ibid., 8.

significant theological contribution of its time in Sydney.[4] Others, since, have also recognized what has been deemed the "Knox-Robinson view" of the church and its influence in Sydney and around the world.[5] In spite of this, the ecclesiologies of these two scholars have never been presented or evaluated at an academic level. In fact, the "Knox-Robinson view" does not exist in any collated ecclesiology, but has only ever been presented piecemeal, as neither Knox nor Robinson ever set out to develop a complete ecclesiology. Yet, in spite of the lack of academic engagement and disparate presentation, the ecclesiological influence of these two scholars continues to shape the Sydney Diocese and wider audiences today.

But what is the "Knox-Robinson view" of the church? Does such a "view" exist? Recent scholarship has argued that while some have contended for such a composite ecclesiology, in fact the ecclesiologies of each of these men remain distinctive.[6] In response it has been suggested that while the origin and actuality of such a conglomerate reality might be questionable historically, there is widespread reception of such an entity and the "view" is legitimate as such; this view must be engaged as it has been received.[7]

Our task in this book is to identify whether or not there is such a view as the Knox-Robinson ecclesiology, and to evaluate whether or not this is a viable theology of the church. We will progress from seeking an understanding of the historical context in which these ecclesiologies were developed, to describing, analyzing, and evaluating each scholar's ecclesiology independently, and finally exploring the idea of a synthesis of the two ecclesiologies. Concluding that such a synthesis is possible, we will offer a few comments on the synthetic "Knox-Robinson" view. The end result will be an academic exposition, analysis, and evaluation of the ecclesiology of Donald Robinson and D. Broughton Knox.

---

4. "The most important theological development was a revision of the traditional concept of the nature of the Church." Judd and Cable, *Sydney Anglicans*, 289.

5. For example: Kaye, "Foundations and Methods in Ecclesiology," 14; Foord, "We Meet Again!," 225–34; Porter, *Sydney Anglicans*, 40–41; Cameron, *Enigmatic Life*, 152–53; Jensen, *Sydney Anglicanism*, 75–89.

6. Loane, "Church," 50; Kaye, "Foundations and Methods," 14.

7. Jensen, "Sydney Anglicanism: A Response," 120.

METHOD

Parameters/Limitations

Before outlining how the study will unfold, we should understand its parameters. Fundamentally we want to understand what Knox and Robinson believed about the nature of the church. We will unpack this by asking, "What is the church?" Involved in this question are the matters of who makes up the church, where the church exists, when the church exists, how the church exists, and for what purpose the church exists. Within the Anglican formularies, the nature of the church is best addressed in Article XIX of the Thirty-Nine Articles of Religion:

> The visible Church of Christ is a congregation of faithful men, in the which the pure Word of God is preached, and the Sacraments be duly administered according to Christ's ordinance in all those things that of necessity are requisite to the same.

The reason for containing this investigation to a study of the nature of the church is twofold. First, the nature of the church addresses primary issues in ecclesiology. Issues of polity and pragmatic matters can only be examined, as secondary issues, once the nature of the church is established. Second, neither Knox nor Robinson developed a full-fledged ecclesiology. The focus of most of their ecclesiological work was the nature of the church.

Furthermore, this study will be limited to the primary subjects, seeking to systematize their ecclesiologies in a clear manner. Analysis and an evaluation of their thought will be given based on questions that arise in the description of their thought. Sometimes there will be other scholars consulted, but there will not be a single antagonist for comparison. The aim is not to measure these ecclesiologies against all other ecclesiologies. There will be points where comparison is helpful, but these will be restricted mostly to those whom the subjects engaged, or those who engaged the subjects.

Finally, the evaluation of the ecclesiologies of Knox and Robinson will be conducted on the basis of terms recognizable by both men. That is, we will seek to establish whether they successfully achieved what they set out to do, and whether the product of their work can stand. Generally, the criteria will be each scholar's fidelity to the text of Bible, the coherence of his argument, and faithfulness to his Anglican heritage.[8] Though these evaluations will come more towards the middle of the book, they embody most of the conclusions we are striving for in this volume.

---

8. It will later be argued that both Knox and Robinson identified with the Anglican tradition. However, being biblical was the ultimate goal, not being Anglican.

Outline of Approach

We will begin in section 1 by discerning the historical and theological milieu of Knox and Robinson. As both scholars were Sydney Anglicans, reared in the Diocese and employed at Moore Theological College, we will examine the ecclesiology of two of the primary theological predecessors at Moore—Nathaniel Jones, principal 1897–1911, and T. C. Hammond, principal 1936–53. For each, we will look into their theological background and their respective ecclesiologies. We also will examine the two major movements that contributed to Knox and Robinson "going public" with their ecclesiology—the ecumenical movement and the campaign for a new constitution for the Church of England in Australia.[9] For each of these movements we will consider how they raised questions of the nature of the church, and how these questions gave rise to issues for theological reflection and development.

We will then proceed to examine the ecclesiology of Robinson and Knox in turn, attempting to listen to each scholar independently for the sake of comparison later. In section 2 will examine the ecclesiology of Donald Robinson and in section 3 that of D. Broughton Knox. We will begin by establishing relevant biographical information, including each scholar's theological education, as well as his acknowledged (and occasionally unacknowledged) interlocutors. We will then consider each man's method of study: for Robinson biblical theology and linguistic analysis and for Knox systematic theology. An understanding of method will provide perspective for how each arrived at his theological conclusions. We will then proceed to describe and analyze the ecclesiological propositions. These ecclesiologies will be presented in logical fashion, collecting and collating data from disparate works to provide a systematic theology of the nature of the church.

Following on from the description and analysis, we will seek to evaluate the core propositions of each ecclesiology. This analysis will generally focus on whether the propositions are biblical, internally coherent, and Anglican. Interlocution will aid the discussion where relevant, primarily engaging those who have offered appraisals and/or critical engagements. Finally, a general appraisal will be offered of the entirety of each ecclesiology, with some constructive suggestions.

In the conclusion, we will seek to determine if there is a "Knox-Robinson view" of the church. To what degree do Knox and Robinson agree on the nature of the church? Where, if anywhere, do they disagree? If there are disagreements, are they irreconcilable? Can we establish which scholar was

---

9. Robinson, "'Church' Revisited," 263–64 (repr. ed.).

more correct? In asking these questions, we will seek to provide a synthesis of the two ecclesiologies. From this synthesis, we will offer an appraisal. The final words will be reserved for constructive comments and suggestions of how this study in ecclesiology might be useful in the current theological conversation.

Goal

The goal of this study is to provide, for the first time, an academic presentation, analysis and evaluation of the ecclesiology of Donald Robinson and D. Broughton Knox. Whether or not their ecclesiologies may be considered as a conglomerate is to be seen, but what is known is the influence the so-called "Knox-Robinson view" has had on the largest Anglican diocese in Australia. Even beyond Australia, Knox and Robinson have had an impact on the theology and practice of many churches, especially as their pupils have gone to serve around the world. Here, their ecclesiology will hopefully be presented in a way that does justice to the authors' original intent, and sets forth their theology in systematic fashion for critical engagement. Are there lessons in the method by which each scholar studied the church? Are there principles that might be helpful for today's ecclesiological dialogue? Are these ecclesiologies helpful for other Anglicans? Would these ecclesiologies serve a wider audience?

SECTION I

Historical and Theological Milieu

1

The Ecclesiological Influence of Nathaniel Jones

IN CONSIDERATION OF THE Diocese of Sydney's ecclesiological developments in the mid-twentieth century, it is appropriate and necessary to investigate the diocese's theological heritage. One of the prominent leaders in the history of the diocese was Nathaniel Jones, principal of Moore Theological College 1897–1911. Jones's influence on the diocese began with his leadership of its theological college and continued through the lives of his pupils and then through their heirs. Reflecting specifically on the topic at hand, this influence was handed down through the lives of such men as D. J. Knox and R. B. Robinson, along with many others,[1] into the lives of their children (D. B. Knox and Donald Robinson) and other diocesan leaders. While traces of Jones's theology and piety continued into the middle of the twentieth century, such as his emphasis on holiness and his passion for the exegesis and exposition of Scripture, the speculation of William Lawton and others about his ecclesiological influence is overstated. In this chapter we will consider briefly the life and ministry of Nathaniel Jones and then move towards an examination of his ecclesiology, concluding with an assessment of the extant literature on Jones and his legacy.

In studying Jones, the primary interlocutor is William Lawton, former dean of students and lecturer in church history and biblical languages at Moore College, whose doctoral thesis included some treatment of the influence of Nathaniel Jones on Sydney Anglican theology. One aim of this

---

1. Some of the other prominent leaders that arose under Jones's principalship include H. S. Begbie, H. G. J. Howe, S. E. Langford Smith, G. A. Chambers, A. L. Wade, S. J. Kirby, S. H. Denman, and J. Bidwell.

chapter is to consider the accuracy of the conclusions proposed by Lawton concerning Jones's ecclesiology and his influence. Most, if not all, scholarly work on Nathaniel Jones has been conducted by, or is heavily indebted to, Lawton's work. The results of his research on Jones were published as *The Better Time to Be: Utopian Attitudes to Society among Sydney Anglicans 1885–1914*.[2] All other published material on Jones cites Lawton's thesis and its published form as their principle sources.[3]

While Lawton's work has been helpful in many areas, especially providing access to biographical information about Jones's life and detail about his ministry and thinking, upon examination, the primary conclusions he reaches about Jones's emphasis on the "little flock" and his connection to Plymouth Brethrenism prove to be unfounded. In fact, surprisingly, nowhere in Lawton's writing does he provide any conclusive evidence to support these claims. The result is that subsequent work on Jones has been based on conclusions that are all but questionable.

We must understand Jones the man if we are to understand his ideas, so we begin with a brief biographical account.

HISTORICAL BACKGROUND

Nathaniel Jones was born in Shropshire, near Oswestry, England, in 1861.[4] He was one of four children born to John Jones, a farmer. Jones came under the pastoral influence of Frederick Cashel, who was vicar in the Diocese of St. Asaph, at a young age. Grace Jones (Nathaniel's wife) wrote much later, "To quote Nathaniel's brother John, he says: 'I think it was the Canon's [Cashel] influence that helped to make my brother the strong evangelical that he developed into.'"[5] It is unknown when Jones became a Christian, though Grace Jones believed that it might have been under the influence of the Open Brethren in Oswestry.[6] However, it may just as well have been from his upbringing in his Christian home.[7] His brother John wrote, "I believe my brother always had a wish to be a clergyman but found it difficult to get his father's consent. About 1880 my father had set him up with one of

---

2. Lawton, "Better Time to Be," and Lawton, *Better Time to Be: Utopian Attitudes*.

3. Dickey, "Jones, Nathaniel," 191–92; Judd and Cable, *Sydney Anglicans*; Piggin, *Spirit of a Nation*, 76–77; Cameron, "Moore College," 96–123.

4. Some have dated his birth in 1863. See Cameron, "Moore College," 98. A more accurate dating places his birth in 1861 as Jones was 49 when he died in 1911.

5. Jones, "Grace Jones' Account," 2.

6. Ibid.

7. Grace Jones mentions the Jones household as "church-going folk." Ibid., 1.

our sisters in a farm called Bronygadfa owned by our father but my brother who used to study Latin whilst following the plough did not make a success of farming. So in 1882 my father decided to send him to Oxford."[8] After training at Oxford, Jones was ordained deacon in 1886. He took his first curacy in Leeds. Shortly after taking this post Jones developed significant health problems, culminating in pneumonia. The common medical advice of the day was to take some time at sea. Jones decided to voyage to Australia. On May 28, 1887, the *Harbinger* departed for Melbourne, Australia. It was on this voyage that Nathaniel met Grace Henderson, the woman he later married.

Jones held several ministry posts in Australia during his lifetime. He began as a curate in Port Arlington, where he was ordained priest in 1888. Later he moved to serve at Tarnagulla. As Jones served in parish ministry, he worked closely with "readers" whom he trained for ministry. It was during this time in the parish that Jones acquired a passion for theological education. He developed what he called a "Reader's Scheme" that "comprised the idea of a period in a hall of residence, where the students were to be taught until they had reached a certain standard, to be followed by parish work."[9] The culmination of this "Reader's Scheme" was the purchase of Perry Hall in 1895, opening formal theological education to students in and around Bendigo. Jones introduced the school to the Cambridge Preliminary Examination, marking a turning point in Australian theological education. Marcia Cameron comments, "Only in raising the standards to equal those of the best theological colleges at home would he [Jones] ensure that colonial clergy were acceptable to their English counterparts, in Australia and in England also."[10] It was this standard of excellence that Jones carried with him in 1897 when he accepted the principalship of Moore College in Sydney. Jones would serve as principal of Moore until his death in 1911.

Jones was not a prolific writer. He was scholarly in his thinking but his output was reflected more in sermons and lectures than in written works. What are published of his works are mostly transcriptions of his sermons at conventions.[11] Jones was one of the founders of the Katoomba Convention, held at Katoomba in the Blue Mountains. These were the primary talks that were transcribed, although Jones taught and preached often in parishes and at the college. He only wrote one theological volume, a short piece on the

---

8. Ibid., 2.
9. Cameron, "Moore College," 100.
10. Ibid.
11. Jones, *Handful of Corn*.

Thirty-Nine Articles entitled *The Teaching of the Articles*.[12] This volume was theological in content but not intended to be rigorous, as might be expected of an academic volume. Jones disclosed his intentions for the book: "It is hoped that the book will be of use to Lay-readers, Bible-class Teachers, and Churchmen generally."[13] There were no claims of originality in what he was presenting. Rather, he acknowledged a debt to the works of H. C. G. Moule, Harold Browne, Thomas Boultbee and Edgar Gibson. Jones hoped that his work would serve as a simplified (and cheaper!) introduction to the greater works that existed on the Articles.[14]

ECCLESIOLOGY

For our interests here, we will consider briefly the format and content of *The Teaching of the Articles* as it pertains to ecclesiology. Of primary concern is the nature of the church, or Article XIX.

Canon Jones moved throughout his exposition of the Articles in a scientific rather than article-by-article fashion.[15] He handled the material based on content and relevance, appropriating the articles into groupings. He addressed the Articles based on their content but expanded the material to include exegetical evidence of how each theological proposition had been derived from Scripture. Jones also allowed for his own beliefs and persuasions to surface in his synopses. Using Jones's work on Article XIX we can observe this methodology.

Jones located Article XIX in the greater group of Articles pertaining to the church, its ministers and sacraments (Articles XIX–XXXIV). He began his exposition with an introductory section on the nature of the church. There he addressed common misconceptions, especially in relation to the invisible and visible natures of the church. He delineated the New Testament uses of the term *ekklēsia*, differentiating between universal and particular (local) references. He separated the visible and invisible in a traditional fashion, commenting on the perfection of the invisible, and the imperfect and uncertain identity of the visible. He interpolated, "On the whole, the term 'ideal' is better than invisible; it describes the Church as it now exists in the mind and purpose of God, but which in the future will have perfect visible expression when Christ shall present it to Himself 'a glorious

---

12. Jones, *Teaching of the Articles*.
13. Ibid., preface.
14. Ibid.
15. Ibid.

Church, not having spot or wrinkle or any such thing.'"[16] Jones understood the two natures of the church to be common knowledge, yet concepts that cause confusion. Therefore, he began with these concepts before moving into direct exposition of the Article, which excludes mention of the invisible church.

William Lawton misquotes Jones's comments concerning the invisible church and misconstrues his preference of the term "ideal" over invisible. Lawton writes,

> He [Jones] shared most profoundly with them [the Brethren] a doctrine of the church as the sanctified gathering of the heavenly Assembly. This is not a classic theology of visible and invisible church derived from mainstream Protestantism; its roots are in Pietism and in Brethrenism. Jones stated quite explicitly that "traditional Reformation terminology inadequately describes 'invisible'; it describes the Church as it now exists in the mind and purpose of God." [The original and correct quote is mentioned above.] This is the same idealistic terminology as used by Brethren. Like them he contrasted Assembly with christendom, urging and practising separation from the world into a Little Flock linked in holiness, bonded as the body of Christ and looking for the appearing of Christ.[17]

By paying insufficient attention to the context, Lawton misquotes Jones in the interests of his argument that Jones's theology was deeply indebted to Brethrenism. More will be said of this later. For now, it is important to restore this quote to its original context and meaning. Jones was not pressing an emphasis on idealism as seen in Brethren theology. He *was* making note of the perfected identity of the invisible church existing with Christ in heaven. He ultimately located this church in the eschaton when the visible and invisible will be one and the same. Jones recognized that the worldly nature of the visible church is imperfect in its membership, as many who take part in the visible institution are not true members of the invisible. This in fact is a common Reformed position on the invisible and visible natures of the church.[18]

Perhaps Jones's beliefs concerning the perfection of the invisible church are best seen in juxtaposition with his views on the imperfection of the visible church. He wrote, "That the word 'faithful' indicates the profession rather than the character of the members is evident from a comparison

16. Ibid., 80–81.
17. Lawton, *Better Time: Utopian Attitudes*, 72–73.
18. See for example the Westminster Larger Catechism, Question 61.

with Article xxvi., where it is stated that in the visible Church the evil are ever mingled with the good."[19] Jones grounded his beliefs about the nature of the church in the Articles. But this grounding was not blind trust in his tradition. Rather, Scripture provided the primary justification of his beliefs. He wrote, "That such was the condition of the Church even in New Testament times, is evident from the rebukes and warnings such as we find in the Epistles to the Seven Churches of Asia (Rev. i–iii.), and in St. Paul's Epistles to Corinth."[20] Jones's ecclesiological conviction was rooted in his tradition, but only insomuch as it accorded with Scripture.

In summary, Jones moved systematically through the Articles offering exposition of each with commentary on how the Scriptures inform their theological propositions. This demonstrates that his ecclesiology was distinctively Anglican, but just as clearly evangelical in the way it was also biblically aware. Jones took care to explain the content of his beliefs, as well as their biblical rationale.

WILLIAM LAWTON ON JONES

The significance of studying the ecclesiology of Nathaniel Jones becomes clear when we observe what has been said of Jones's influence on the leadership that came after him in the Diocese of Sydney. William Lawton makes a bold estimate of the extent of Jones's influence. The connections Lawton draws are seen implicitly in his doctoral thesis and explicitly in his chapter for the Festschrift presented to D. B. Knox, *God Who Is Rich in Mercy*. It is worth considering two lengthy quotes to understand these connections that Lawton makes between Jones and Knox. First, he writes,

> Broughton Knox is one of his [Jones] spiritual heirs. He shares with Jones the same commitment to the text of Scripture, the same concern for careful exegesis, the same doctrine of the Church and the same passionate expectation of Jesus' return. It is not surprising that this should be so. His father, David John Knox, fired with zeal by Jones' lectures, spoke from the same convention platform and carried Jones' theology into his parochial ministry. The diaries of D. J. Knox reveal the intensity with which he followed the teaching of his master.[21]

---

19. Jones, *Teaching of the Articles*, 82.
20. Ibid., 82.
21. Lawton, "Nathaniel Jones," 361. There appears to be a mistake in this quote, making reference to David John Knox. The appropriate reference is David James Knox.

This connection is partly true. Jones was passionate about the text of Scripture and the exegesis of Scripture being the driving agent in preaching and teaching. However, the proposition that Jones and D. Broughton Knox share the same ecclesiological views is unfounded. Jones in fact greatly influenced D. J. Knox, Broughton Knox's father, as he was his pupil at Moore College. However, the theological connections Lawton asserts between D. J. Knox and Jones lack support. At times, Lawton quotes from sources ambiguously in a paragraph in which Knox or other students are the subjects. These citations mislead the reader to believe that they are the view of the subject of the paragraph, when in fact there is no support for this connection.[22] This unhelpful presentation of material is unwittingly deceptive, as it gives the impression of endorsement or logical relation.

Later, Lawton draws further connections between the theology of Jones and leaders of the diocese in subsequent generations. He writes,

> When Jones came to Sydney, he almost single-handed drew together men of common outlook. His oratory was born of evangelical zeal, his wisdom was circumscribed by the Scriptures. His view of prophecy did not survive past the early years of the twentieth century, but his doctrine of the Church, formed by Brethrenism, has continued to disturb Sydney Anglicanism. Those of the same spiritual stock, and sometimes with the same family connections, continue to lead the Diocese and theological education.[23]

The hints he makes at the "same family connections" are references to the Knox and Robinson families. His statement about the disturbance this ecclesiology has caused refers to the disquiet he and others felt at what would become known as Sydney Anglican ecclesiology or "The Knox-Robinson doctrine of the church." Lawton recognizes that a distinctive ecclesiology has gained traction in the Diocese of Sydney—the ecclesiological conclusions proposed by D. B. Knox and Donald Robinson—and he is working on a hunch concerning its origins. Based on inference, he assumes this thinking has been handed down through generations because of the genealogical connections in the leadership of the Diocese of Sydney. Jones had a number of Brethren friends and connections, and the popular ecclesiology of the

---

22. See Lawton, *Better Time: Utopian Attitudes*, 86–87. In a paragraph with D. J. Knox as the subject, he cites C. A. Auberlen without any introduction, leading readers to believe that it is the position of Knox. This kind of ambiguity exists elsewhere in Lawton's work. He often puts forward the position of Brethren scholars and then connects it to non-Brethren Anglicans as if they are of one accord. See *Better Time: Utopian Attitudes*, 76.

23. Lawton, "Nathaniel Jones," 364.

1960s and beyond seemed to most closely resemble that theological pedigree. Unfortunately, there is no extant evidence to support this thesis.

Lawton draws a connection between the ecclesiology of D. B. Knox and Donald Robinson and that of Nathaniel Jones's identification of the church as the "Little Flock." The suggestion is not entirely far-fetched. Knox and Robinson placed a heavy emphasis on the gathered community of believers as the true visible manifestation of the church. In consideration of this theology it is quite natural to ask, "From where did it come?" and this is precisely the investigation that Lawton has undertaken.

Lawton repeatedly claims that Jones believed in a "Little Flock" theology consistent with Brethren thinking.[24] This has already been observed in a previous quote, but it is also worth observing again in other places. Lawton writes, "Jones's and Archdall's enthusiasm for holiness, prophetic fulfillment, Jewish resettlement of Palestine and futurist eschatology bound them into the ideals of Brethrenism. Biblicism fired their imagination for a purified Little Flock and a coming 'ideal' world where the 'body of Christ' would rejoice as 'the bride of Christ.'"[25] Again later he writes,

> Their [Jones and Archdall's] theology turned its back on the world, emphasising a division between sacred and secular that characterised so much of late nineteenth century Protestantism. They both—Jones openly and Archdall by implication—endorsed a Brethren view of the church, gathered and separate from all worldliness. The "Little Flock" needed guidance, encouragement and correction. They intended to rebuild the church from within, settling it on the foundations of biblical literalism, personal conversion and holiness.[26]

It is clear that Lawton is not entirely sympathetic and that he identifies Jones's core theology with Brethrenism. More specifically, he links Jones's

---

24. Lawton at one point says that Jones never abandoned the influence of Brethrenism in his thinking. He writes, "At no time, however, did Jones resile from his Brethren beliefs; his faith was enthusiastic but entirely grounded in the tenets of his early upbringing, distinguishing him both from Welsh revivalism and from the later charismatic movements. His theology of Scripture as unfulfilled prophecy and his expectation of the immediate return of Christ came directly through the Brethren." Lawton, *Better Time: Utopian Attitudes*, 72.

25. Ibid., 75. Note that Lawton connects the thinking of Jones with that of Archdall. Jones and Archdall were good friends in the Diocese of Sydney. However, what is said conclusively about the thinking of Jones is often done by association rather than by evidence. Even here, what is said of Jones and Archdall is said without support of the writings of either. At one point Lawton does refer to the writing of Archdall, with Jones as his editor, but even here the connections are weak. Ibid., 73.

26. Ibid., 76.

ecclesiology to his association with Brethren thinking and a premillennial (or as Lawton puts it, "premillennarian") eschatology. There is evidence to support the claim that Jones was a Premillennialist.[27] This eschatology would certainly have influenced Jones's ecclesiology. However, at this point we are firmly in the realm of speculation. There is very little, if any, evidential material to support a theology of an otherworldly reclusive community inherent within Jones's ecclesiology. On the contrary, we can know with near certainty that Jones did not propagate a "Little Flock" theology, as it is nowhere found in any of his published or extant handwritten materials.

Sir Marcus Loane—another former principal of Moore College, archbishop of Sydney and primate of Australia—took issue with this characteristic appended to Jones's theology. He wrote, "Canon Jones was undoubtedly a preacher whose emphasis was on personal holiness, but did he ever use the term 'Little Flock' to describe the Church? Even though the idea of a 'gathered community' may have been prominent in his teaching, the terminology about the Little Flock was not."[28] Again later Loane expressed his concern with the attachment of the "Little Flock" theology, especially as Lawton sees it handed down through influential leadership in the Diocese of Sydney. Loane named the most influential men trained under Principal Jones and clearly dismissed any connection to this theology. He wrote,

> The ten who were to play the most prominent role in Diocesan life [with the year of their ordination] were as follows: H S Begbie [1898]; D J Knox [1899]; H G J Howe [1900]; S E Langford Smith [1900]; G A Chambers [1901]; A L Wade [1904]; S J Kirkby [1905]; S H Denman [1907]; J Bidwell [1908]; and R B Robinson [1911]. . . . I grew up when these men were at the height of their ministry and influence in the 'twenties and 'thirties, and I knew them all in more or less degree. I never heard any of them, in the pulpit or in private, speak of the "Little Flock." It is a disservice to Evangelicals to label them in this way.[29]

Considering Loane's own influence in the diocese and the fact that he was trained under the leadership of Jones's pupils, his objection to Lawton's thesis must command attention. Jones did not promote a "Little Flock" theology.

The greatest challenge to Lawton's theses, however, is his faulty method. He draws conclusions from associations and assumptions rather than from evidence. Often the conclusions proposed about Jones's theology refer to a source other than Jones and claim his endorsement of such views without

---

27. Jones, *Teaching of the Articles*, 27–33.
28. Loane, review of *Better Time to Be*, 42.
29. Ibid., 42. Notice the mention of both D. J. Knox and R. B. Robinson.

demonstrating any evidence of him affirming such a position.[30] At one point he does seem to recognize the uncertainty of his claims concerning Jones's theology. He writes, "Whilst his endorsement of these ideas could have been derived from mainstream Anglican Evangelicalism, his constant association with leading Brethren families makes their influence much more likely."[31] It is precisely this kind of reasoning that leaves Lawton's work unconvincing.

CONCLUSION

Nathaniel Jones left a strong legacy in the Diocese of Sydney. He worked hard to bolster theological education and bring it up to par with the training found in the UK. He also encouraged many through his platform preaching at Katoomba, his regular parish and college sermons, and his written works. He cared deeply about his own holiness and the holiness of others. He lived expectantly, hoping in the near return of the Lord. His legacy was a spiritual legacy marked by the concern to present everyone mature in Christ.

It has been demonstrated in this chapter that Nathaniel Jones's legacy was not, however, an ecclesiological legacy. William Lawton has propagated the theory that Nathaniel Jones had deep ties to Plymouth Brethren theology and this carried with it influential ecclesiological commitments. This lies at the heart of Lawton's thesis: Jones's association with Plymouth Brethrenism issued in a commitment to seeing the church as the "Little Flock." We have seen repeatedly that this argument is unfounded. Lawton has worked towards a historical explanation of a popular ecclesiology that he opined has "continued to disturb Sydney Anglicanism." Despite the debt owed to Lawton for making helpful material on the life and thought of Nathaniel Jones accessible, his thesis about Jones's Brethren beliefs and his "Little Flock" ecclesiology needs to be corrected for the purpose of accurately and appropriately understanding Jones's own theology and the theology of those after him.[32]

We must draw two conclusions here. First, Jones did not have as clear a connection to Plymouth Brethrenism as Lawton has suggested. There is no evidence of Jones holding to a "Little Flock" ecclesiology. Second, there

---

30. Lawton, "Nathaniel Jones," 365. Here Lawton cites Teulon, *History and Teaching*, 97, claiming this citation to be a position Jones affirmed without any reference to anything written by Jones himself. For other examples, see *Better Time: Utopian Attitudes*, 76, 86–87.

31. Lawton, "Nathaniel Jones," 365.

32. Some helpful and thorough research has been conducted by John McIntosh for his PhD at the University of New South Wales. McIntosh, "Anglican Evangelicalism in Sydney."

is no demonstrable tie between the ecclesiology of Jones and that of D. W. B. Robinson and D. B. Knox, especially not a "Little Flock" ecclesiology. There are certain genealogical ties that can, at best, support inferences but there is no evidence that either Robinson or Knox had any ecclesiological convictions indebted to the theology of Jones. Neither of them made any mention of Jones in their work, or of any "Little Flock" ecclesiology. We conclude, against Lawton, that Jones had no explicit influence upon Robinson or Knox.

2

The Ecclesiological Influence of T. C. Hammond

As we continue to investigate the ecclesiological formation of Robinson and Knox, we now move to consider a more immediate theological predecessor at Moore College, T. C. Hammond. Hammond was principal and lecturer in doctrine when both Robinson and Knox began teaching at the college. He is not remembered for any groundbreaking theological conclusions or the development of any distinctive school of theological thought.[1] Nevertheless, he contributed a timely intellectual voice for Evangelicalism. In the UK his handbook on theology, *In Understanding Be Men*, played a critical role in the evangelical renaissance of the 1930s and 1940s. In Australia, he aided Moore College in rediscovering the school's evangelical heritage and gave it intellectual depth. On both continents, Hammond's lasting impact was the strong voice that he offered conservative evangelicals and the battles he fought in the name of Evangelicalism against liberal and Roman Catholic opponents. Ecclesiology is a noteworthy doctrine in Hammond's thought, as it was the doctrine of the church that served as the battleground for much of his ministry. This chapter is an exploration of Hammond's ecclesiology, with concern for how it served as a defense for evangelical Protestantism, with the aim of showing how it contributed to the development of Robinson's and Knox's ecclesiologies. We will begin with a brief examination of Hammond's historical and ecclesiastical heritage, moving to understand his theological method, then to detail some major emphases in his ecclesiology, concluding with a statement on his ecclesiological influence on Sydney.

1. Nelson, *T. C. Hammond*, 107–8.

HISTORICAL AND ECCLESIAL CONTEXT

Thomas Chatterton (T. C.) Hammond was born 20 February 1877 in Cork, Ireland.[2] His Christian conversion came in 1892. He was ordained as deacon in 1903, and as presbyter in 1905. Prior to his ordination he studied at Trinity College Dublin where he excelled in philosophy and won the Downes (1902) and Wray (1903) prizes, and graduated with the Gold Medal. Years later, Archbishop Marcus Loane reflected on Hammond's passion for philosophy: "His own lifelong approach to Theology always emanated from the background of Philosophy. He saw Philosophy as the handmaid of Theology; he saw Theology as the Queen of the Sciences."[3] It was a skill that served him well throughout his ministry, in street preaching, debates and theological instruction.

Much of Hammond's early ministry set the tone for his work later in life. After ordination he served at St Kevin's Church in Dublin, first as a curate (1903–10) and then as rector (1910–19). He left the parish to become superintendent, and later general superintendent, of the Irish Church Mission. He spent much of his time on the streets of Dublin preaching, directing most of his sermons towards a Roman Catholic audience. During these years of service in Ireland he saw over five hundred people converted from Roman Catholicism, at least twenty-five of whom were priests.[4] This concern for evangelism and the defense of the Protestant faith remained the focus of the rest of his life in ministry. His priority was equipping people in the truth found in Scripture and training them to defend it. His passion arose from a deep conviction that Roman Catholicism had distorted this truth.

Hammond left this ministry in Ireland to accept a call to be principal at Moore Theological College in 1936.[5] The Anglican leadership in Sydney was already acquainted with Hammond from his visit to Sydney in 1926 as a part of a lecture tour sponsored by the Vickery Trust. This tour of Canada and Australia was planned in the wake of attempts to revise the 1662 Book of Common Prayer in an Anglo-Catholic direction.[6] Hammond's academic

---

2. There are several biographical references available for Hammond's life: Nelson, *T. C. Hammond: Irish Christian*; Nelson, "T. C. Hammond"; Thompson, "Hammond, Thomas Chatterton"; Loane, *Mark These Men*, 70–76; Judd and Cable, *Sydney Anglicans*, 232–40; Cable, "T. C. Hammond"; Davis, *Australian Anglicans*, 89–163; Loane, *Centenary History of Moore Theological College*, 139–53.

3. Loane, *Mark These Men*, 71.

4. Ibid., 72.

5. Nelson, *T. C. Hammond: Irish Christian*, 88–90. The call came from Sydney in 1935; Hammond occupied the position in 1936.

6. Nelson, "T. C. Hammond," 151.

ability and his firm stance against the Church of Rome, along with his quick wit and rigor in debate, made him a favorable candidate for principal. These skills would be highly valued in a context where Anglo-Catholicism threatened the traditionally evangelical Anglican theology of the Sydney Diocese.

The first three decades of the twentieth century tested the integrity of Sydney's evangelical tradition. In 1909, Archbishop Saumarez Smith died and a new archbishop was to be elected. The principal of Moore College, Nathaniel Jones, worked hard to have W. H. Griffith Thomas, then principal of Wycliffe Hall, Oxford, elected to this office. However, others advocated John Charles Wright and through some tactful politicking by F. B. Boyce, archdeacon of Sydney, Wright was elected.[7] Wright claimed to be an Evangelical and stood against Tractarianism; however, he favored liberal theology and theologians more than his predecessors. His sympathies became apparent when he appointed David John Davies as principal of Moore College upon Jones's death in 1911. Marcus Loane describes Davies, who was principal during Loane's student days, as "a Protestant in churchmanship, a Liberal in scholarship."[8] This appointment created a division amongst the clergy concerning the inspiration and authority of the Bible. In 1933 Archbishop Wright died. Conservatives, both lay and clerical, decided that the new archbishop needed to be more concerned with preserving the evangelical heritage of the diocese. Howard West Kilvington Mowll was elected archbishop in 1933 and arrived in 1934 from West China, where he had served as a bishop.[9] Soon after his arrival, Archdeacon Davies died and a new principal of Moore College had to be appointed. Mowll called upon T. C. Hammond to fill the position. His theological expertise and direction of Moore College complemented the leadership of Archbishop Mowll. Together, they would re-establish the unambiguously evangelical identity of Sydney Anglicanism.[10]

Hammond's scholarly work consisted in both published writing and public addresses. He produced more than half a dozen books. The three best known are *In Understanding Be Men* (theology), *Perfect Freedom* (ethics), and *Reasoning Faith* (apologetics). In addition to these volumes, he wrote many small booklets and articles during his Sydney years.

His public addresses include lectures in the classroom, public debates, and contribution to a biweekly radio program. At Moore College, Hammond lectured to students preparing for ministry on a wide array of topics across multiple disciplines such as New and Old Testament, Philosophy of

---

7. Dickey, "Nathaniel Jones," 192.
8. Loane, *Centenary History of Moore College*, 137.
9. Judd and Cable, *Sydney Anglicans*, 228.
10. Piggin, *Spirit of a Nation*, 130–31.

Religion, and Prayer Book.[11] Outside the classroom he participated in debates of different sorts, ranging from public street-side disputes to formal moderated debates at Sydney University.[12] The biweekly radio program was broadcast on Sydney's 2CH on Sunday evenings and was sponsored by the Council of Churches in conjunction with the Loyal Orange Institution of New South Wales (of which Hammond was grand chaplain from 1943–47, 1950–61 and grand master in 1961).

During his time as principal of Moore College, Hammond brought his Protestant doctrine to bear on the ecclesiastical issues of the day. Two examples stand out. In 1943 Bishop A. L. Wylde of the Diocese of Bathurst authorized the printing and limited distribution of a book that was red in color, entitled "The Holy Eucharist," incorporating part of the Roman Catholic order of service.[13] Some of the practices introduced were "the use of decidedly medieval catholic actions such as the ringing of a sanctus bell, making the sign of the cross, and implicitly encouraging belief in 'the real presence' (in the Roman Catholic sense)."[14] When Archbishop Mowll, as metropolitan of the province of New South Wales, requested the removal of the book, Bishop Wylde refused and the case ended up in the Supreme Court. The case lasted for four years with the decision ultimately in favor of the Evangelicals. The "Red Book" was withdrawn, but was replaced almost immediately by an only slightly less controversial "Green Book." The controversy became known as the "Red Book Case" and brought to the forefront questions of the Australian Church's loyalty to the Book of Common Prayer and the Church of England. Prayer Book revision seemed necessary, but would not be possible until a new church constitution was drafted and agreed upon.

In the wake of this controversy, Hammond became involved in the drafting of a constitution for the Church of England in Australia (from 1971 the Anglican Church of Australia). Judd and Cable have commented about the Evangelical victory in the "Red Book Case" and its ramifications for constitutional revision:

> The success, however limited, of Evangelicals in any negotiations for a new Constitution could be neither steam-rollered nor ignored. Any workable Constitution had to take considerable

11. Nelson, *T. C. Hammond: Irish Christian*, 101.

12. One of the most well-known debates was against John Anderson, professor of philosophy at Sydney University, in 1941. Donald Robinson, then a student and later archbishop of Sydney, arranged this debate. Ibid., 112.

13. Judd and Cable, *Sydney Anglicans*, 253–55; Cable, "T. C. Hammond," 368; Breward, *History of the Australian Churches*, 137–38. On the Red Book Case, see Knox, *What Is "The Red Book"?*; Galbraith, "Just Enough Religion to Make Us Hate."

14. Nelson, *T. C. Hammond: Irish Christian*, 115.

account of their views and position. That meant that, far from being an embattled minority, Sydney Evangelicals were in a position of strength in the fresh constitutional debates of the early 1950s.[15]

Constitutional drafting, debate and revision took place until a consensus was achieved. The final form of the constitution, agreed to by Hammond, was not what his younger Evangelical friends in Sydney (including D. W. B. Robinson and D. B. Knox) had hoped for, especially with regard to what they perceived as its inability to protect the doctrine of the church.[16] Nevertheless, Hammond believed it to be the best possible outcome given the political realities of the day.

Hammond's activity for and on behalf of the church in Sydney was shaped by his ecclesiological convictions. These convictions were hardly novel; rather, they were thought through carefully by a man with a first-rate mind and were sharpened by his years of sectarian debate.

THEOLOGICAL METHOD

The areas Hammond treated theologically were most often those relevant to the battles he was fighting. Hammond did not pursue innovation in his scholarship. Rather, he worked to expound and cultivate thinking rooted in the Protestant Reformation. Nelson comments, "As a teacher he was no innovator. He started no school of theology nor did he give the world fresh insights. He expounded Christian orthodoxy, presenting the historic and classic core of the faith as it has come down through the centuries, serving it up in Anglican dress."[17] It is hardly surprising, then, that Hammond grounded his teaching in the creeds and the Thirty-Nine Articles. He offered theological insights from these historic sources, reinforcing the traditional

---

15. Judd and Cable, *Sydney Anglicans*, 255.

16. Ibid., 256. On the constitutional debate, see Davis, *Constitutions*, 131–79. For Hammond on the constitutional developments, see: [TCH], "Synod and the Constitution," 8; [TCH, as edited by DBK], "One View on the Draft," 12. The challenges to Hammond and the new constitution came from Robinson and Knox in articles and editorials submitted to the Australian Church Record. See the following: [DBK], "New Constitution," *ACR* (11 Mar 1948) 3–4; [DBK], "Look Before You Leap!," 8–9; [DBK], "Constitutions New and Old," 8; [DBK], "Constitution," 8–9; [DBK], "Sydney's Eight Amendments," 2; [DBK], "New Constitution," *ACR* (13 May 1954) 4–5; [DWBR & DBK], "Contradictory Principles," 2; [DBK], "Retain the Ancient Catholic Principle," 2; [DBK], "Draft Constitution," 3; [DBK], "Evils of the Proposed Constitution," 7; [DBK], "Profit and Loss," 3; [DBK & DR], "Need to Examine," 2–3; [DR], "Present Constitution," 6; [DBK], "Diocese of Sydney," 6. [DBK], "Four Fatal Flaws," 8; [DBK], "Need for Unanimity," 2. [DBK], "Sydney Accepts Constitution," 1, 15.

17. Nelson, *T. C. Hammond: Irish Christian*, 107–8.

Evangelical view, and then extended arguments against perceived misunderstandings, distortions and departures from evangelical doctrine.

At Moore College, the Thirty-Nine Articles provided a rough syllabus for Hammond's lectures. He began a term or lecture series with logical questions that opened discussion and provided justification for further theological dialogue. This time of introduction also provided a broad survey of the material for the series. For example, in his lectures on the doctrine of the church, Hammond opened with questions such as: What are the sources for our doctrine of the church? Did Jesus teach concerning the church? When was the church founded? And, are there two natures of the church (visible and invisible)? From these questions others naturally followed, such as: If Jesus did not teach directly concerning the church, as some maintain (Eschatologists), did he use any cognate terms (as opposed to *ekklēsia*) that pertained to ecclesiology? Does the church have a corporate life? And, if there are two natures of the church, visible and invisible, are there two churches?[18] Using these questions as a stimulus, Hammond proceeded into examination of creedal truths and then followed the structure of the Thirty-Nine Articles, thus progressing from introduction to general Christian orthodoxy (the creeds) to narrower convictions of the Anglican tradition (Thirty-Nine Articles).

Integrated into his doctrinal elucidation was a pointed defense against departures from Protestantism. In his teaching on the church, Hammond explicitly addressed issues such as the nature of the church, the unity of the church, and the authority of the church. His target was invariably the Roman Catholic Church and the Anglicans who wished to join them.

One feature of Hammond's theological approach is the philosophical rigor that he brought to issues. Marcus Loane commented,

> This was something that he shared in common with the German and Scottish theologians, but it was in contrast with the English writers whose studies were always rooted in sound exegesis rather than in philosophy. Few men of his generation in the Anglican Communion were so genuinely at home in the literature and modes of thought of the medieval schoolmen.[19]

Hammond's fascination with the intersection of philosophy and theology is evidenced in the study he undertook throughout his life of Robert Bellarmine (1542–1621). This study served as ammunition for his engagement with

---

18. Hammond, *Verbatim Notes*, 1–14. The only available notes from T. C. Hammond's lectures on doctrine are his ecclesiology lectures, which exclusively cover Articles XIX–XXIV. Thus, these notes are the only available source for typecasting his lecture format. Hereafter referred to as *Notes*.

19. Loane, *Mark These Men*, 71.

Roman Catholic doctrine, as Hammond was well versed in Counter-Reformation reasoning and thought. Interacting with Bellarmine in his writing and lectures provided him with credibility and gave his enunciations a certain rhetorical force, as he frequently pointed to a prominent Catholic authority on doctrine.

Hammond's preference for theology did not produce a lack of regard for exegesis of the Bible—far from it. Philosophy was simply where he was most at home. He thought in terms of logic and systems. In his explanations he chose reason as his means of constructing an argument, often employing analogy or illustration to make his point. One example of this is an analogy he utilized in his excursus on the visible and invisible nature of the church. He compared the visible nature of the church to an institution such as a government and the invisible nature of the church to an association or society. Institutions, such as governments, he argued, have visible markers such as flags and symbols that mark them physically. However, what bonds people within an institution is a personal allegiance that is invisible.[20] It is this sort of analogy that Hammond would use to make his point in collaboration with the biblical evidence.

It could be argued that Hammond assumed too much and relied too heavily on reasoning rather than justifying his conclusions in the teaching of Scripture. For example, in *In Understanding Be Men* Hammond surveys Protestant theology, providing readers with a clear, concise, and systematic overview of the Christian faith. However, the role of the Bible in the text appears to be marginal. Scripture passages are provided at the conclusion of each chapter rather than being integrated into his discourse, and therein failing to demonstrate how each theological proposition is arrived at biblically. However, elsewhere, in his *One Hundred Texts*,[21] there is clear evidence of the primacy of Scripture in his theological method. As its name indicates, this volume is a treatise on one hundred key texts aiming to establish and defend Protestant doctrine. Beyond this volume, Hammond's lectures and discussions contain other small indications of his exegetical abilities and his high esteem for the Bible.[22]

In the classroom Hammond primarily engaged with other Anglicans as interlocutors for his lectures. In his biography of Hammond, Warren Nelson

---

20. Hammond, "The Church" (radio address). This analogy appears to be one that Hammond adopted and modified from E. J. Bicknell. Hammond never credited this to Bicknell, but the similarities are too great. See Bicknell, *Theological Introduction to the Thirty-Nine Articles*, 298–99.

21. The selection of texts predates Hammond, dating back as far as the mid-nineteenth century, but its genesis is uncertain.

22. E.g., see Hammond's discussion of the ordination of Presbyters in *Notes*, 60–61.

identifies W. H. Griffith Thomas' *Principles of Theology* as the primary textbook for Hammond's doctrine courses.[23] However, notes from his second year lectures in doctrine from 1943 indicate that E. J. Bicknell's *Theological Introduction to the Thirty-Nine Articles of the Church of England* was the common text for discussion.[24] When he disagreed or was unsatisfied with Bicknell, such as on the charter of the church,[25] he would turn to other Anglican theologians such as Richard Hooker to fortify his argument.[26] All three of these interlocutors—Thomas, Bicknell and Hooker—demonstrate Hammond's anchoring in the Anglican tradition and his priority of expounding that tradition.

Hammond also possessed a deep knowledge of wider church history, citing Ignatius, Clement, Irenaeus, Tertullian, and Gregory Nazianzen amongst others. His reference to historical figures served the purpose of demonstrating the roots of doctrine. For example, in his case for episcopacy he cites Ignatius of Antioch as the first writer to mention the term "episcopacy" in the modern sense (AD 110), and from the Ignatian Epistles he builds a case for the legitimacy of episcopacy in ecclesial polity.[27]

Overall, Hammond's theological method cannot be divorced from his circumstances, first as a Protestant apologist in Ireland and later as a defender of evangelical orthodoxy as principal of Moore College. The context in which his teaching and writings took shape, whether in Ireland or Australia, was often defined by controversy and contention. Nelson wrote of Hammond,

> He had come [to Australia] when the evangelical cause was weak and lacking in theological depth, and when Roman Catholicism had its eyes set on turning Australia into a Catholic country. He had come when the hollow fruits of modernism and the bitter attacks of ritualism were in danger of changing the character of the Diocese of Sydney, and he helped to turn back the tide.[28]

Hammond saw evangelical theology under attack on two fronts, from Catholicism and Liberalism, and for this reason his work and tone were often polemical; he worked tirelessly to see the future of the Anglican Church in Sydney (and abroad!) as one marked by evangelical doctrine.

---

23. Nelson, *T. C. Hammond: Irish Christian*, 101.

24. Jensen, "Broughton Knox," 23 (repr.).

25. Hammond, *Notes*, 16–20.

26. Hammond (or his stenographer) left no record of the works he was citing, but undoubtedly the reference is to Hooker, *Of the Laws of Ecclesiastical Polity*.

27. Hammond, *Notes*, 63–64.

28. Nelson, *T. C. Hammond: Irish Christian*, 130.

MAJOR EMPHASES IN HAMMOND'S ECCLESIOLOGY

Three major ideas occurred often in T. C. Hammond's ecclesiology: the visible and invisible nature of the church, the unity of the church, and authority in the church. These three themes are prominent in the Thirty-Nine Articles, but they were also critical in Hammond's intellectual battle with Roman Catholicism. As we explore each of these themes in turn, the connection with this polemical context will be evident.

Visible and Invisible

The first theme is the most prominent in Hammond's ecclesiology: the visible and invisible nature of the church. Hammond wrote and taught on this theme throughout his ministry, most often anchoring his arguments in Article XIX.[29] The most forthright address he gave on the topic came at some point during his ministry in Sydney, likely towards the end of his career.[30] Some Roman Catholic accusers attacked Protestant ecclesiology, claiming Protestants subscribed to a deficient understanding of the church, reducing it to an invisible reality.[31] Hammond responded with a radio address devoted to a rebuttal of this accusation. He began,

> It may sound to many of my hearers like casuistry, but I am anxious to point out the position of the Protestant Church when, she maintains there is an invisible body as well as a visible body, or perhaps to speak more correctly, that the bond that unites men to Jesus Christ is not sensible, not capable of being expressed accurately and fully by any visible sign or form or adhesion. But that it is nevertheless a real bond which finds expression in the organisations of communities for worship of God and the service of Jesus Christ our Lord. That is the position that the Protestants adopt. The church of God is known to God only in its fullest, truest and widest sense. The adhesion to certain fundamental principles that are laid down in the Sacred Scriptures.[32]

---

29. See Hammond, *In Understanding Be Men*, 162; Hammond, *Notes*, 8–13.

30. The ambiguity surrounding the timing of this attack exists because neither the attacker nor the context in which the attack arose is disclosed. The likelihood of the date being later in Hammond's life is related to the date of the radio address, 10 April 1960.

31. Hammond, "The Church." Hammond quoted his opponents as saying (in effect), "The Church has become obscured by the errors of the Protestant belief, that they have caused it to fade away into nothingness. They have reduced their belief to the existence of an invisible Church."

32. Ibid.

Hammond recognized that the bond that unites men to Christ, and therein unites Christians to one another, is not something that can be expressed fully in visible form. This does not discount or discredit the visible manifestation of this bond—in fact it affirms it—but recognizes there is something deeper than the superficial visible markers, especially since the visible markers are not always accurate; there are many who appear to be members of the visible church who are not in fact united to Christ. He was careful not to be guilty of the critique of his accusers; the church is not merely an ethereal reality, rather the visible is real and meaningful. However, the truest form of the church is an ethereal reality that finds visible expression.

Hammond turned to historical authorities to justify his conclusions. Concerning the visible church he looked to the Thirty-Nine Articles, arguing that the visible church is identified where the Word of God is preached and the sacraments are duly administered. Where the Articles are silent, particularly concerning the invisible church, he depended on the *Westminster Confession of Faith* for theological support. The main thrust of his argument concerning the invisible church was its timeless nature. In short, the visible church is manifested worldwide relating to Christians in space, and the invisible church is timeless relating to Christians throughout all of time.[33]

This defense of the visible and invisible natures of the church targeted an underlying conflict with the Roman Catholic notion that the Roman Church is coextensive with the invisible church.[34] One of the primary angles Hammond took was to critique this line of thinking in relation to the concept of church unity. He wrote,

> But the vast body of believers, who have been chosen of God from the foundation of the world, cannot, by the very limitation of time and space, so exhibit unity. The unity which they possess, is that which has been contributed to them by God, and they must, in obedience to His mind and will, exhibit it, some in the glory, praising His name to all eternity and some in time, sometimes enduring great hardness, because of their faith in Him.[35]

In other words, the Roman Catholic Church cannot be coextensive with the invisible church simply because the visible does not fully express the invisible; the present, visible church in the world, does not represent all believers for all time. More so, the Roman Church is not representative of all who have placed faith in Jesus Christ, especially since the Protestant Reformation.

---

33. Ibid. This summary is drawn from Hammond's expression of the dichotomy in Christian worship of some expressing worship in time and others in glory (eternally).

34. See Hammond, *In Understanding Be Men*, 162.

35. Hammond, "The Church."

Conversely he stated, "The Visible Church is never co-extensive with the Church Invisible even on earth, because there are often attached to communities of professing Christians those who do not really belong to them (1 Jn. ii. 19). There may thus be membership in the Visible Church which does not secure membership in the Invisible."[36] The existential reality of "tares among the wheat," or unbelievers amongst believers in the visible church, is further rationale for the invisible church. Not only is the church bound by time and space, but also its true membership is not known on earth or in time.

What is lacking in Hammond's development of the visible and invisible church is a sustained reflection on the cohesion of the two concepts. A careful reading of his work, at places, leaves the reader with the notion that the visible and invisible are mutually exclusive. He was explicit in his lectures on the church that there are not two distinct churches. He taught, "The Visible Church is the expression in sensible form of the Invisible. What we call the Invisible may otherwise be described as the secret bond that unites believers to the Lord. . . . The Visible Church never represents completely the Invisible. On the other hand, the Invisible is never without visible manifestation."[37] However, he seemed to indicate that the visible and invisible operate independently, one across space (visible) and the other across time (invisible). He wrote, "The Church is something that is independent of time, it does not consist merely of the members who are present [sic] constituted as a visible assembly, it consists of those who reposed faith in Jesus Christ and passed into eternal judgment."[38] This statement is clear and an appropriate description of the invisible and visible church. However, Hammond continued to discuss how the boundaries of time and space then cause division between the visible and the invisible. As we have seen already, Hammond wrote, "The unity which they possess, is that which has been contributed to them by God, and they must, in obedience to His mind and will, exhibit it, some in the glory, praising His name to all eternity, and some in time, sometimes enduring great hardness because of their faith in Him."[39] While he was clear to say that the two coincide, he did not fully address how the visible is a spatial manifestation of the timeless invisible church. Hammond argued that simultaneously some believers participate in the visible, while others participate in the invisible. But how can the New Testament claim that Christians are presently already seated with Christ in the heavenly places (Eph 2:6)? Is there a sense in which the visible is participating in

---

36. Hammond, *In Understanding Be Men*, 162.
37. Hammond, *Notes*, 10.
38. Hammond, "The Church."
39. Ibid.

the heavenly/invisible? These questions were never answered by Hammond, but would be considered and developed later by some of his successors, such as D. B. Knox.[40]

In his radio address, Hammond took care to recognize it is the place of no man to determine who belongs to the true church. He wrote concerning the Catholic Church, "We dare not communicate concerning sundry [sic] her gross and grievous abominations, yet touching these main parts of Christian truth, wherein they constantly still persist, we gladly acknowledge them to be of the family of Jesus Christ."[41] Regarding Hammond's embrace of Roman Catholics as Christian brothers, the question that naturally arises is, "Why crusade against the Roman Church?" Hammond saw a distinction between fighting for doctrine and determining who belonged to the church. Poor doctrine does not necessitate exclusion from the church.[42] Hammond wrote,

> All who profess a living faith in Jesus Christ are united in the visible [invisible?] body which is called His Church, even though unhappily, through the sin of men, and many misconceptions, they may err grievously concerning the faith. It is our duty to point out these difficulties and differences, and it is our obligation to insist as firmly as ever we can, upon the maintenance of the truth as it is revealed in Sacred Scripture, but it is no part of our province to pass judgment upon other people, and to assume that because they are, in our judgment, manifestly in error, therefore they are entirely rejected from the body of Christ.[43]

Underlying all of his critique of Roman Catholic doctrine was a genuine passion for reform and a desire for unity. Hammond did not believe that the notion of Protestant and Roman Catholic unity was absurd. Rather, he deeply believed it already existed in Christ and he longed for a visible unity that could come from the "adhesion to Jesus Christ, and . . . hope of eternal

---

40. See Knox, "De-mythologizing the Church," 26–27 (repr.).

41. Hammond, "The Church."

42. In his unpublished document "Article XIX," Hammond wrote, "The expressed confessions of faith, where they may be had, afford a suitable standard by which we can judge the Church. That body which imposes, as articles of faith, that which cannot be established by God's Word, or that body which fails to observe the necessary requirements in the administration of the sacraments, is shown to have departed from the character of a visible church" (p. 2). Hammond wrote these words with regard to church authority and individual choice in places for fellowship. His concern in this statement appears to be more the corporate rather than the individual. This is rationale for the Protestant Reformation.

43. Hammond, "The Church." Here Hammond is drawing from Hooker.

salvation only in him."[44] Hammond believed this desire and demeanor of longing for unity was the posture every Protestant should have in regard to Roman Catholics.

Unity

The second major theme in T. C. Hammond's ecclesiology is the unity of the church. Hammond's concept of unity was deeply entrenched in his thinking about the nature of the church. Hammond disagreed with Bicknell's argument that "you cannot divide an invisible body."[45] Hammond believed that both the visible and the invisible church are currently divided. He wrote, "The divisions of the invisible church are present imperfections within the body which will finally be surmounted; the divisions in the visible church are twofold: Divisions due to imperfections, and divisions to the incrustations of alien elements."[46] Disunity, however, does not mean destruction. Hammond attributed much of the current disunity in the church as the lesser of two evils, the greater evil being a suppression of conscience.[47] Hammond believed in and endorsed the right of individual conscience, as was necessitated by his Protestantism (and perhaps also his Irish background!). He argued that nonconformity does not always produce disunity, and that multiple expressions and manifestations of churches may actually be united even in disagreement.

In order to define and defend his views of unity, Hammond employed an analogy of nations.[48] He wrote, "They [nations] consist of separate individuals, with varying outlooks, which sometimes attain very large dimensions, and threaten national integrity. But underlying the difference, there is a common spirit, and a broad common inheritance."[49] Like a nation, Hammond identified similar uniting forces within Christianity. Externally, Christians are bound by their common inheritance through faith, a common environment of worship, and general moral and spiritual principles. Internally Christians share the bond of the regenerating power of the Holy

---

44. Ibid.
45. Bicknell, *Thirty-Nine Articles*, 303. See Hammond, *Notes*, 19–20.
46. Hammond, *Notes*, 20.
47. Ibid.
48. Hammond obtains this analogy as well as similar analogies with the same purpose, of the family unit illustrating unity, from Bicknell. See Bicknell, *Thirty-Nine Articles*, 298–99.
49. Hammond, *Notes*, 23–24

Spirit.[50] Hammond contended that, above all, the locus of the church's unity is in its headship—Jesus Christ.[51]

Several questions arise about Hammond's view of the divided invisible church. First, how do imperfections such as division remain if the invisible church comprises the saints in glory? Are these imperfections rooted in the visible manifestation of the invisible? If so, to what extent does the invisible depend on the visible? Is the earthly church to be given primacy over the heavenly? Second, do both the external and internal uniting bonds of Christianity necessitate a united invisible church? Is the believer's existential membership in the invisible church not the realization of this unity and the full expression of these bonds? These questions return to the inadequacy of Hammond's consideration of the present spiritual reality of believers being seated in the heavenly places (Eph 2:6).

Hammond worked to provide bridges for unity, as seen in the inclusive nature of *In Understanding Be Men*, written for evangelical Protestants rather than Anglicans exclusively. He deeply hoped and longed for the unity of the church. However, he recognized that disunity was a matter greater than issues of polity and other functional and superficial disagreements. Should the Roman Church rescind its claims of exclusivity, the Church of England still could not reunite with Rome on the basis of polity alone, even with a similar view of episcopacy. The Reformation took place because of desperate need for doctrinal reform. Hammond's place as a theologian was one in continuation of this spirit of the Reformation.

Authority

The third major theme of T. C. Hammond's ecclesiology is the authority of the church. Hammond, in many ways, treated this issue as prolegomena to the rest of his consideration of the church, understanding the Bible to be the ultimate authority over the church.[52] The authority of the church is grounded in Scripture and this authority extends only so far as Scripture permits. Hammond contended that the church's fidelity to Scripture is essential to its purpose. He wrote, "The primary function of the church is that of witness. This leads directly to the place of Holy Scripture. We maintain that the church is the servant and not the mistress of her message."[53] The question that must be answered is, "What is the Word of God?" The Roman Church's

---

50. Ibid.
51. Hammond, *In Understanding Be Men*, 163.
52. Hammond, *Notes*, 1. Notice his introduction to ecclesiology.
53. Ibid., 31.

elevation of tradition to position alongside Scripture in the scheme of divine revelation is a major point of contention. Hammond was not dismissive of obvious questions that arise from this controversy, addressing issues such as: "Who decides what section [denomination/faction] of the church has authority?" and, "Who gave it this authority?"[54] Not avoiding these questions, but answering them on a different level, Hammond proposed, "The authority of the church is real, but not absolute."[55] He argued that corporate authority is the norm, however, in extreme circumstances the enlightened conscience may challenge corporate authority. This conscience, of course, must proceed prudently and only stand against the corporate if there is an imposition of mandates lacking scriptural warrant. With this point, Hammond again demonstrated his theological grounding in the Thirty-Nine Articles.[56]

For Hammond, the most relevant battle over the issue of the authority of the church is the Roman Church's imposition of extra-biblical doctrine. This imposition has largely been carried out under the authority ascribed by apostolic succession. Hammond's view of apostolic succession is as follows: "The essence of apostolic succession is found in the Christian deposit. That is the gauge by which everything must be tested. The authority of the apostles is not due to an accident in time, nor to their inherent genius, but to the fact that they were the recipients of the message of Christ."[57] The misunderstanding of this doctrine has allowed for many other non-biblical practices to be carried out in the church under false authority. This is, perhaps, most explicitly seen in the sacerdotal priesthood. Hammond believed that Rome has both misunderstood and abused the notion of apostolic succession and the "power of the keys," using this as a power play and an afterthought to accommodate her *ex opere operato* view of the sacraments. He concluded with a warning against sacerdotalism, writing, "The idea that the Christian minister is in any sense a mediator between God and man is 'repugnant to holy Scripture.'"[58] It is in opposition to such a doctrine that Hammond

54. Ibid., 30–31.

55. Ibid., 31.

56. Hammond's comments on limits to ecclesial authority, especially over doctrine, are rooted in Article XX: "The Church hath power to decree Rites or Ceremonies, and authority in Controversies of Faith: And yet it is not lawful for the Church to ordain anything contrary to God's Word written, neither may it so expound one place of Scripture, that it be repugnant to another. Wherefore, although the Church be a witness and a keeper of holy Writ, yet, as it ought not to decree any thing against the same, so besides the same ought it not to enforce any thing to be believed for necessity of Salvation."

57. Hammond, *Notes*, 27.

58. Hammond, *In Understanding Be Men*, 172.

would have argued for the intervention of the scripturally informed individual conscience.

HAMMOND'S ECCLESIOLOGICAL INFLUENCE

The great contribution of T. C. Hammond's ecclesiology was the intellectual depth it provided to evangelical thinking in these areas. His ecclesiology emerged from his Anglican heritage, finding its grounding in the Thirty-Nine Articles and the creeds. However, Hammond was not naïve. He asked questions of his tradition and engaged with voices of other traditions. His doctrine was shaped in the face of opposition and therefore articulated in contrast. The juxtaposition of Protestant ecclesiological convictions over against Roman Catholic doctrine served as a powerful tool in bolstering the Evangelical cause. For him, these claims against Catholic doctrine were not academic exercises. Hammond demonstrated clearly why the Church of England departed from the Roman Church and why there was continual doctrinal disagreement.

The three main themes we have explored in his ecclesiology—the nature of the church, the unity of the church, and the authority of the church—served for him as case studies for the contradistinction between Protestantism and Catholicism. While Hammond's thought was not innovative, it served his context well in recovering and re-establishing an evangelical foundation. His successors would not find agreement with all of his ecclesiology, especially regarding the connections between the visible and invisible church. His legacy was not so much in the ecclesiological details as it was in a retrieval of evangelical Protestantism. He arrived in Sydney when liberalism threatened orthodoxy, and Anglo-Catholicism and the Roman Catholic Church threatened Protestantism. Upon the completion of his ministry, the Diocese of Sydney was undeniably evangelical and confident rather than defensive. With fewer dogmatic battles left to fight, he paved a way for fresh thinking on the doctrine of the church in response to the emerging ecumenical movement.

3

Ecumenism and the World Council of Churches

ALONGSIDE THE CONTINUING LEGACIES of influential men like Jones and Hammond, a number of broader ecclesiastical and theological currents provided the critical background for Robinson and Knox in the 1950s and beyond. Here, we will investigate how the ecumenical movement and the advent of the World Council of Churches contributed to the development of the ecclesiologies of Donald Robinson and D. Broughton Knox. In order to assess this influence we will briefly survey the history and aims of the ecumenical movement, the development of the World Council of Churches and its goals for accomplishing ecumenical ideals, and finally the engagement of Sydney Anglicans in the ecumenical movement in the mid-twentieth century. We will conclude with a statement of the movement's ecclesiological influence on Robinson and Knox.

THE RISE OF THE ECUMENICAL MOVEMENT: WHEN AND WHY?

Stephen Neill opened his account of the involvement of key leaders in the ecumenical movement, *Men of Unity*, with these words: "The ecumenical movement exists to work for two great aims—the unity and the renewal of the Church."[1] Disunity has been a perceived problem area for the Christian church throughout its entire history, not least since the East-West schism of the eleventh century and more recently the Protestant Reformation in the

---

1. Neill, *Men of Unity*, 7.

sixteenth century. The pains of Christian factions became acute in the late nineteenth century as evangelistic efforts were being organized by parachurch societies, such as the Young Men's Christian Associations (YMCA) and the Student Christian Movement. In the early 20th century, these societies claimed that the denominational divides were hampering mission activities, as greater evangelistic achievement required a united witness and effort.

By 1910, the vision for ecumenical action had been a dream for more than a century. William Carey had proposed a decennial gathering of denominations to discuss missionary partnership as early as 1810.[2] However, the official beginning of the modern ecumenical movement is most commonly associated with the International Missionary Conference in Edinburgh, Scotland on June 14, 1910.[3] This conference differed from others before it because its membership was composed of official emissaries from missionary societies, whereas previous conferences consisted of an open membership. The official delegates of the various societies conferred to discuss strategies for achieving world mission, not writing policies to be enforced in each society, but conversing about prudent plans to be taken back to them.[4] The conference chose as chairman John Mott, the founder of the World Student Christian Federation (WSCF; later the Student Christian Movement), as he had already contributed a great vision for ecumenism through the WSCF.

The priorities of the ecumenical movement were developed in the years following 1910 in the lead up to what would be the World Council of Churches. These priorities were fourfold:[5]

1. *Common Service* in promoting justice in the world and working cooperatively to provide interchurch aid to victims of calamity, war, poverty, oppression.

2. *Common Fellowship* in a common apostolic faith, a mutual recognition of members and ministers, and working towards the removal of barriers to sharing the Eucharist.

---

2. Latourette, "Ecumenical Bearings," 355.

3. Van der Bent, *Historical Dictionary of Ecumenical Christianity*, 3. Also see Latourette, "Ecumenical Bearings," 355–57.

Brian Stanley argues that this conference in 1910 is given too great an emphasis in the origins of ecumenism as it was not very diverse nor was it representative of denominations, rather it was comprised of some mission societies from around the globe. However, we are arguing here that it was this conference that spawned the ecumenical activities that eventuated into the WCC in 1948. See Stanley, "Edinburgh 1910."

4. Latourette, "Ecumenical Bearings," 357–58.

5. Kinnamon and Cope, *Ecumenical Movement*, 2.

3. *Common Witness* in cooperative mission and evangelism.

4. *Common Renewal* in the transformation that comes through receiving the gifts which others contribute in the body of Christ.

These aims testify that the ecumenical movement has historically aimed at achieving something beyond a superficial or political interdenominational harmony, or even simply common cause in missionary endeavors. Rather, the movement is driven by common action that is *both* inwardly and outwardly focused. Inwardly, the movement recognized the broader Christian faith and tradition to which all who call on the name of Christ belong and sought spiritual unity on those bases. Outwardly, it called Christians to serve a broken world's tangible and spiritual needs.

Without jettisoning other priorities of the movement, it is worth noting the evangelistic zeal of ecumenists. It is this mission for the world to know the Lord Jesus that led to the inception of the movement. Indeed, this missionary and evangelistic purpose would become a benchmark of the ecumenical movement as the World Council of Churches developed in 1948. But while there was a shared passion for *common witness*, how would these different churches unite to share a gospel about which they disagreed? There was no dispute about the common creedal confessions on the person of Christ, but there was (and remains) great diversity of beliefs about the work of Christ and how that work is experienced in the life of the Christian. Surely if there was to be a common witness it would require an agreed soteriology.

Undergirding the priorities of the ecumenical movement is the biblical and theological conviction that the church should be united. Ecumenists ground their belief in the necessity for unity in Jesus' high priestly prayer (John 17) and in Paul's exhortation to maintain unity (Eph 4:1–7). Veli-Matti Kärkäinen writes,

> To rightly understand this goal of ecumenism, one must keep in mind the fact that this concept seeks to preserve the distinction between God-given unity as gift and the human response to God's action and desire. Consequently, it is not the task of the ecumenical movement—or any other human organization for that matter—to create unity between the churches, but rather to give form to the unity already created by God. In other words, since God has created one church of Christ on earth, let Christians then live up to that fact in empirical life.[6]

---

6. Kärkäinen, *Ecclesiology*, 85.

But the pursuit of unity, God-given as it may be, is difficult because various parties define it differently. This difference in conviction about the essential nature of the church's ecumenicity is a problem ultimately of divergent ecclesiologies. That is, few would dispute the oneness of the church, but they would dispute the location of this unity, whether it is earthly or heavenly.

The ecumenical movement did not develop without challenge. Some of the most important theologians and church leaders of the twentieth century drove the ecumenical agenda.[7] But there were also those who opposed the movement on ecclesiological grounds. Most notable was the early refusal of participation by the Roman Catholic Church, though this changed after Vatican II. Still others, while sympathetic to the movement, cautioned against seeking a return to an idealistic form of the pure church of history. Ernst Käsemann wrote,

> No romantic postulate, however enveloped it may be in the cloak of salvation history, can be permitted to weaken the sober observation that the historian is unable to speak of an unbroken unity of New Testament ecclesiology. One sided emphasis, fossilized attitudes, fabrications and contradictory opposites in doctrine, organization and devotional practice are to be found in the ecclesiology of the New Testament no less than among ourselves. To recognize this is even a great comfort and, so far as ecumenical work today is concerned, a theological gain.[8]

Thus, while the unity of the church is a priority because of biblical and theological convictions, the ecumenical task is not now, nor has it ever been, simple. Factions have existed since the inception of the church. Thus, while some may see the ecumenical task as a biblical mandate, one should not presuppose that there was once a unity belonging to a glorious moment in history.[9]

---

7. We might include in this list Barth, Schlink, Nygren, Torrance, MacKinnon, and Michael Ramsey among others. The scope of this book prohibits us from exploring further why each scholar was involved in the ecumenical dialogue and how their respective ecclesiologies compare to the conclusions of Robinson and Knox. Robinson and Knox did not pursue a dialogue with these scholars in a capacity that we might have hoped, but this would be a useful task for future scholarship.

8. Käsemann, *New Testament Questions of Today*, 256–57; cited in Kinnamon and Cope, *Ecumenical Movement*, 97.

9. Käsemann later (on the same page) argues that the unity of the church is an eschatological reality.

THE FORMATION OF THE WORLD COUNCIL OF CHURCHES: MOMENTUM FOR ECUMENICAL IDEALS

The ecumenical movement gained momentum in the decades following the International Missionary Conference in 1910. On January 10, 1919, the Church of Constantinople issued an invitation for all Christian churches to form a "league of churches"—"an initiative without precedent in church history"[10]—in its "Unto the Churches of Christ Everywhere" *Encyclical of the Ecumenical Patriarchate*. Nathan Söderblom, archbishop of Uppsala, and J. H. Oldham, secretary of the continuation committee of the World Missionary Conference, put forward similar proposals within a year. In an effort to continue the ecumenical efforts, a committee for Faith and Order met first in 1927 in Lausanne and later in 1937 in Edinburgh where the Life and Work Movement proposed the development of the World Council of Churches (WCC). In 1938 the World Council of Churches in Process and Formation was set up to organize the first gathering of the WCC. World War II delayed this gathering until 1948 when the first meeting was held in Amsterdam, bringing together representatives from 147 churches. Subsequent to the first meeting in 1948, there have been nine other council meetings: 1954 in Evanston, Illinois; 1961 in New Delhi; 1968 in Uppsala; 1975 in Nairobi; 1983 in Vancouver; 1991 in Canberra; 1998 in Harare; 2006 in Porto Alegre; and 2013 in Busan.

Of the WCC meetings, the 1961 New Delhi Council set out to define the nature of the unity that the council seeks. The definitive statement produced at that gathering stated:

> We believe that the unity which is both God's will and his gift to his Church is being made visible as all in each place who are baptized into Jesus Christ and confess him as Lord and Saviour are brought by the Holy Spirit into one fully committed fellowship, holding the one apostolic faith, preaching the one Gospel, breaking the one bread, joining in common prayer, and having a corporate life reaching out in witness and service to all and who at the same time are united with the whole Christian fellowship in all places and all ages in such wise that ministry and members are accepted by all, and that all can act and speak together as occasion requires for the tasks to which God calls his people.[11]

---

10. Visser 't Hooft, *Genesis and Formation*, 1.

11. "Report on the Section on Unity," *Third Assembly of the WCC, New Delhi 1961*, in Kinnamon and Cope, *Ecumenical Movement*, 88.

In an exposition of this statement, the rationale for the usage of "fellowship" was explained.

> The word "fellowship" (*koinonia*) has been chosen because it describes what the Church truly is. "Fellowship" clearly implies that the Church is not merely an institution or organization. It is a fellowship of those who are called together by the Holy Spirit and in baptism confess Christ as Lord and Saviour. They are thus "fully committed" to him and to one another.[12]

This statement of the third meeting of the WCC served to materialize the doctrinal commitments and objective aims of the council. The unity of the church is an essential property of the nature of the church. Therefore, the pursuit of such unity is a fundamental Christian mandate. The objective expression of unity requires a common message, mission, Communion, and organization. Though the exposition of the statement declares that unity is greater than institutional unity, council members believed that it is not less than institutional solidarity.

Dr. W. A. Visser 't Hooft, the first general secretary of the WCC, presented a retrospective summary of eight of the main motives and convictions that gave the World Council plan its substance and form.[13]

1. The purpose of the planners was to persuade the churches to accept full responsibility for the fulfillment of the ecumenical task.

2. The plan for the World Council was based on the conviction that the mandate of the ecumenical movement had two aspects that were closely related. It was an attempt to encourage the churches to cooperate in service to each other and to the world.

3. The plan was motivated by the conviction that the unity of the church is based on the action of the Lord Jesus Christ who gathers his people together.

4. The plan was not considered an end in itself or as a definitive solution for the problem of disunity, but as a method of mobilizing the churches for a common effort to pursue that goal.

5. The plan sought to provide an instrument through which the solidarity of the churches might find clear expression.

6. The plan provided for that mutual encouragement and exhortation which was such a prominent feature of the early Christian churches, as

---

12. Ibid., 89.
13. Taken from Visser 't Hooft, *Genesis and Formation*, 87–93.

described in the letters of St. Paul. The ecumenical significance of this paraklesis is clearly described in the message of the first assembly of the World Council: "As we have talked with each other, we have begun to understand how our separation has prevented us from receiving correction from one another in Christ. And because we lacked this correction, the world has often heard from us not the Word of God but the words of men." (Later: "In other words, the existence of the World Council provided the opportunity to set in motion once again that exchange and sharing of the *charismata*, the diverse spiritual gifts which St Paul described in the twelfth chapter of the First Epistle to the Corinthians.")

7. The plan sought to express the dimension of wholeness in the calling of the churches. (Here, Visser 't Hooft defines "ecumenical" as "everything that relates to the whole task of the whole Church to bring the Gospel to the whole world.")

8. The plan sought to enable the churches to render their common witness to the world.

This list attests to the fact that the WCC was formed for the purpose of achieving the priorities of the ecumenical movement. The unity that is sought by the WCC is dynamic rather than static; in other words, the WCC seeks unity in mobility—churches sharing common activity in pursuit of a singular mission.

SYDNEY ANGLICANS AND THE WORLD COUNCIL OF CHURCHES

Sydney Anglicans participated in the World Council of Churches from a relatively early stage. In 1946 Howard Mowll, archbishop of Sydney and primate of Australia, became the president of the Australian Council for the World Council of Churches. This council was developed in anticipation of the first gathering of the World Council of Churches and focused on common action between churches in Australia. Mowll later served as a senior delegate to the first gathering of the WCC in 1948. It was his ecumenical fervor that encouraged other Australian Anglicans, especially other Sydney Anglicans, to be involved in the WCC and other ecumenical endeavors.[14]

Broughton Knox became involved in the WCC at the request of Archbishop Mowll. Knox attended the Faith and Order Conference in Lund,

---

14. Judd and Cable, *Sydney Anglicans*, 252.

Sweden, in 1952, where he was elected to serve on the Geneva Faith and Order Commission of the WCC. His position on the Faith and Order Commission led him to participate in the second assembly of the WCC in 1954 at Evanston, Illinois. Knox remained on the Faith and Order Commission for a few more years after Evanston, but did not attend any more conciliar gatherings. Even before Evanston, reservation about the council was expressed by leading evangelicals in Sydney. Donald Robinson commented,

> Our position in the World Council is so far only by tacit agreement, resting largely on the initiative of some individual church leaders. Our synods have never discussed the questions of participation in the W.C.C. and how Anglican members of the various conferences come to be described as "fully accredited representatives" is something of a mystery.[15]

It was clear that it was the drive of Archbishop Mowll that promoted Sydney Anglican participation in the WCC. The participation of Sydney Anglicans in formal ecumenical activities dwindled with the conclusion of Knox's participation with the WCC and the death of Archbishop Mowll in 1958.

However, the position of Sydney Anglicans, especially of Robinson and Knox as set forth in the *Australian Church Record*, was not entirely critical of the WCC. It would be fair to say that they maintained a charitable posture in their engagement, but they were not optimistic about the council's seemingly grandiose ideals; it was their ecclesiology that prohibited them from fully endorsing the WCC. Robinson explained their position as follows:

> For our part, we welcome the opportunities provided by the W.C.C., and especially the Commission on Faith and Order, for the mutual discussion of theological agreements and differences. We believe that, while there are dangers in this, rightly undertaken it opens up some prospect of those who profess and call themselves Christians holding the faith in unity of spirit and the bond of peace. From this point of view we should be glad to see even Roman Catholic representatives in the World Council.
>
> On the other hand, we have little sympathy with the exaggerated and misleading doctrines of "Christian unity" promulgated by many World Council leaders and publications which speak of "the coming World Church." The New Testament knows only one unit of the Visible Church, namely, the local worshipping community. Thus, we do not believe that our Saviour's prayers

---

15. [Robinson], "WCC," *ACR* (22 Jul 1954) 4.

for the spiritual unity of His disciples in the truth has anything directly to do with the formation of the world councils.[16]

Robinson believed that Christian communication about the Word of God is a very helpful exercise and can be very fruitful because of the common Spirit by which Christians share a bond (Eph 4:1–7). However, Robinson believed that the fundamental beliefs expressed by the WCC were erroneous concerning the nature of the church and the location of unity. The error of these beliefs became most apparent to Robinson and others as ecumenism materialized in Australia in the formation of the Joint Commission on Church Union.

The Joint Commission on Church Union

In 1957 the Joint Commission on Church Union was established by several different denominations—the Congregational Union of Australia and New Zealand, the Methodist Church of Australia, and the Presbyterian Church of Australia—in order to pursue the union of these different denominations. The Commission produced several key documents, including *The Faith of the Church* (1959) and *The Church: Its Nature, Function and Ordering and Proposed Basis for Union* (1964). These documents detailed theological agreement between the denominations and a rationale for uniting, as well as the means by which unity could be achieved. The end result of the commission was the formation of the Uniting Church in Australia in 1977.

The advent of the Uniting Church raised the profile of ecumenism in Australia, moving beyond abstract ideals to concrete application. With the formation of this union many asked "to what end?" The formularies of the Uniting Church tell of several reasons for pursuing union. First, there is both weakness of faith because of division and division because of weakness.[17] Thus, to bolster faith there is to be the pursuit of unity. This is to be accomplished through the confession of weakness identified as the cause of division. Second, there cannot be faithful proclamation of the gospel to the world and therein evangelism if there is disunity. A church that is divided cannot proclaim justification by faith, as division expresses preference over against identification with the grace that gathers sinners into one family.[18]

---

16. Ibid.
17. Joint Commission on Church Union, *Faith of the Church*, 30.
18. Ibid., 41.

Ecumenism and the Ecclesiologies of Robinson and Knox

Donald Robinson identified the ecumenical movement's discussions of the nature of the church to be one of two leading influences on both his and D. Broughton Knox's ecclesiologies.[19] He noted, "In all this ecumenical discussion large claims were being made for 'the church,' allegedly on the basis of biblical truth, which did not always stand up to exegetical scrutiny."[20] Robinson and Knox asked questions of their own ecclesiologies and of those of the ecumenical movement. For instance, is mission the locus for unity? Does mission belong to the church? Is the church larger than a local gathering? Has Jesus' prayer for unity been waiting for an answer in the form of an ecumenical rallying of the churches of the world? Has there been a failure in mission that can be attributed to ecclesial divisions?

Robinson and Knox sought to be sympathetic with the movement, but ultimately found they arrived at different ecclesiological conclusions from the ecumenists. In an interview with Marcia Cameron in 2002, Donald Robinson commented,

> We thought, particularly in all the ecumenical discussions, that were very active in the 1950s and 1960s—they were building up and giving theological punch to concepts of denominations and concepts of church councils, and they said "This is the Church!" You see, they were transferring biblical assertions about the church "I will build my church" which were quite unjustified. We were trying to get our students to start thinking. . . . In the New Testament you can see that the church at Corinth or the church somewhere else can be the place that God is using, through which he speaks and says "Separate for me Barnabas and Saul." . . . The church itself is not the mission agent. The apostle is the mission agent.[21]

Robinson's critique of the movement demonstrates the impetus for his and Knox's biblical investigations into the nature of the church. It is not to say that they believed the WCC and other ecumenical groups were seeking to be unbiblical in their positions. In fact, Knox praised the WCC gathering for its esteem of the Scriptures as God's authoritative Word. He wrote, "[a] welcomed feature of the discussions was the unanimity among the delegates (many of whom are leading theologians in their churches) in the treatment

---

19. The other influence was the movement for a new church constitution for the Church of England in Australia, discussed in chapter 4 below. See Robinson, "'Church' Revisited," 263–64 (repr.).

20. Ibid., 264.

21. Cameron, *Enigmatic Life*, 153.

of the Bible as the supreme standard on which discussions were to be based. This was no doubt the secret of the spirit of Christian unanimity present in the conference."[22] Although they appreciated the WCC's pursuit of biblical truth, Robinson and Knox believed that the conclusions of the WCC were turgid, ascribing more to the church than was biblically warranted.

Later, we will see that Robinson and Knox both gave priority to the questions raised by the ecumenical movement. In particular, what is the nature of the church? Can the church have a visible expression if it is a global entity? Are denominations churches? Is disunity epitomized in the discord of denominations? Is unity a fundamental property belonging to the church or something for which the church must work? For now, we recognize that the ecumenical movement gave rise to great ecclesiological inquiry across the globe into which context we place the contribution of Robinson and Knox.

---

22. Knox wrote, "A welcomed feature of the discussions was the unanimity among the delegates (many of whom are leading theologians in their churches) in the treatment of the Bible as the supreme standard on which discussions were to be based. This was no doubt the secret of the spirit of Christian unanimity present in the conference." Knox, "Impressions of Lund," 3.

4

The Australian Church Constitution

IN THE TWENTIETH CENTURY Anglicans in Australia sought various constitutional revisions that would grant them a clearer and more defined autonomy from the Church of England.¹ Here we will detail a few of the features of the proposals and the achievement of a national constitution for Anglican churches in Australia, seeking to demonstrate the relevance of the constitution to the development of Robinson and Knox's ecclesiologies. We will see that Knox and Robinson were dissenting voices, advocating a reformed evangelical ecclesiology, in the formulation of a new church constitution and the establishment of the Anglican Church of Australia.²

There were two parties—Evangelicals and Anglo-Catholics—advocating change in the Anglican Church constitution in Australia, both with different agendas.³ The Evangelicals had thought that their links with the Church of England safeguarded their theology, but found themselves disillusioned, as a revision to the Prayer Book—submitted to Parliament in the

---

1. The Church of England in Australia had relative freedom in decision-making previously, with church law being passed in local synods since the 19th century. However, it remained under the ultimate authority of the Church in England. Therefore, "the effect of the constitution was to create a new church. Before the constitution, the various dioceses were part of the Church of England but following its enactment, the dioceses became part of the autocephalous Anglican Church of Australia." See the Anglican Church of Australia, "Constitution."

2. The "new Church" was created in 1962 with the implementation of the new constitution, though it did not assume change from the Church of England in Australia to the Anglican Church of Australia until 1981. Provision for the name change was included in the constitution from its inception (sections 66 & 67).

3. These parties expressed their differences in two prominent periodicals, the *Anglican*, representing much of the Anglo-Catholic party, and the *Australian Church Record*, representing much of the Evangelical party.

1920s—condoned Anglo-Catholic ritual.[4] Though the revised Prayer Book was defeated in Parliament, the threat of encroaching Anglo-Catholic practice caused concern among Evangelicals that their doctrine was no longer safe in the hands of the English Church. On the other hand, Anglo-Catholics felt entitled to certain ritualistic expression and feared that the Evangelicals would prohibit their practices.[5] Thus, the fight for an Australian Anglican identity ensued.

Proposals for change in the constitution began in the 1920s but did not amount to an accepted draft until the 1950s. The "Red Book Case" in 1949 caused a great deal of confusion about the nature of church authority and raised key questions:[6] Who has authority to approve or deny church practice? Can the state courts exercise judicial authority over the churches? Along with the question of authority, once again issues of doctrine and practice came to the fore: What is permissible practice in church services? Is practice decided locally, nationally, or internationally? What doctrine exists at the core of Anglican identity? With so many questions arising, the 1950 General Synod agreed to the drafting of a new constitution. Geoffrey Fisher, archbishop of Canterbury, played a very significant role in securing this decision. Fisher attended the 1950 General Synod, held at a point at which it appeared the draft would be rejected, and preached the opening sermon. In it he urged the Anglicans in Australia to consider seriously a redrawn constitution, seeing it as essential to stabilizing the Anglican Church in Australia.[7] Indeed, Fisher took it upon himself to initiate the process by composing a first draft of the constitution on his journey back to England.[8]

During the last decade of constitutional drafting—the 1950s—there were several significant points of contention that caused concern; it was thought that moving forward with the draft would only produce a *guise* of Anglican unity in Australia, while in reality there were *two* churches. At the heart of the argument remained questions of doctrinal norms and varieties of practice. Regarding doctrine, there was pressure to remove the Thirty-Nine Articles and the 1662 Book of Common Prayer from the Fundamental Declarations section of the constitution. This concerned the Evangelicals, as

---

4. The concern for doctrine was preservation of Reformation doctrine and practice as seen in the 1662 *Book of Common Prayer*, the *Ordinal*, and the *Homilies*.

5. Anglo-Catholic practice gained influence during the 19th century with the rise of Tractarianism.

6. Details of the "Red Book Case" may be found in our chapter on T. C. Hammond's ecclesiology (p. 17 above).

7. Davis, *Constitutions*, 131.

8. Much of Fisher's draft of the constitution remained in the final draft of the constitution.

they saw the fundamental theological basis for their Anglicanism residing precisely in these formularies.[9] Regarding practice, there was pressure to maintain the reservation of the sacrament for the communion of the sick and for prayer for the dead. These practices had been endorsed by some Anglo-Catholics but were of grave concern for Evangelicals who saw them as strange and foreign to biblical Christian ministry, as provided for in the Book of Common Prayer (BCP) and the Ordinal.[10] In the 1955 draft there was compromise. The Anglo-Catholics agreed to remove the reservation of the sacrament from the constitution, and the formularies (Thirty-Nine Articles and BCP) were put back into the constitution, albeit in a later section.

Beyond the primary difficulties of doctrine and practice, there also existed disagreements about the finality of the constitution, the opportunity for revisions, and the nature of the church and church government. Many Evangelicals believed that the new constitution sought the establishment of a kind of coercive authority.[11] If the government of the church was centralized, then the national church could impose standardized doctrine upon all the dioceses, irrespective of their theological and ecclesiastical commitments.[12] It was believed that comprehensiveness would amount to compromise; therefore, it was thought that the only sensible conclusion was the protection of diocesan autonomy.[13] The alternative, the legislative protection of diocesan autonomy, only validated the concerns of some about legitimizing continuing division amongst Australian Anglicans.

Amongst Sydney Evangelicals there was difference of opinion about the constitution. On the one hand, T. C. Hammond endorsed the constitutional revisions, working on behalf of Archbishop Howard Mowll. Hammond believed that the concessions of the draft from both the Anglo-Catholics and Evangelicals were as good as they would get. He also believed that this was the last chance that he would have—after many years of hard work—to secure the draft. Indeed, Hammond died in 1960 shortly after the constitution was approved in 1957, but before it took effect in 1962.

On the other hand, younger Evangelicals like Donald Robinson and D. Broughton Knox stood against Hammond and those who advocated acceptance of the constitution.[14] Both Robinson and Knox believed that

---

9. Davis, *Constitutions*, 138, 148–50.
10. Ibid., 146–48.
11. Knox, "Government by Consent," 2.
12. See Knox, "Safeguard Not Adequate," 7.
13. [DBK], "Undefined Comprehensiveness," 2.
14. For a listing of *ACR* articles and editorials from Robinson and Knox, see our ch. 2, n16.

the constitution conceded too much and would ultimately amount to the demise of evangelical theology amongst Australian Anglicans. In particular, they detailed "Four Fatal Flaws in the Draft Constitution" in an article for the *Australian Church Record*:[15]

1. The doctrines of the 39 Articles had been removed from first section and placed later in section 4. This is representative of a diminishment of authority of the articles in governing doctrine. This would allow for the doctrine of the 39 articles to be ignored or side-stepped, thus reneging Reformation doctrines. In fact, if there was a three-quarters majority of the dioceses, the articles can be removed altogether.

2. The Queen's court would no longer be allowed to interpret laws of the church. This interpretation would be reserved exclusively for the Appellate Tribunal.

3. The authority of the bishops was increased to an unbiblical position. The inside cover of the constitutional document read, "the authentic decision" "in matters of faith" is "given by the whole body of bishops."

4. The church removed uniformity of worship allowing each diocese to determine which prayer book to use for worship. Therefore, illegal "Anglo-Catholic" practices (i.e., ringing of sanctus bell, incense, mass vestments) could be authorized.

In all of these matters, Knox believed that "the draft radically alters the character of the church, away from the Reformation, in a medieval direction."[16] Ultimately, Knox and Robinson, along with others who shared their concerns, protested the new constitution for fear of the loss of Reformation doctrine. They believed that a new church under a new constitution was unnecessary at best and most likely to be undesirable, especially as it appeared to represent an abandonment of doctrinal foundations.

Ultimately, a complete draft constitution was agreed upon at General Synod in 1955. A major factor in the approval of this draft was the endorsement of T. C. Hammond, which won the support of many Evangelicals.[17] By 1957 all of the dioceses of Australia had approved the draft at their local synods. The new constitution was instated in 1962. One contributor to the *ACR* said,

> This constitution is an awkward compromise between groups which intend to remain divided on fundamental questions of

15. [DBK], "Four Fatal Flaws," 8.
16. Ibid.
17. Davis, *Constitutions*, 131–32.

doctrine and worship, regardless of whether it is adopted. The Anglo-Catholic group desire a power of change consistent only with the retention of basic Christian doctrine. The evangelical group desire to restrict the power of change to preserve the Reformation formularies. The complexities of the draft show that it was negotiated predominantly with reference to these conflicting ideas of change.[18]

The constitution represented a great compromise between two parties who seemed determined to disagree. Therefore, its passage did not mean that it enjoyed universal support. The younger generation of Evangelicals complained that the draft was approved by the older generation, who would not have to live under the new regulations. While relative peace and unity seemed to exist at the inception of the constitution and the Anglican Church of Australia, the younger generation feared it would not last.

An expression of the younger generation's rejection of the constitution surfaced in November 1960. After Mowll and Hammond died (in 1958 and 1960, respectively), Broughton Knox, principal of Moore College, and Donald Robinson, vice-principal of Moore, along with J. R. L. Johnstone and K. N. Shelley—members of the diocesan Standing Committee—wrote to the attorney general with regard to the preparation of the Constitution Act for state parliament. They sought to delay the process and ultimately have the constitution modified. They detailed their theological objections, along with legal concerns about institutional oversight, regarding the formation of a "new church." The archbishop of Sydney, Hugh Gough, responded to these men with a letter expressing his disappointment in their "going behind his back," and his consequent "distrust" of them. They tried to defend themselves in responding letters, but could not make themselves understood.[19] Ultimately, divided opinions remained as the new constitution was instituted. Concerns for unity were addressed at the first General Synod of the new church in 1962. At that Synod one of the first items of discussion was Prayer Book Revision. This set in motion a project that ultimately resulted in *An Australian Prayer Book* (1978).

Ecclesiology was not at the fore in conversations concerning a new church constitution, but ecclesiological *concerns* were. As a new church emerged, questions were asked about the nature of the church, in particular

---

18. P. W. Henderson quoted in *ACR* (19 July 1956) 7; as cited in Davis, *Constitutions*, 160.

19. Davis, *Constitutions*, 162–63. For further information regarding Gough's response, see Loane, *Men to Remember*, 82.

what the church is and where it is to be found.[20] Australians were seeking autonomy from England, but should they, they wondered, seek relative autonomy from *one another*? If so, should autonomy extend to dioceses or to local churches? Thus, coinciding with questions pertaining to the place of the church were questions about power. How and where should authority be expressed in the church? In all of these queries, we can see that a great concern in the reconstitution of the Anglican Church of Australia was ecclesiology.

As we look to the ecclesiology of Donald Robinson and D. Broughton Knox, we can discern certain developments in their thinking in and through the constitutional debates of the 1950s. In particular, we can see that both Robinson and Knox had established themselves in reformed evangelical doctrine and practice at the time. But as we will see later, most of their ecclesiological writings, especially those that seem to move beyond (but not away from) classic Protestant ecclesiology, took place *after* 1962. Therefore, we might conclude the following: Robinson and Knox focused their ecclesiologies on traditional reformed Anglican doctrines during the development of the new constitution. After the constitution was instated, they moved towards further developments in their own theologies about the nature of the church, without necessarily abandoning the principles they discerned in evangelical Anglicanism.[21] In one sense, the battle—*their* battle—was lost. With the constitution now in place, and there being less opportunity to press hard for an embedding of reformed evangelical doctrine in the Australia-wide body, Knox and Robinson now had nothing to lose in ecclesiological exploration. Thus, in the 1950s they had fought for local diocesan autonomy.[22] Eventually, however, they went further and defined the church as a gathering in a particular locality—the congregation. They also further developed their beliefs about the nature of authority in the church, built upon their theology of the place and time of the church. A sympathetic reading of their thought might still recognize even here a resonance with the Reformation: just as Martin Luther was freed to more radical questioning of Roman Catholic doctrine after being anathematized by the Pope Leo X in 1521, so too Knox and Robinson enjoyed a new freedom of ecclesiological inquiry after the enactment of the new Anglican constitution.

---

20. These questions are evidenced in Robinson and Knox, "Contradictory Principles," 2.

21. We will see later that both Knox and Robinson held the Thirty-Nine Articles in high esteem throughout their ministries.

22. In 1955 Knox wrote, "The ideal of one voice speaking for the whole Church continent-wide, or world-wide, is attractive to many minds. It is the papal ideal. But a truer Christian ideal is local autonomy, with a General Synod to speak nation-wide on those points on which the Church is unanimous." [DBK], "Government by Consent," 2.

SECTION II

Donald William Bradley Robinson

5

The Ecclesiology of Donald Robinson

THIS CHAPTER SEEKS TO present the ecclesiology of Donald W. B. Robinson in an analytical and descriptive manner. As a presentation of his thought, and in an attempt to hear him in his own words, this chapter will present Robinson's thought from his own pen where appropriate. This will entail longer quotes where necessary to capture the essence of his theology. The aim of this chapter is to draw ecclesiological threads together from the many pieces Robinson authored throughout his ministry. In order to properly understand his thought, some attention will be given to his life and his interlocutors. Evaluation will be reserved for chapter 6.

The presentation of Robinson's ecclesiology will progress as follows: First, we will consider briefly those elements in his background that may have contributed to the development of his ecclesiology; second, we will attend to Robinson's chief ecclesiological interlocutors; third, we will outline his methodology in ecclesiology, namely a particular construal of biblical theology; fourth, we will examine key areas in his ecclesiology related to the nature of the church; finally, we will draw conclusions from the analysis and anticipate issues for evaluation in the final chapter.

DONALD W. B. ROBINSON[1]

Donald William Bradley Robinson was born on November 9, 1922. His father, the Reverend Richard Bradley Robinson, was rector of the Anglican

---

1. There has been very little biographical information published on Robinson. The best available may be found in these articles: Thompson, "Donald William Bradley

parish of Lithgow on the outskirts of the Sydney Diocese, and was later to become archdeacon and honorary canon of the St Andrew's Cathedral. Donald Robinson was raised in a home dedicated to evangelical ministry. As a young boy he participated in the Crusader Union at school and later participated in the Evangelical Union at the University of Sydney. It was this upbringing in his home, and these further influences in the student unions, which nurtured Robinson's deep evangelical theological convictions.

Robinson's higher education focused on the disciplines of linguistics and New Testament. He graduated from the University of Sydney with a BA in classics, having worked closely with G. P. Shipp, a philologist with a particular focus on semantic studies. After graduating from Sydney, Robinson travelled to the University of Cambridge to read for the Theological Tripos at Queens' College. There he was supervised by C. F. D. Moule. It was Moule who taught him to value linguistic details in exegesis. Robinson was also instructed by others steeped in the Cambridge exegetical tradition. C. H. Dodd's New Testament seminar taught Robinson to examine the biblical narrative in terms of the theme of "promise and fulfillment."[2]

During his final year at Cambridge, C. H. Dodd taught the special New Testament doctrine, which for that year was "the church." Robinson attended this seminar with several scholars whom he would later engage, including R. Newton Flew and J. Y. Campbell. Robinson admits that he was at first disappointed by the subject matter. He writes, "I had hoped for the opportunity to study a New Testament doctrine closer to the heart of my evangelical priorities. But 'the church' it was, and I began to read around the subject."[3] During the course of this seminar Robinson began to apply his linguistic skills to ecclesiology and to draw conclusions that were further explicated in his academic career at Moore College.

After completing his theological education at Cambridge in 1950, Donald Robinson returned to Australia where Archbishop Howard Mowll ordained him. He served two brief curacies before he was appointed as lecturer in Old Testament at Moore Theological College in 1952. Initially he lectured part time while continuing to serve as principal T. C. Hammond's curate at St Philip's, York Street. By 1954 he became a full-time lecturer in New Testament, as well as teaching Prayer Book and Liturgiology. His expertise was broad, as he had knowledge of both Greek and Hebrew, and he possessed a particular interest in the relationship of the Testaments, which allowed him a wide range of suitable teaching opportunities.

Robinson"; Cameron, "Donald William Bradley Robinson: An Appreciation."

2. Robinson, "'Church' Revisited," 261.

3. Ibid., 260.

It was during his years of lecturing at Moore College that Robinson developed most of his ecclesiology.[4] His first lectures in exegesis, on the book of Acts, largely focused on Luke's use of the word *ekklēsia*. Later, he taught a special doctrine course on ecclesiology. This course examined the development of ecclesiology in the biblical canon, particularly examining how promise and fulfillment—even covenant—provided greater clarity to a biblical theology of the church. Though Robinson did not ultimately settle on a covenantal view of the church, his teaching explored how these covenantal themes applied to the church, recognizing the place of the church in the greater scheme of God's purposes for redeeming the elect.[5]

In 1959, D. Broughton Knox was appointed principal of Moore College, succeeding Marcus Loane who had become an assistant bishop in the Diocese of Sydney. Knox appointed Robinson as his vice-principal. Robinson continued teaching full time at Moore until 1973 when he left to serve as bishop of Parramatta. He continued to teach part time during his years at Parramatta, but the ministry demanded much of his time and slowed his academic career significantly. In 1982, Robinson was elected archbishop of Sydney, a position he held until retirement in 1993.

Robinson encountered several ecclesial issues during his tenure at Moore College and his episcopal ministry that demanded practical ecclesiological assessment and evaluation. Chief among these ecclesial issues were the ecumenical movement and the need for a new constitution for the Church of England in Australia.[6] Robinson comments on the significance of these events and their impact on the development of his ecclesiology:

> What precipitated the attempt of some of us in Sydney not only to define "the church" more accurately in the 1950s but also to "go public" was not any sort of interest in promoting a polity of congregational independency, or a desire for particular congregations to develop their own characteristics, such as appeared in the wake of experimentation in liturgical revision in the mid-1960s. It was rather the challenge of two ecclesiastical activities: the ecumenical movement, and the movement for a new constitution for the Church of England in Australia. The nature of the church, and "the nature of the unity we seek," dominated the establishment of the World Council of Churches in 1948 and the two subsequent General Assemblies at Evanston, 1954 and New

---

4. Ibid., 262–70.

5. This distinction will be examined further below in the section on Robinson's interlocutors.

6. These have been examined in greater detail in chapters 3 and 4 (respectively), but are worth revisiting here briefly once more.

Delhi, 1961. The first (and so far the only) National Conference of Australian Churches met in Melbourne in February 1960. . . . In all this ecumenical discussion claims were being made for "the church," allegedly on the basis of biblical truth, which did not always stand up to exegetical scrutiny.[7]

As these two ecclesiastical activities unfolded, Robinson drew upon what he had learnt at Cambridge and forged a biblical theology of the church in conversation with others.

INFLUENCES AND INTERLOCUTORS

Having examined the movements within Donald Robinson's life that contributed to his scholarship, we now turn to examine the influences on his thinking from within the academy. Here as elsewhere, an important source is an autobiographical article that Robinson submitted to the *Reformed Theological Review* tracing his own recollection of the development of his ecclesiology.[8] In this article he identified numerous scholars, publications and movements that contributed to his own thought. The following is a summary of that intellectual trajectory with detail given to each of the sources Robinson engaged.

Linguistic Influences and Interlocutors

Robinson's study began at the University of Sydney under the tutelage of G. P. Shipp, whose philological studies taught Robinson to reflect carefully on semantics, not just as they developed over time (Shipp's particular interest) but also as they differed and developed between authors and texts.[9] He reflected on his learning,

> From Shipp I learned a little about how to assess the actual semantic value of words as they are used by individual writers and in particular contexts, without simply importing a dictionary meaning into them with a heavy hand. . . . I began, in my theological studies, to discover that many commentators and theologians tended to read more into the meanings of words than either context or usage warranted, and did not allow for

---

7. Robinson, "'Church' Revisited," 263–64.
8. Ibid., 259–71.
9. Another, later but significant, voice in Sydney discussions on ecclesiology was William Dumbrell who also studied under Shipp. Dumbrell, *Meaning and Use.*

subtle changes of meaning of words from one writer to another or even from one context to another in the same writer.[10]

Robinson applied this careful and contextual semantic examination to his study of *ekklēsia* throughout the canon, both in the New Testament and the LXX. This study provided an important foundation for his ecclesiological conclusions, as he ultimately understood the theological and conceptual parameters of the church to be determined by the linguistic parameters of *ekklēsia*.

Several scholars aided Robinson in his thinking on the semantic value of *ekklēsia*. F. J. A. Hort's *Christian Ecclesia* is the book that Robinson claims "undoubtedly set the lines of my study."[11] The first page of this text declared, "The English term *church*, now the most familiar representative of *ecclesia* to most of us, carries with it associations derived from the institutions and doctrines of later times, and thus cannot at present without a mental effort be made to convey the full and exact force which originally belonged to *ecclesia*."[12] Hort examined the historical development of the term, and indeed the concept of, *ekklēsia* in the canon. He began with an overview of its use in the Old Testament, examining the LXX use of *ekklēsia* against the Hebrew correlate *qāhāl*. Hort also took notice of the alternative words employed for congregation, *synagōgē* in the LXX and *ēdâh* in the Hebrew text. He noticed a distinction of usage between *ekklēsia*/*qāhāl* as exclusively descriptive of a human gathering and *synagōgē*/*ēdâh* which is often descriptive of a gathering, but also used to describe the Israelite people as whole, particularly as their representative heads gathered.[13] He then moved to consider the development of thought around *ekklēsia* throughout the New Testament, with particular emphasis on the developments in the early church in the Epistles. His conclusions slightly vary from those eventually reached by Robinson, particularly with regard to the singularity of the church on earth. Hort concluded that later usage of *ekklēsia* in the New Testament is used to describe more of the new society that had been created in Christ, the singular church on earth, than exclusively describing singular (local) congregations.[14] Robinson would not deny this broader use, but did not understand this as a description of an earthly reality; rather he believed this

10. Robinson, "'Church' Revisited," 261–62.

11. Ibid., 260.

12. Hort, *Christian Ecclesia*, 1.

13. Ibid., 5.

14. For example, Hort says, "It is a serious misunderstanding of these Epistles to suppose, as is sometimes done, that the Ecclesia here spoken of is an Ecclesia wholly in the heavens, not formed of human beings [on earth]." Ibid., 148.

broader use described the heavenly and eschatological gathering. While arriving at different conclusions, Hort's methodology had a significant influence on the way that Robinson later examined the use of *ekklēsia*, namely in seeking to discern the meaning of the word from context.

Other members of the conversation at Cambridge included R. Newton Flew and J. Y. Campbell.[15] Flew had published *Jesus and His Church*, which argued that the church was the new People of God, true Israel. He wrote, "The Ecclesia of God is the People of God, with a continuous life which goes back through the history of Israel, through Prophets and martyrs of old, to the call of God to Abraham; it is traced back farther still to the purpose of God before the world began. The origin of the Ecclesia lies in the will of God. All that Israel had from God the Church has through Christ."[16] This position might be likened to what is today known as the supersessionist view, in which the church now replaces ancient Israel as the new Israel of God and inherits all of her privileges.[17] Robinson disagreed with Flew's conclusions, seeing Israel still maintaining a distinct identity from the church. His basis for maintaining that distinction was the clear presence of both Jew and Gentile evidenced in the New Testament, especially in the two apostleships (Peter's Jewish apostleship, Paul's Gentile apostleship).[18]

Differing from Flew, and originally published ten years later, Campbell's article "The Origin and Meaning of the Christian Use of the Word ΕΚΚΛΗΣΙΑ,"[19] drew the conclusion that there is no textual support for the *ekklēsia* being representative of or synonymous with the Israel of God. Campbell wrote, "There is no good evidence for the generally accepted view that in using the word ἐκκλησία [*ekklēsia*] the early Christians were borrowing an Old Testament term in order to express their claim to be the true people of God, the legitimate successor of the Israel of the Old Covenant."[20]

---

15. Robinson also cites K. L. Schmidt as an interlocutor for his readings of Flew and Campbell. See Schmidt, "ἐκκλησία." There is no apparent influence that Robinson expressed regarding Schmidt's work, other than Schmidt's value of discerning *the* particular meaning for ἐκκλησία. Robinson expressed his own concern of Schmidt (and others practicing "Biblical Theology") to find a singular meaning for a word, at the expense of understanding how the word was used and developed throughout the biblical canon. See Robinson, "'Church' Revisited," 261.

16. Ibid., 253–54.

17. Vlach, *Has the Church Replaced Israel?*

18. See Robinson, "Distinction between Jewish and Gentile," 133 (repr.). Here Robinson describes the "two ministries, one gospel." Robinson believed that these two ministries ultimately produced two types of churches, Jewish and Gentile.

19. Campbell, "Origin and Meaning," 41–54 (repr.).

20. Ibid., 54.

Robinson sided with Campbell's conclusion, against Flew, that the church did not replace (supersede) Israel.

It is worth taking notice of the extent of Campbell's influence on Robinson. In his autobiographical piece Robinson mentions Campbell but does not specify the extent of his influence.[21] Upon investigation, it is clear that the conclusions drawn in Campbell's article are fundamental to Robinson's ecclesiology, as will be argued later in this study. Campbell effectively carried out the semantic studies that Robinson himself would conduct during his ministry. For instance, Campbell wrote, "In ordinary Greek . . . ἐκκλησία [ekklēsia] means a single meeting; when the meeting breaks up, that particular ἐκκλησία [ekklēsia] ceases to exist. This is also true of the *qahal* in the Old Testament generally."[22] Campbell supported this thesis through detailed linguistic work exposing the usage of *ekklēsia* throughout the canon. Following his conclusion, he pressed the opposing view to demonstrate its lack of coherence:

> The actual use of the word ἐκκλησία [ekklēsia] in the New Testament affords no support to the view that it expressed the Christians' claim to be the true people of God. If it did, it would follow at once that its primary application must have been to the Christian community as a whole (*die Gesamtkirche*), and its application to particular local "churches" must have been a secondary development. But in fact the word is used in the New Testament much more often of the local community than of the Church as a whole.[23]

This conclusion is very similar to that to which Robinson later arrived in his study. It is undeniable that Campbell had a significant influence on Robinson. However, the extent to which Campbell's linguistic study coincided with Robinson's own conclusions, and how much Robinson depended on Campbell for in his own linguistic study, is undetermined.

Alongside Campbell's investigation into the origins and meaning of *ekklēsia*, Robinson found insight through the work of his friend Edwin Judge. Judge published "Contemporary Political Models for the Interrelations of the New Testament Churches" in the *Reformed Theological Review* of October 1963. The standout contribution of this article to Robinson's

---

21. This may be because of the nature of Hort's work, which accomplished similar things to Campbell's. Robinson has explicitly stated that Hort had a great impact on the direction of his thought. Campbell may have simply confirmed conclusions at which Robinson had already arrived.

22. Campbell, "Christian Use of the Word ΕΚΚΛΗΣΙΑ," 49.

23. Ibid., 50–51.

thinking was a careful examination of the relationship of a general Church concept to the local church. Judge wrote, "We should . . . expect to find that everything that can be said about the *ecclesia*, can be said equally and fully of each *ecclesia*, and that there will be no other way of using the term, except by deliberate and conscious extension of the self-evident meaning."[24] Judge continues,

> We must ask whether even the most all-embracing claims made by St. Paul for the church are not being made with nothing more in mind than the church he happens to be addressing, and of course, each other of the multiplicity of churches in its turn. Or, to put the matter positively, we should expect quite plain verbal indications before accepting the view that he has at any point translated the term from its concrete sense to some supernal parallel.[25]

Robinson, like Judge, would question the application of *ekklēsia* to any broader, or supernal, reality than the local church because of the regular employment of the term for a local reality. Judge's understanding provided Robinson with a robust conception of the local church, recognizing the full expression of the church in the local church.

Finally, Robinson engaged K. L. Schmidt's article on *ekklēsia* in *Theological Dictionary of the New Testament* as an interlocutor for the work of Hort and Campbell. Like the other authors, Schmidt believed that it was imperative to understand the full scope of how *ekklēsia* functioned throughout the Bible.

Methodological Influences and Interlocutors

Methodologically Robinson's influences were scholars who sought to understand the Bible as a whole. This school of thought cares for thematic developments within the canon, especially in what can be identified as "promise and fulfillment,"[26] and is best known as "biblical theology."[27] The

---

24. Ibid., 74.
25. Ibid., 75.
26. Robinson, "'Church' Revisited," 263.

27. This is not the same biblical theology that came under scrutiny by James Barr in the mid-twentieth century. That sort of scholarship ascribed a limited theological meaning to particular words, most clearly evidenced in the volumes edited by Gerhard Kittel. While Robinson would face accusation of this sort of semantic fallacy by Kevin Giles, Robinson easily refuted this sort of accusation by clear demonstration of his method, as will be demonstrated later in this chapter.

most potent influences on Robinson's thought in this area included R. Newton Flew, C. H. Dodd and Gabriel Hebert. Robinson understood this biblical-theological method as a complement to, or companion of, sound exegesis. Proper exegesis requires contextual and ultimately canonical location, leading to intertextual dialogue. Robinson took note of the continuity of the Bible's message, with special emphasis on its soteriological purposes.[28] Robinson presented a scheme for biblical theology that was later popularized by Graeme Goldsworthy.[29] At its heart was the recognition of a threefold vision of Scripture. Robinson wrote,

> We enunciated a biblical "typology" using the three stages in the outworking of God's promise to Abraham, that is, (a) the historical experience of the fulfilment of God's promise to Abraham through the exodus to the kingdom of David's son in the land of inheritance, (b) the projection of this fulfilment into the future day of the Lord, by the prophets, during the period of decline, fall, exile and return, and (c) the true fulfilment in Christ and the Spirit in Jesus' incarnation, death, resurrection, exaltation and in his parousia as judge and saviour in a new heaven and new earth.[30]

Robinson recognized that Dispensationalists also divided the Bible according to perceived epochs, though he did not interact with Dispensational scholars in the development of his own scheme, nor did he arrive at the same conclusions.[31]

Robinson discovered that Gabriel Hebert, an Anglican monk in South Australia, had developed a similar threefold division of Scripture. In his

---

28. Robinson's soteriological emphases in the narrative of the canon were not necessarily the same as what some scholars have called *Heilsgeschichte*, though loosely this term might encompass the focus of Robinson's work. *Heilsgeschichte*, literally "salvation history," has caused confusion and debate over the past century. There has been a divide amongst scholars about the reliability and place of history in these studies. Therefore, it is best not to ascribe this term to what Robinson was concerned with in his studies. It is better to think about *biblical theology* as a general overarching term for Robinson's position. Biblical theology, as method, can certainly be applied to different systems of theology, but never being far from the way these systems interact with God's soteriological purposes.

29. Graeme Goldsworthy has written several volumes on biblical theology that have implemented and popularized Robinson's schema, for example: *Gospel and Kingdom* and *According to Plan*. In his recent volume, *Christ-Centered Biblical Theology*, Goldsworthy expresses his indebtedness to Robinson for his own biblical-theological method (see the dedication and pp. 19–26).

30. Robinson, "Origins and Unresolved Tensions," 9.

31. Ibid., 9–10.

autobiographical piece, he did not recall any direct influence of Hebert on his own scheme, but noticed the similarities after his scheme was formulated.[32] He acknowledged that there was an ongoing friendship with Hebert throughout his career, in which many theological and methodological issues were discussed constructively. In their dialogue about method, Robinson recognized particular congeniality in Hebert's typology. Both understood true biblical types to be those that occur throughout each of the three dispensations of the biblical narrative.[33]

Theological Influences and Interlocutors

Donald Robinson is an exegete, linguist and biblical theologian. He is not, and never presented himself to be, a systematic theologian. His academic interests involved how the Bible uses language to develop themes and how these themes are understood in context of the canon. Of his own theological education, he said,

> I went to England banging the drum for the IVF [InterVarsity Fellowship] basis of belief and I was taught exegesis and I didn't go to any theology lectures—there weren't any! You did that in other courses, but not the Tripos. You did Old Testament—a limited amount of that. The theory was if you knew a certain part of the Old Testament or New Testament very well, you could work out the rest of it for yourself.[34]

Despite his lack of a more specifically theological education, Robinson did engage with systematic theologians during his career. Special mention should be made of Karl Barth and J. I. Packer.

Robinson encountered Barth's ecclesiology through the latter's essay for the 1948 World Council of Churches.[35] Barth's recognition of the activity bound up in the concept of church provided added stimulus to Robinson's developing thought. Barth made use of the linguistic considerations that Robinson had observed in his own study. Barth wrote, "The Church is neither the invisible fellowship, nor the visible community, of all those who believe in Christ; nor is it a monarchial, aristocratic, or democratic form of the

---

32. Robinson writes, "It is not easy for me to trace any direct influence of his [Hebert's] views on the contents of our course [at Moore College], although, as I shall show, we had a close affinity in one important feature of our hermeneutical principles." Ibid., 4.

33. Ibid., 10–11.

34. Donald Robinson cited in an interview dated 25 February 2002 in Cameron, *Enigmatic Life*, 137.

35. Barth, "Living Congregation."

latter. The Church is the 'event' in which two or three are gathered together in the name of Christ. . . . The primary, normal, and visible form of this event is the *local congregation*."[36] Robinson had found support for his thesis from a respected systematic theologian. The conclusions that Robinson had arrived at linguistically, Barth had reached theologically.

Robinson's other theological interlocutor of mention was his friend J. I. Packer. Throughout their teaching ministries Packer and Robinson corresponded via post, discussing a potential writing project to address liturgical revisions. Robinson mentions Packer's theological influence at the juncture of systematic and biblical theology, namely Packer's covenant theology.[37] Though Robinson's biblical theology did not fully endorse the traditional covenant theology schema, to which Packer subscribed,[38] he benefited from Packer's theological insight. He wrote,

> [Packer's covenant theology] gave me the necessary framework in which to integrate my thinking and the fruits of earlier reading. "The church" as such was subsumed under the wider theme of God's creative purpose for Adam, his promise to Abraham and his seed, the elect people of Israel and the promise to the nations beyond and through Israel. "Covenant" proved less comprehensive than I had at first thought; I came to see it rather as a means of conveying (and appropriating) a promise, promise being the primary concept.[39]

Robinson recognized the value of "covenant theology" especially as it helped to highlight the nature of promise and fulfillment in the Bible. Covenant served to situate his understanding of the metanarrative of the canon, but remained a subset of this narrative rather than its primary principle.

Friends and Acquaintances

A final category of interlocutors for Robinson's ecclesiological developments is the group of friends and acquaintances with whom he had regular

---

36. Ibid., 73.

37. Robinson writes, "I was stimulated by an article of Jim Packer on the place of 'covenant' in the overall theme of Scripture. I cannot now recall where this article appeared, but both Broughton Knox and I knew Jim Packer, and I remember our discussing his article and our agreeing on its importance." Robinson, "'Church' Revisited," 262–63.

38. Robinson found particular disagreement with the ecclesiological tenet of covenant theology that understood the church as the new Israel. Ibid., 263.

39. Ibid.

interaction. Many of the names previously mentioned could be repeated in this category. Here we draw attention to those not already identified.

There were several friends with whom Robinson discussed theology during and after his time at Cambridge. Alan Cole and Robinson knew each other before Robinson's studies at Cambridge, but their friendship and conversations deepened during Cole's visits to Cambridge while Robinson was a student.[40] Both had a particular interest in ecclesiology and eventually wrote on the subject, though approaching differing topics within the discipline.[41] Cole's approach to ecclesiology involved engagement with independent metaphors for the church. This was not to deny the multitude of metaphors for the church, but rather to examine major biblical images for the church and build an ecclesiology through those lenses. In reading both of their studies it is clear that Cole and Robinson arrived at different conclusions, especially with regard to the nature and location of the church, denominations and unity.[42] Neither scholar directly engages the other's work in his own ecclesiological work.

Robinson also became acquainted with Alan Stibbs while in the UK. Stibbs was one of the leaders of the evangelical resurgence in the UK in the mid-twentieth century and authored two small though influential books on ecclesiology.[43] Stibbs and Robinson found great agreement on the nature of the church. Stibbs wrote,

> To sum up the two sides of our Lord's teaching about the church, we may say, on the one hand, that the one great church of God exists invisibly in the heavenly places. It is to Christians an object of faith, not of sight. On the other hand, the only thing that exists visibly in the world as an earthly counterpart to this heavenly fellowship is the local churches, the meeting together in many places of those who profess the faith of Christ.[44]

40. Ibid., 262.

41. For instance, Cole authored *The Body of Christ: A New Testament Image of the Church* and *The New Temple: A Study in the Origins of Catechetical "Form" of the Church in the New Testament*.

42. In summary, Cole believed that the church had an extended presence on earth beyond a local reality. He also had hope that there would be a reunion of the church that is currently divided in the world. This reunion he believed would be a spiritual reunion, rather than an institutional one. For more on Cole's position see Cole, *The Body of Christ*. Robinson, on the other hand (as will be evidenced in this chapter) did not believe there was a church on earth beyond the local reality gathered. He believed that efforts for church unity on earth were frivolous as the church is a united reality as the body of Christ, and this united reality is ultimately gathered in the heavenly places.

43. Stibbs, *God's Church*; Stibbs, *Church Universal and Local*.

44. Stibbs, "New Testament Teaching," 234 (repr.).

Like Robinson, he concluded that the visible church on earth is exclusively a local reality, and conversely the invisible church is exclusively a heavenly reality. These conclusions on the nature of the church led Stibbs, like Robinson, to find the notion of an ecumenical earthly church unbiblical. He wrote,

> There is . . . no scriptural ground for looking for the emergence of one ecumenical or worldwide church as a visible earthly organization, having like an earthly empire a geographical centre and a human head. The great invisible church's one mother-city is the heavenly Zion, not Rome, nor Canterbury, nor Geneva. The great invisible church's one Head is Christ Himself, not some human pope or primate or moderator.[45]

Though Robinson and Stibbs were friends and found clear agreement on the nature of the church—conclusions that are seemingly unique in Anglican circles—there is virtually no engagement with the other in either of their writings.

The most significant relationship in Robinson's ecclesiological development was his friendship with D. Broughton Knox. Indeed, though not mentioned above, Knox was the greatest theological influence on Robinson. This friendship occurred in and around Moore Theological College. The two had offices on the same hall and were often found in each other's company discussing theological concepts, especially ecclesiology. They also worked together to author editorials and articles for the *Australian Church Record* during the 1950s. Knox and Robinson worked so closely on the doctrine of the church that it became common to identify their thinking about the church collectively as the "Knox-Robinson Model of Church."[46] However, Robinson has insisted that though the coupling was prevalent, this grouping of their thinking is actually a misnomer as they had differing views on the matter and approached the topic from different directions.[47] Though they may have differed in their views, and we shall investigate this further in a later chapter, there is no denying that Knox and Robinson had a significant impact on one another's ecclesiological development.[48] While

---

45. Ibid., 235.

46. One of the tasks of this book is to determine if there is indeed an appropriate synthesis of their thought, or an ecclesiological model to be identified. This will be addressed in the conclusion. The comment here is not a premature evaluation, but rather recognition of common perception.

47. Cameron, *Enigmatic Life*, 152.

48. Cameron assesses, "Donald Robinson's sharp mind, engaging lectures and stimulating approach was a great asset to the college. He and Broughton Knox were excellent foils, Broughton tossing ideas to Donald and Donald assessing them in terms

analyzing Robinson's ecclesiology in this chapter, we will leave attention to a detailed analysis of Knox's ecclesiology to a later chapter.

METHODOLOGY

Biblical Theology

We turn now to consider Robinson's preferred method for unfolding ecclesiology: biblical theology. As a biblical scholar, Robinson cared most about how theological themes developed in the narrative of the canon. As we have already noted, Robinson identified a threefold scheme for the progression of the biblical narrative. The overarching dynamic he observed within the canon was one of promise and fulfillment. With this overview in mind, Robinson developed his thinking on the doctrine of the church, examining the movements of God to gather a particular people to himself.

Robinson did not simply superimpose this biblical-theological scheme on his ecclesiology as a hermeneutical framework. Rather, his biblical-theological approach developed in tandem with his ecclesiology. It was Robinson's investigation into the concept of God gathering people to himself that sent him searching the Scriptures, seeking to identify a coherent movement of God amongst his people. What Robinson discovered in the process was a recurring pattern in the biblical canon: the metanarrative of the Old and New Testaments was the story of God's engagement with humanity. Before creation God set forth soteriological purposes for humanity. These purposes were initially presented in the form of promise, namely the promise given to Abraham and his descendants, ultimately finding fulfillment in the person of Jesus Christ. This fulfillment gathers not just the Hebrew people, but also the nations, to God. This fulfillment in Christ brings hope to the nations and will ultimately be realized at the eschaton.

The method of biblical theology, identifying unfolding continuities and discontinuities, may be applied to any theme represented in the canon. The discipline seeks to understand how themes are developed through the movements of God in his interaction with his people. For instance, in ecclesiology, how has the theme of "gathering" developed in the canon? This stands in distinction to biblical studies (or actually the "biblical theology" movement which did much the same) that have traditionally understood themes or concepts within particular books, authors or genres. It also stands in distinction to systematic theology that seeks to tie together common

---

of scholarly, meticulous exegesis. Donald's mind was iron to sharpen Broughton's iron. In him Broughton had an intellectual equal." Ibid., 137.

threads from the canon to present a normative account. Biblical theology seeks to examine concepts across the canon and present conclusions in relationship to the metanarrative of God's soteriological work. Robinson recognized that God does not redeem people to a vacuum of purpose. Instead, God redeems people to fellowship *with* himself. Ecclesiology is intrinsic to the soteriological purposes of God. God saves people in order to gather them to himself, as is evidenced in the biblical narrative of God's actions towards his people. At the heart of this "salvation history" is the person and work of Jesus Christ. It is towards Jesus that all of God's promises look, and it is in Jesus that all of God's promises find their fulfillment.

Ecclesiology was, therefore, integral to Robinson's hermeneutic not just historically (they arose together in his thought) but conceptually. He understood the church to be central in the biblical narrative, particularly as ecclesiology cannot be divorced from Christology. If Christ is the hermeneutical key, featuring as the centerpiece of Scripture, to whom all Scripture points and through whom all Scripture is properly understood, then those "in Christ" are not far from the center. Robinson wrote,

> The New Testament recognizes, therefore, two levels of fulfilment for Old Testament prophetic anticipation—in Christ and in His Church. But these are perhaps not two levels at all for the Church is "in Christ," its members are all baptised "into Christ" (Romans 6; Gal. 3:27). It is in Christ and His Church that "the manifold wisdom of God" in saving a people for Himself is fully displayed before men (Eph. 3:1–12).[49]

This biblical-theological observation elevates ecclesiology to a position of systematic prominence in Robinson's thought. Ecclesiology is not a secondary doctrine. To understand Christology properly, and the entire narrative of the biblical canon (with Christ at its center), one must understand the church which is "in Christ." The person and work of Christ go hand in hand. And the work of Christ—redeeming a particular people—then becomes integral to the person of Christ, as those redeemed—believers, who gather—effectively become "in Christ."

Semantic Study of *Ekklēsia*

A key feature of Robinson's ecclesiology is his semantic study of *ekklēsia*. It is difficult to discern which came first for Robinson: his semantic work on *ekklēsia* or his conceptual investigation of the "new man," otherwise

---

49. Robinson, "Biblical Doctrine of the Church," 209 (originally written 1962).

understood as Jew-Gentile relations in Christ.[50] It is best to consider first the semantic work as it has bearing on the rest of Robinson's ecclesiology. It may well have been that his conceptual inquiry spawned the semantic investigation. Nevertheless this semantic work must be understood as the foundation of his thought because his semantic work ultimately influenced all of his ecclesiological conclusions.

From his earliest writings through to the end of his academic career, Robinson argued that *ekklēsia* almost always meant "gathering" or "assembly" in the Bible.[51] His interest in the usage of the word was grounded in his recognition of the semantic shift that occurred between the ancient meaning of *ekklēsia* and the use of "church" in modern English. He repeatedly drew attention to two primary errors that have arisen in the modern discussion. The first is applying the word "church," originally rendered from *ekklēsia*, to refer to a building or place. He wrote,

> The English word "church" is derived from the Gk. adjective *kyriakos* as used in the phrase *kyriakon dōma* or *kyrakē oikia*, meaning "the Lord's house," i.e., a Christian place of worship. "Church" in the NT, however, renders Gk. *ekklēsia*, which mostly designates a local congregation of Christians and never a building. Although we often speak of these congregations collectively as the NT church or the early church, no NT writer uses *ekklēsia* in this collective way. An *ekklēsia* was a meeting or assembly. Its commonest use was for the public assembly of citizens duly summoned, which was a feature of all the cities outside Judaea where the gospel was planted (e.g., Acts 19:39); *ekklēsia* was also used among the Jews (LXX) for the "congregation" of Israel which was constituted at Sinai and assembled before the Lord at the annual feasts in the persons of its representative males (Acts 7:38).[52]

The second common error in modern English is the use of *ekklēsia* to identify a people. Robinson wrote, "'Church' is not a synonym for 'people of God'; it is rather an *activity* of the 'people of God.' Images such as 'aliens and exiles' (1 Pet. 2:11) apply to the people of God in the world, but do not

---

50. Robinson seems to allude to the fact that the semantic work came first and gave rise to his inquiry into the "the last adam," therefore confirming my hypothesis and method for analysis. See Robinson, "'Church' Revisited," 269.

51. Robinson left room for an "extension of meaning to designate 'the persons who constitute an assembly' (especially in Acts)." Robinson, "Church and Evangelism," 114 (repr.; originally, "Letter to the Editor").

52. Robinson, "Church," 222 (repr.; originally in *New Bible Dictionary*).

describe the church, i.e., the people assembled with Christ in the midst (Matt. 18:20; Heb. 2:12)."[53] Later he recognized the linguistic nuance of such usage:

> The Greek word *ekklēsia*, which is the word translated *church* in the New Testament, meant a *meeting* or an *assembly*. It did not mean *a society* or an *institution* in our modern sense. In a Greek city-state, the citizens, the *demos*, came together in regular assembly for certain purposes. This assembly was the *ekklēsia* of the *demos*. The terms were not synonymous. The *demos*—the people—was a constant, on-going thing. But the *ekklēsia* was an *intermittent function* of the people.[54]

Robinson associated these two errors with transference of meaning from other Greek concepts. With the building/place misconception, Robinson argued that the usage is more akin to the meaning of *kyriakos*—"belonging to the Lord," or "the Lord's."[55] Likewise, with the demographic misconception, Robinson argued that the usage is more akin to the meaning of *dēmos*—"people," "populace," or "crowd."[56] Both misconceptions possess an understanding of "church" that is associated with an identity. It is either the people of God or the place where the people of God meet. But Robinson is clear that based on a proper understanding of *ekklēsia*, "church" actually functions grammatically as a verbal noun, identifying an activity of the people of God (e.g., the gathering or assembling), but not the people of God themselves. He is explicit, "[the church] is the *gathering together*, the actual *meeting*, of Christians in a certain place. It is not a word for Christians generally, or even for Christians in a particular locality; but rather for Christians seen or considered as *gathered together*."[57]

As noted earlier, it is uncertain from the extant literature how much of Robinson's work on *ekklēsia* is indebted to the influence of others (Hort, Flew, Schmidt, and Campbell). His conclusions are steeped in detailed linguistic analysis, but it is unknown how much of this work was entirely his own. Nowhere do we have a record of Robinson's textual analysis or notes from his semantic work. We see clear conclusions presented that required this sort of detailed work, but we cannot know when Robinson conducted this work. This is largely due to the fact that this sort of textual analysis would not have suited the audiences for which he was writing. We can state with great probability that his work drew upon that of F. J. A. Hort and

---

53. Ibid., 223.
54. Robinson, "Church of God," 231 (repr.; originally *Church of God* [1965]).
55. BDAG, "κυριακός," 576.
56. BDAG, "δῆμος," 223.
57. Robinson, "Church of God," 232.

even more heavily upon J. Y. Campbell. Even if he did his own independent analysis, he certainly found great support for his conclusions in their work.

ECCLESIOLOGY

Having traced the influences upon Robinson's thought and outlined his methodology, we now turn to consider the major ecclesiological conclusions in his thought. The central themes we have considered are prominent throughout the corpus of Robinson's ecclesiological work, but they come together in his consideration of the nature of the church. The most significant of these themes are: when and where church exists; unity; Jew and Gentile relations; authority; and the purpose of the church.

Church: When and Where?

One of the oldest questions concerning the nature of the church is "when and where does the church exist?" As early as the fifth century, in the face of the Donatist schism, Augustine addressed the imperfections of the "visible church" on earth and the perfection of the "invisible church," only to be revealed at the eschaton.[58] Since then, the church has been referred to as both visible and invisible, though the questions of how these two aspects are related and precisely where and when the church occurs have remained.

Augustine's great concern was the perfection of the church. Need the visible church stand perfect in its being? Could this perfection ever be realized before the eschaton? Is there a place for the apostates who have lapsed under persecution? Robinson picked up these questions,

> The Fathers had a saying, *extra ecclesiam nulla salus*, "no salvation outside the church." This is indeed true. "The ark of Christ's Church" is the only place of security for men from eternity to eternity. There is no salvation except for those whom Christ has incorporated into His holy Church. No man has ever seen this church, but its reality and its holiness in Christ are revealed truths of scripture, and so when the Apostles' Creed came to be formed in the second century men affirmed: "I believe in one holy church." It is an article of faith, not of sight. This church is a heavenly, not an earthly reality, and it is already complete and

---

58. See Augustine, *Writings in Connection with the Donatist Controversy*.

glorified in the purposes of God. It is "the church of the firstborn sons whose names are written in heaven."[59]

Robinson, like Augustine, recognized that the true church in its purest form exists in heaven. However, for Robinson, the inquiry into the nature of the church was not incited by a question of the perfection of the church, as it was for Augustine, but rather of the locus of the church.[60] Robinson's conclusion was that the church is primarily a heavenly and eschatological reality, though not without earthly form.

Robinson traced three distinguishing characteristics between the visible and invisible church, distinctions centering on questions of place (location), form (number), and continuity (time). He wrote,

> An important distinction now needs to be drawn between the church in its heavenly aspect and the church in its earthly aspect. Not only is the church on earth *multiform*, that is, it may be seen wherever two or three are gathered together in Christ's name; but it is also *intermittent* and not continuous in character, since its every meeting involves the necessity of dispersal when the time comes for the *ite, missa est*. The Church in heaven, on the other hand, is *uniform*, existing only in one place, and it is a *continuous* assembly, offering perpetual praise as it hears without intermission the name and glory of God declared in its midst by Christ. But on earth the church comes and goes, having no abiding city or temple. Christians never know exactly whom they will meet at their next assembly; and no church has any certainty that it will ever meet again. In the midst of life it is in death.[61]

The following table demonstrates Robinson's conclusions.[62]

	Visible	Invisible
Place	Earthly	Heavenly
Form	Multiform	Uniform
Continuity	Intermittent	Continuous

59. Robinson, "Church Universal," *ACR* (2 Feb 1956) 3.

60. Robinson and Augustine had different emphases because they each faced different issues in their own time and context.

61. Robinson, "Church of God," 236.

62. It should be noted that Robinson does not himself employ the categories of visible and invisible. He restricted these categories to place: earthly and heavenly. However, the categories are employed here in a way that is true to Robinson's thought, but helps to relate his work to the broader ecclesiological conversation. This will be particularly important later in the final evaluative chapter.

Place

Robinson observed the binary locale of the church in Scripture. That is to say, the church is both on earth and in heaven. These are not two distinct churches, as we will come to see in a later section, but rather the earthly gives expression to the heavenly. Robinson wrote, "These churches [local] are, again, not *societies* but *meetings*, and each one of them, if rightly convened, constitutes a visible expression of that great meeting in the heavenly places where Christ is for ever head of His assembled body."[63] The earthly church is representative of the heavenly church.[64]

The essential constitutive element of the church is its position in relation to Christ. Robinson wrote, "The church is where Christ is. On earth, that is where two or three are gathered together in His name (Matt. 18:20); in heaven, it is where He is seated at the right hand of the throne of God and sings praise to the Father ('in the midst of the church,' Heb. 2:12)."[65] Matthew 18:20 is a very significant verse in Robinson's ecclesiology, for it describes what he believed to be purpose for the church: namely, believers gathering together in the presence of Christ. A church is not any meeting of people for any occasion; the church is the meeting of believers "in the name of Christ" where Christ promises his presence.

Inherent within the concept of church is the ability to congregate. On earth the gathering of believers happens in particular locales. In heaven the church is the gathering of believers around the throne of Christ. Robinson wrote,

> There is another use of the word "church" in the NT which is not local, or at least not capable of multiplication: a church which is one and only, undivided and without blemish. This church is not ecumenical, as is commonly supposed, but is supernal. That is to say, the church is, in this aspect, a reality "in the heavenly realm," *en tois epouraniois* (Eph. 1:3; 1:20; 3:10; 6:12). Its locality is determined by the presence of Christ in its midst.[66]

---

63. Robinson, "Church of God," 233.

64. Our evaluation of Robinson's thought will address this seemingly dualistic nature of the church. Many have accused Robinson here of platonic dualism, and therefore written off his ecclesiology on this basis (Kevin Giles). However, it is likely that Robinson was not suggesting the earthly mirrors the heavenly, but rather that the heavenly will be the eschatological manifestation of the earthly. This of course opens up further the discussion of time and its relevance to location. These issues will be examined in detail in our evaluation.

65. Robinson, "Church in the New Testament," 213 (repr.; originally read to the theological seminar at St Mark's, Canberra, May 1959).

66. Ibid., 212–13.

So, whether on earth or in heaven, the constitutive element of the church is the presence of Christ; his presence is promised "where two or three gather in my name" (Matt 18:20). These numbers, "two or three," are not meant to indicate a quorum, but rather to identify that there is no minimum number of persons gathered for Christ to be present; if only two or three gather in his name, even with those few, he is present.[67]

Form

Concerning the form of the church, Robinson identified the church on earth as multiform and the church in heaven as uniform. This is connected to the places of the gatherings. On earth, there are many gatherings in many places. Therefore, the church has multiform expression. The multiform expression of the church is seen in the Bible, not just in various locales, but also in a single location. Robinson wrote,

> The situation in the New Testament, to judge from the few hints we have, was that, in a given city, the church existed on two levels. There was the believing household which also had the character of the church as it was assembled for prayer and instruction and (need we doubt?) the breaking of bread.... At the second level there was the meeting of believers from the whole city.[68]

The primary expression of the *ekklēsia* in the New Testament era was a gathering in a local place, most likely in a city or town. However, even within these singular locations, there were many smaller gatherings of believers, primarily in their households with family members and servants. The church, then, can be multiform even in a singular location.

Robinson believed that *ekklēsia* is never used of anything other than a local assembly when speaking of the church on earth. He wrote, "Here, in a local assembly of believers, is the visible, historical form of the church. The church of God on earth, as we see it in the New Testament, is neither national, nor regional, nor ecumenical, but local. The word 'church' is never applied to any visible, earthly body larger than a local congregation."[69]

---

67. Alan Stibbs expands this reading of the text by noting that the Jews required ten to twelve circumcised males to open a new synagogue. Stibbs, "New Testament Teaching," 233.

68. Robinson, "Church of God," 247.

69. Robinson, "Church Universal," *ACR* (16 Feb 1956) 9.

One might question how a passage such as Acts 9:31 is to be reconciled with this understanding of a multiform expression.[70] Doesn't Acts 9 identify a singular expression across multiple regions? Robinson anticipated this objection and answered contextually from the Acts narrative:

> One occurrence of *ekklēsia* is worth special mention. In [Acts] 9:31 we read, according to the best texts, of "the church throughout all Judaea and Galilee and Samaria." At first sight this looks like the one example in the whole NT of a regional, as distinct from local, use of "church." In fact, however, as the context beginning at 8:1 reveals, this is still the Jerusalem church, attenuated or dispersed through persecution. But the conception of a church which extends territorially while remaining the same church, however it may appeal to our modern frame of mind, has no further development in the NT.[71]

Robinson believed this is the only passage in the New Testament of its kind, and the reference to a singular expression in multiple locations may be explained contextually.

In heaven, the church is singular in its location and therefore in its expression. Robinson took particular exegetical interest in Heb 2:12 and 12:22–24.[72] He wrote,

> The two uses of *ekklēsia* in Hebrews (2:12 and 12:23) both imply a gathering-together of the children of God in heaven. In the first, Christ is in the midst of the many sons He has brought to glory.... Church, we might say, is in progress in heaven. There is preaching and praise in the assembly. Christ is in the midst of those gathered in His name. In chapter 12 the readers are reminded that their coming is no longer to the *ekklēsia* of Israel as it had assembled at Mt. Sinai, but to "the general assembly and church of the first-born sons who are enrolled in heaven" (12:23). The picture throughout is that of the *qehal Yisrael*, the congregation of Israel, as it is actually assembled "to meet God"

---

70. Acts 9:31: "So the church throughout all Judea and Galilee and Samaria had peace and was being built up. And walking in the fear of the Lord and in the comfort of the Holy Spirit, it multiplied."

71. Robinson, "Church in the New Testament," 216–17.

72. Heb 2:12: "I will tell of your name to my brothers; in the midst of the congregation I will sing your praise" (cited from Ps 22:22).
Heb 12:22–24: "But you have come to Mount Zion and to the city of the living God, the heavenly Jerusalem, and to innumerable angels in festal gathering, and to the assembly of the firstborn who are enrolled in heaven, and to God, the judge of all, and to the spirits of the righteous made perfect, and to Jesus, the mediator of a new covenant, and to the sprinkled blood that speaks a better word than the blood of Abel."

at Sinai for the making of the covenant between them, through the mediatorial work of Moses. Believers have now, however, come to a better assembly, a better Moses, a better covenant.[73]

This gathering in heaven is uniform in its expression because it is in the physical presence of Christ. Like the gathering of the nation of Israel before the Lord, this gathering in heaven is all of the redeemed in Christ gathered *in toto*. However, this gathering exceeds the original gathering because it is not through the mediation of a prophet, but through God himself in the Person of Christ.

Continuity

The matter of the continuity of the church, like form, is also relative to place. The church on earth is intermittent because it meets and scatters. However, the church in heaven is continuous because it is constantly gathered in the presence of Christ. Continuity is connected to the actuality of the gathering occurring. On earth, this gathering happens occasionally, while in heaven the gathering is unceasing.

The identity of believers arises within this discussion of continuity of the church. Are "Christian," "believer," and/or "people of God" synonyms for "church?" In other words, does the church (and its members) still have an identity as the church when it is not meeting? Robinson addressed this question:

> It is not too much to say that the church on earth does not exist, or is not visible, except in the actual assembly of believers. This does not mean that believers have no apprehension of the church except when actually meeting together. Believers may regard themselves as *continuously* partaking of the life of the church *above* inasmuch as they are already risen with Christ, are part of His body, and have their minds set on things above where He is exalted (Col. 3:1–4). We may even say that the heavenly church exists on earth in the persons of true believers; but we cannot equate them, at any time, with the church, nor does the heavenly church appear *as a church* in them. They may also look upon fellow believers, and pray for them, as members of the heavenly or catholic church throughout the world. On the other hand, believers cannot think of themselves as in the same way *continuously* partaking of the life of the earthly church; for although an earthly church is an expression of the heavenly

73. Robinson, "Church of God," 235.

church, it has this character only in so far as, and only as often as, there is an actual meeting.[74]

Robinson recognized legitimacy in the claim that Christians are constantly connected to, and may be identified with the church. However, this claim must be qualified with the recognition of this being a spiritual, and not a physical (and therein earthly), reality. Christians are spiritually present and active in the heavenly gathering, which is presently occurring, insomuch as they are in Christ (Eph 2:4–7; Col 3:1–4). Therefore, believers have some sense of continual belonging to the church—that is, the heavenly church—because they are in Christ. But to speak of a constant identity concerning the church on earth, that is a local assembly, is a misconception.

Unity

Having understood the basic conclusions of Robinson's ecclesiology concerning the time and place of the church, we now turn to consider the church's unity. It might be said that the unity of the church was Donald Robinson's ecclesiological preoccupation. He believed—if not explicitly, then implicitly—that the ecumenical conversation was the most misguided of ecclesiological colloquies, and therefore the most prone to error. Therefore, much of Robinson's ecclesiology was expressed in a polemical manner, addressing the concerns he had with the doctrine driving the ecumenical movement.

Robinson began by examining key texts that have been used in the history of the ecumenical conversation to appeal to a need for unity. The Epistle to the Ephesians is one of the primary documents in ecumenical discussion. Robinson engaged with the epistle and concluded that the unity discussed in the letter is something already existing, not something to be sought after.[75] The unity of the church is bound to the church's position in Christ. Paul, in the epistle, identifies the church as the metaphorical body of Christ (Eph 1:22–23; 2:14–16; 3:4–6; 4:4–6, 11–16; 5:23, 30). Of the theological implications of this metaphor, Robinson wrote, "The unity of the church is a fact because there is one Lord or head of the church, who convenes it, and one God above all (Eph 4:4–6). If the church is related to Christ at all, then it is one. If it is not related to Christ, then it is not His church, whatever it

---

74. Ibid., 236.

75. For example, Eph 4:3—σπουδάζοντες τηρεῖν τὴν ἑνότητα τοῦ πνεύματος ἐν τῷ συνδέσμῳ τῆς εἰρήνης: "Do your best to keep the unity of the Spirit in the bond of peace." Unity is mentioned in this passage in a sense that it is already existent/possessed. The exhortation is to work to maintain/keep/guard this unity.

may look like to the observer."[76] Robinson recognized the ontological connection of the church to Christ; because Christ is one, and the church is in Christ, then the church cannot be divided. He continues,

> It is *as a body* that the church is (and not merely strives to be) "one." Whether in heaven or on earth, the church, being a body, is, by its very nature, one. It is a coherence of parts and members. He who does not partake of the unity of the body does not partake of the body at all. This means that the church can never be larger than, or thought of as larger than, the body which is *actually one* in the coherence and mutual relationship of its parts. To say (as some do) "we are divided members of the same body" is a contradiction in terms.[77]

Robinson also addressed the creed, the locus of ecumenical agreement. He wrote, "It is to be noted . . . that, when we speak of 'the unity of the church,' we speak of a truth to be believed, a reality to be acknowledged. 'We *confess* one church.' Oneness is not a mere attribute of the church which may or may not be present, nor is it something to strive for, a state of perfection yet to be realized. Oneness is of the *esse* of the church: it is basic to its nature."[78] Robinson identified the unity of the church as a confessed reality. If believers, of all backgrounds, can regularly confess that there is one church, how can this be done with integrity if it is actually believed that the church is divided? Church unity is something that is, not something that should be.

Unity is an essential property of the church. Robinson wrote,

> There is a spiritual bond between "all that call upon the name of our Lord Jesus Christ in every place, their Lord and ours" (1 Cor. 1:2). This bond exists despite human sin and earthly divisions. We affirm its existence as often as we say, "I believe in the communion of saints," which means the fellowship of all who are members of the holy people of God. Nothing can destroy this unity of the Spirit, for it is created "in Christ."[79]

Once again, Robinson addressed the creed, but this time examining the next clause—"the communion of saints." We confess that we believe in "the holy catholic church" and "the communion of saints" because there is an undivided spiritual unity shared amongst believers because they are "in Christ."

76. Robinson, "Church of God," 233.
77. Ibid.
78. Ibid.
79. [DR], "Unity of the Spirit," 2.

This conclusion is grounded not only in the declaration of the creed, but also in Robinson's exegesis of Ephesians 4.

One of the driving issues for ecumenists is the pursuit of a global unity of all who call upon the name of Christ. Current disunity is most often perceived in discord surrounding the origin and existence of denominationalism. Robinson recognized that this conversation came close to home in the redrafting of the church constitution for the Church of England in Australia. He disagreed with the opening paragraph of the constitution that claims the Church of England in Australia as "a part of" the one Holy Catholic Church. For Robinson, this is "theologically untrue." He wrote, "The church of the Colossians and Ephesians is not a visible, earthly entity at all: it is transcendent, heavenly, invisible. Its existence, character and unity are truths of revelation, not of observation. It is part of the new creation, not the old."[80] Robinson identified what is the likely cause of this error:

> The thing we call "the church in the New Testament" or "the primitive church" is not called "the church" in the New Testament. For when we speak in a general way of "the church" we usually mean the sum total of all Christians or Christian bodies in the world (with or without its fringe of *haereseis*) forming a *corpus* which we take to be its true, or at least its ideal, form; even though we know such an ecumenical unity does not, and never has, existed.[81]

So, when addressing the church in its earthly expression, it is never appropriate to speak in terms of a global church. This is a misnomer because there is no actual assembly of Christians worldwide. This is not to say that there are no ecumenical ideals. Robinson clarified,

> The only strictly ecumenical concepts in the NT are those of a world-wide mission of the gospel, and of saints in every place calling on the name of the Lord. But the concept of "church" (*ekklēsia*) is, by definition, of something capable of assembling, something *epi to auto* (see Acts 2:44; 1 Cor. 11:20; 14:23), something gathered together, and therefore something visible and local and organised. By far the greatest number of uses of the word *ekklēsia* in the NT relates to such a local body, either generically or with particular reference.[82]

---

80. Robinson, "Church in the New Testament," 220–21.
81. Ibid., 212.
82. Ibid.

The Church of England in Australia, or the Anglican Church of Australia as it has come to be, is not the church or a part of the church. This institution, at best, is a fellowship of churches. The church on earth is always a gathering.

Here again Robinson returned to his conclusions about the place, form, and time of the church. How is it that the earthly and the heavenly relate? He wrote, "The local church (and there is no national or ecumenical church in the New Testament) is the earthly, historical embodiment of the supernal church. 'Now ye are the body of Christ,' Paul tells the Corinthians (1 Cor. 12:27). The church at Ephesus is the 'church of God which he purchased with his own blood' (Acts 20:28)."[83] The local church is *the* expression of the heavenly church. This does not mean that the earthly church is less significant that the heavenly church, for "it is the means whereby we apprehend the reality it represents and embodies in earthly form."[84] How then can the relationship between the two be explained? Robinson wrote, "In God's purposes there is only one church, one gathering of all under the headship of Christ. But on earth it is pluriform, seen wherever two or three gather in his name. There is no need to explain the relation between the one and the many. Like the believer, the church is both local and 'in heaven.'"[85] The already/not-yet realization of the *ekklēsia* is one that is beyond full explanation. It is a reality in which believers have a physical and a spiritual participation: physically, believers congregate on earth occasionally in local assemblies; spiritually, believers congregate in Christ around the throne of God continuously in heaven.

John 17 is another text that is prominent in the ecumenical conversation. Robinson addressed this text early in his ecclesiological writing, recognizing the significance of the theological claims by the World Council of Churches that are anchored in this passage. In an editorial for the *Australian Church Record*, Robinson argued,

> The World Council of Churches, despite its carefully phrased official statements, seems constantly to be guided by a false conception of the church and consequently of church unity. It frequently gives the impression that Christ's prayer of John 17—"that all may be one"—has not yet been answered, and that we should look for its answer in the direction of church union schemes. Church union schemes may, indeed, be a bond of peace by which the unity of the Spirit is maintained, but there is no guarantee that they will. The church on earth has never been

---

83. Ibid., 221.
84. Ibid.
85. Robinson, "Church," 223 (repr.).

visibly united. The unity of the Spirit resides in common faith, not common order, and the bond of peace is not necessarily the bond of outward church union.[86]

Robinson believed that the unity of the Spirit is something possessed by all who call upon the name of Christ, as we have already seen demonstrated in Robinson's conclusions derived from Ephesians 4. Christ's prayer is John 17 is one that was answered fully after the ascension of Christ when the Spirit came upon all believers (Joel 2:28–32; Acts 2).

Robinson offered a brief exposition of John 17 vis-à-vis the ecumenical understanding of the chapter:

> It is sheer wishful thinking to refer this to the relationship of churches to each other. The popular ecumenical exegesis of John 17 is extremely superficial. Without embarking on a full exposition of the chapter here, the following points may be noted: a) The nature of the oneness prayed for is defined by the words "even as we are one" (verse 22; cf 17 and 21). This "oneness" of the Son with the Father is plainly an allusion to 10:30, "I and the Father are one," which is the only other place in the Gospel where "one" is used of the Father and the Son . . . b) The prayer for the unity of the apostles (17:11f) is a prayer that they, the first to believe, may all be spiritually secure (i.e., that "not one of them be lost")—not that they may exhibit some sort of visible union with each other; c) The prayer "that they may *all* be one" is a prayer for the unity with the apostles of those who shall believe through their word. This unity is to be of the same sort as binds the "sent" Son to the Father "who sent Him." . . . This has no necessary connection at all with the visible relationship of believers to each other laterally, apart from their mutual love.[87]

Robinson was careful in his exposition to show the vertical elements of John 17. It is only from the vertical—namely Jesus' oneness with the Father and believers' oneness with Christ by faith—that any horizontal (relational) implications can arise. The emphasis in John 17 is not dissimilar to the emphasis of Ephesians, in particular believers' identity "in Christ."

Robinson was concerned that ecumenists read into the text what they observe in the world, and therefore begin with a presupposed problem. He wrote,

> The question ["what is the nature of the unity we seek?"] . . . is not very well framed, for it assumes that "the unity" (that is,

86. Robinson, "Unity of the Spirit," 2.
87. Robinson, "Church of God," 243–44.

of the church) has been lost or does not yet exist: for why else should we seek it? Whereas, in terms of the biblical and credal doctrine of "one church," unity is not something to seek at all, but is the very nature of the church, never absent wherever Christ meets with His people.[88]

He continues,

> What the framers of the question are really seeking is, not the unity of the church in the biblical and credal sense, but a way by which churches (such as at present are comprised in various groups and denominations) can establish proper relations with each other. This is, without doubt, an important question and pressing concern, especially for denominationally-conditioned Christians, who are the real "we" mentioned in the question. But a solution to this problem would not mean that "the unity of the church" had been discovered. Nor would a failure to find a solution make any necessary difference to the unity—and I mean the visible unity—of the Church of God on earth.[89]

Is Robinson then, dismissive of inter-congregational relationships in the world? Are the relationships between congregations, or even Christians, beyond the local gathering then insignificant? No, he believed that these relationships are very significant. He wrote,

> The relationship between such local churches is a concern of highest importance. It is little dealt with in the New Testament because there was little threat to complete mutual recognition and acknowledgement. Their "inter-communion" was taken for granted. This is our great practical problem today. But it will not be solved unless we have a proper assessment of the true character of the local church and of its relationship to that heavenly reality which is "the fulness of him that filleth all in all" (Eph. 1:23).[90]

So, the relationships between Christians and congregations do matter, but they must be understood in their proper theological context. There is no visible institutional unity to be sought *between* churches on earth. True unity is already existent in the supernal church and ought to characterize the local church. Aside from ecclesial unity, there is a bond of mutual love and concern to be expressed between Christians everywhere.

---

88. Ibid., 239–40.
89. Ibid., 240.
90. Robinson, "Church in the New Testament," 221.

How then should the multiplicity of churches and denominations be understood? Robinson believed that the presence of many churches in any given area is a normal expression of Christian society.[91] In fact, Robinson believed that a fixation on ecumenism and denominationalism often overshadows a focus on the local church. He believed that this overshadowing emphasis is detrimental to the testimony of true church unity. He wrote,

> The unity of the church, at whatever level it meets, in earth or heaven, derives from the Lord of the church, who is its one Head, and from His Word, confessed in our one faith and baptism. Let us take heed that we do not despise the true "church of God" (1 Cor. 11:22), or give it any occasion of stumbling (1 Cor. 10:32). We will certainly be in danger of this if we exalt ecumenism, or denominationalism, or diocesanism above the unity of the local church, forgetting that Jesus builds His church only where men confess Him as Lord (Matt. 16:16—18:20).[92]

The church is united because it is in Christ, and Christ himself is the guarantor of church growth and unity. To presuppose disunity is to indirectly presuppose the absence of Christ. And where Christ is not, his church is not.

Jew and Gentile

We now turn to consider the issue of unity that is most prominent in the New Testament, that of Jew and Gentile relationships. As we mentioned earlier, Robinson's method shaped his ecclesiology. He expressed great care and concern for how the church fits within God's greater soteriological purposes. In particular, Robinson wanted to understand how Israel and the Gentiles relate as the new man. Does the church supersede Israel? Are the promises to national Israel still intact and awaiting further fulfillment (e.g., restoration of the land)? Robinson's ecclesiology must be understood in the context of how he understood God's movements of drawing a particular people to himself. In matters of ecclesiology, this is best expressed in the question "is there continuity in God's salvific purposes, especially with regard to the 'people of God'?"

Robinson documented his methodology and the relevance of the Jew–Gentile question to ecclesiology, as well as the theology that arose from the application of his method:

---

91. Robinson writes, "I believe that our multiplicity of churches in the same area is not of necessity an evil to be reformed, but is, on the contrary, a normal if variegated expression of Christian society." Robinson, "Church of God," 249.

92. Ibid., 251.

> As early as 1951, having satisfied myself of the linguistic limitations of the New Testament usage of church, which took its start from the Epistle to the Ephesians and from the related but not identical concept of the church in Hebrews. Both of these views of the *ekklēsia* seemed to me to have their basis in the creation of Adam, and *ekklēsia* seemed to be a term to express the fulfilment of God's creative purpose in Christ, *ho eschatos Adam*, "the last adam" or "Adam at last." The church, then, in the Ephesians (and less probably Hebrews) sense is a reality related to creation, redemption, and the restoration of all things. To explain why the term *ekklēsia* should be used to express the final transcendent reality of the new man in Christ it was necessary to turn to the history of salvation, and, as I set out in my Canberra paper of 1959, the doctrine of the church in the New Testament could not be understood apart from the history of Israel and of God's purpose of salvation through Israel to the Gentiles. At least it must be noted that, what appears as merely an ordinary term first for the assembly of Israelites and then for the assemblies of Christians, can be taken to indicate (a) the engagement of God's people corporately with him, when they hear his word and see his glory, with Christ in the midst, and (b) in the case of New Testament assemblies, the place of reconciliation of Jews and Gentiles in Christ, i.e., a demonstration of mankind (Adam) renewed in Christ.[93]

As is evidenced in his autobiographical account, Robinson recognized a shift in God's soteriological activity. He articulated this shift as follows:

> In Acts, James, 3 John, Revelation and the earlier Pauline letters, "church" is always a particular local congregation. . . . But in the later Colossians and Ephesians Paul generalizes his use of "church" to indicate, not an ecumenical church, but the spiritual and heavenly significance of each and every local "body" which has Christ as its "head," and by which God demonstrates his manifold wisdom through the creation of "one new man" out of all the races and classes.[94]

No longer is God's primary emphasis on the one nation of Israel, but in Christ he is welcoming people from the nations, just as promised through the prophets. The chosen and redeemed people always have constituted the people of God. In the Old Testament this people was the nation of Israel,

---

93. Robinson, "'Church Revisited," 269.
94. Robinson, "Church," 222–23 (repr.).

while in the New Testament that people was no longer ethnically but faith based and inclusive of the nations.

This concept of the "people of God" has been a source of great confusion in ecclesiological conversation, even for Robinson's readers. Graham Cole, in his article "The Doctrine of the Church: Towards Conceptual Clarification," argued that a helpful distinction needs to be made in Robinson's thinking allowing a conceptual separation between "people of God" and "the church." This is a helpful assessment of Robinson's work, as his thinking on the topic on occasion can be unclear. Contributing to the lack of clarity is an apparent shift in Robinson's thought in the course of his ministry.[95] Robinson ultimately expressed agreement with Cole's position in his autobiographical comments on ecclesiology.[96]

Early in his ministry, Robinson was equivocal in his description of the people of God in relationship to the church. For example, in 1956 he contributed a series of articles to the *Australian Church Record* on the nature of the church that were very clear about the church's position in the soteriological purposes of God. However, they were less clear on the relationship of the people of God to the church. For example, Robinson wrote, "The continuity of the people of God in the New Testament with the people of God in the Old Testament is obscured for English readers by the fact that different words are employed to express what is essentially the same ideal: the people of God. In the O.T. we have the 'congregation,' and in the N.T. we have 'the church,' but the concept is one and the same."[97] Robinson is correct in recognizing the obscurity concerning continuity with regard to the people of God in the Old and New Testaments. However, Robinson does not help his readers by identifying the people of God with the congregation in the OT and the church in the NT. It is not necessarily incorrect to speak of the church and the people of God together, but there must be a distinction made between people and the activity of that people.

Later in his ministry, Robinson explicitly stated that "church" is not coterminous with "people of God." He wrote, "'Church' is not a synonym for

---

95. The shift appears to take place in 1962. In one article written in 1962, Robinson wrote, "Thus the Church, founded upon Christ and His Apostles and Prophets (Matt. 16:18; 1 Cor. 3:9; Eph. 2:20; Rev. 21:14), experiencing and acknowledging God's rule in Christ, is represented in the New Testament as the new 'People of God,' the new 'Jerusalem' and 'Temple' (1 Cor. 3:16, 17; 6:19; 2 Cor. 6:16; Gal. 3:25, 26; Heb. 12:22, 23; Rev. 21:1–5, 9–14) to which all people some and attach themselves as the OT prophets had said they would." Robinson, "Biblical Doctrine of the Church," 209. In another article written in 1962, Robinson wrote, "'Church' is not a synonym for 'people of God'; it is rather an *activity* of the 'people of God.'" Robinson, "Church," 223 (repr.).

96. Robinson, "'Church' Revisited," 269–70.

97. Robinson, "Church Universal and Its Earthly Form: 2," 9.

'people of God'; it is rather an *activity* of the 'people of God.' Images such as 'aliens and exiles' (1 Pet. 2:11) apply to the people of God in the world, but do not describe the church, i.e. the people assembled with Christ in the midst (Matt. 18:20; Heb. 2:12)."[98] Robinson came to understand the people of God as the broader identity of the redeemed, with church as a fundamental activity of these people.

By way of summary, we shall consider the major turning point that Robinson observed in the narrative of the Acts of the Apostles. This turning point identifies the shift in salvation history that wrought the theological implications we have seen articulated in Robinson's ecclesiology, namely the nature of the church with regard to place, form, and number.

> At this stage [the Acts of the Apostles], the new form of the church was still within the womb of the old. It did not immediately become apparent even to the apostles that a new "body" was coming to birth which was entirely distinct from the old "body." Nor, until the realization was forced upon them by the working of God Himself, did they realize that the old "church of Israel" was ceasing to be "the church of God" and that this solemn prerogative was now resting on the new body which, externally, was still a sect within the church of Israel.
>
> Here, [Acts] 7:1 [actually, 8:1], we are told that on the day of Stephen's death "there arose a great persecution against the church which was in Jerusalem." The new body was being violently ejected from the womb of the old, and it was the new body, not the old, which was called "the church." It was the first great schism. Israel after the flesh persecuted Israel after the Spirit (Gal. 4:21–31). The old church excommunicated the new church. As Jesus had said, the house of the Jews was left to them desolate, and the church of God was "scattered abroad" to take a new and hitherto unsuspected form.
>
> From now on, or at any rate from the time the Gentiles were clearly recognised as members with the Jews of the one "people of God," we encounter a surprising new fact: the form of the church is no longer one—as it had been throughout the Old Testament—but many. There is "the church which was in Jerusalem" (Acts 11:22), but there is also the church at Antioch! (Acts 11:26, 12; 13). The first missionary journey resulted in the formation of many "churches" (14:23, 15:16). And so the story goes on. We may take this terminology for granted now, but we should not overlook the astonishing change which this terminology represents. To the old Jew there was, there could be, but

---

98. Robinson, "Church," 223 (repr.).

> one church on earth, the visible congregation of Israel. But now that august and holy title, the church of God, belonged to groups of believers in many places.[99]

The shift that has occurred is the inclusion of the Gentiles. As the church is no longer closely tied to national Israel and a singular gathering, the church is now multiform, taking its place all over the globe in local gatherings. This shift has opened up the reality of the heavenly and eschatological dimension of the church.

What should be made, then, of the church's relationship to Israel? Has Israel been replaced by the church? Robinson believed that Israel is preserved as an identity (ethnic?) in the church as a demonstration of God's wisdom in bringing together Jews and Gentiles (Eph 3:6–10). Robinson believed that while the church is the gathering of the people of God, there is good reason why it is not called "Israel." He wrote,

> It is doubtful if the New Testament writers ever refer to the Church as "Israel" (Gal. 6:16 may simply refer to converted Israelites). Nevertheless, Old Testament descriptions of Israel are constantly used of the Jewish-Gentile churches in the New Testament (notice in addition to the above examples Gal. 3:7; Phil. 3:3; 1 Pet. 2:1–10). The reason for this may be that the word "Israel" would tie the Church to Jacob and not to Christ and may also give it too national a character. Israel was called and summoned to be "the Church of God" and it is this description and status (along with many others) that is applied to the disciples of Jesus. Within this Church Israelites fulfil their destiny (notice Isa. 42:6; 49:6 and Luke 2:30–32; Acts 13:47).[100]

In the scheme of salvation history, Israel failed in covenantal fellowship with God and therefore in purpose of being a light to the nations. Robinson believed that it is only through Christ—true Israel—that people can fulfill their calling as the people of God, as it is Christ who has fulfilled the old covenant. Those who are joined to Christ by faith are the people of God, a people inclusive of the nations.

While Israel is not superseded in the church, there remains a place of prominence for Israel in the salvific purposes of God. Robinson believed the church at Jerusalem (consisting of Israelites) was the dispenser of grace to the nations.[101] Robinson elaborated on Israel's dispensational role in his article "The Church in the New Testament." There he wrote,

---

99. Robinson, "Church Universal and Its Earthly Form: 2," 9.

100. Robinson, "Biblical Doctrine of the Church," 209.

101. Robinson writes, "The church at Jerusalem holding a primacy which was not

I make the suggestion that the famous promise of Matthew 16:18, "I will build my church" (being Jesus' reply to Peter's confession of His messiahship) belongs to this same theology. Not only, as Hort[102] long since pointed out, does "my *ekklēsia*; carry something of the idea of "my Israel": the promise, "I will build it," is really the promise to "restore" Israel in the remnant of those who truly confess Him as *kurios* and *christos*. Thus it is not, in the first instance at least, a conception of "church" any wider than that which we have seen in the first chapter of Acts— the remnant of believing Jews who were being saved. But the restoration of Israel was always with a view to the salvation also of the gentiles, and so Peter was given the keys of the kingdom of heaven. Here, following the building, or rebuilding, of the church, is the gentile mission. In this context, kingdom is far wider than church. It is as if Jesus said to Peter, "It is too light a thing that thou shouldest be the rock on which I shall build again the restored of Israel; thou shalt also be the dispenser of the good things of the gospel to all who shall come from the east and the west, the north and the south, and sit down in the kingdom of Heaven."[103]

The fulfillment of God's promises to Israel also brought fulfillment of God's blessing to the nations (Gen 12:3). It is first and foremost through Christ, the true Jew and true Israel, that salvation comes to the Gentiles. But it is also through those initially redeemed from Israel that the church continued to spread to the wider world. Finally, it is through the rejection of Israel that the gospel is advancing amongst the Gentiles (Rom 11).

Having considered the unity of the church and Jew-Gentile relationships with respect to continuity in salvation history, we now move to consider the task of the church. If the church is an activity of the people of God, what is this activity intended for and what is involved in this activity?

The Task of the Church

Purpose

The task, or purpose, of the church is difficult to discern because it can easily be muddled with the task of Christians. However, as Robinson insisted,

---

merely chronological but (having in mind God's *oikonomia*) dispensational." Robinson, "Church in the New Testament," 216.

102. Hort, *Christian Ecclesia*, 10–11.
103. Robinson, "Church in the New Testament," 217–18.

the church is not synonymous with the people of God, but rather is an activity of the people of God. Therefore, the task of the church is specific to the action of assembling Christians. The question "What is the task of the church?" can therefore be rephrased this way: "Why do Christians gather together?" Robinson identified this distinction as follows:

> The highly significant term *ecclesia* has connotations which do not and cannot apply to anything but an assembly or meeting. It is a very great pity that the term "church" has been allowed over the years to be applied to activities and organizations, which, though perfectly legitimate, are simply not "the church" in any sense in which the Bible uses the word, and which therefore should not be invested with the dignity or prerogatives which the New Testament assigns to the church which is Christ's body. The church is where God's people meet in the name of Christ and with the promise of his presence in their midst.[104]

The task therefore is limited to a particular people, in a particular place, for a specific amount of time. Developing this notion, Robinson wrote,

> "The church" is not just another word for Christians, or for the people of God. It is, quite specifically, the *assembly* of the people of God. There is high significance in this activity of gathering together, though it is not the whole story of what Christians are or do in the world. The church is the ever recurring activity whereby believers gather together to meet God in their corporate character. Its prototype is the assembly of Israel at Mount Sinai, and at other times at the festivals at Jerusalem. There the Lord is among them, and there he promises his blessing. There they hear his word, and renew their covenant with him. There they feast before the Lord and share their food things with the poor and needy.[105]

Therefore, the church's task is bound to its corporate nature. It is the people of God assembling around the Word of God.

Robinson was quite happy to embrace the Thirty-Nine Articles' position on this matter, namely that of Article XIX. He wrote,

> In our Articles of Religion we accept a definition of the visible church of Christ—based on New Testament truth—as "a congregation of faithful men, in which the pure Word of God is

---

104. Robinson, "Doctrine of the Church," 110 (repr.); originally written for and read at a Conference on Evangelism in Sydney, NSW, 1974.

105. Ibid., 109.

preached, and the sacraments be duly ministered according to Christ's ordinance in all those things that of necessity are requisite to the same." This can easily be extrapolated. Clearly it belongs to the function of the church to be a place of ministry, of the offering of prayer and praise, of nurturing "little ones" in the faith, of sharing in the things of God. It must be a primary goal of congregations acting corporately to care for each other in the effectual functioning of each as "the visible church of Christ" in that parish.[106]

Article XIX supports Robinson's thesis that the church is the gathering of believers and its task is bound up in that activity.[107] Robinson drew attention to the Articles' emphasis on the corporate nature of the church. The gathering is of multiple believers together, in fellowship around the Word, expressing common faith and that faith's implied care for others.

Commenting further on the corporate nature of the church's task, Robinson wrote, "The purpose of the *ecclesia* is that God's children, ordinarily scattered in the world, might strengthen one another's hands in the sharing of ministries to their mutual edification, and be renewed and inspired for godly living in their ordinary avocations. But the church as such has no *face* to the world, and is not therefore a direct agent in evangelism."[108] Christians, in gathering, are in a sense being fueled for Christian living. They are dependent on the corporate fellowship for support in the Christian life. The church is an inward looking activity. It seeks to develop, edify, and care for those within its body. However, the church's task, as the church, begins and ends with the gathering. At the adjournment of the gathering, believers return to their individual lives in the world. This does not mean that there is no dependence on Christian fellowship apart from the gathering, but it does mean that the church's task ceases with the scattering of its members. The activities that normally occur outside of the gathering (e.g., evangelism) cannot be ascribed to the church. They may belong to the people of God, who at some point or other are gathered as church, but the tasks themselves belong to the scattered people of God, not to the gathered people.

---

106. Robinson, "Diocese of Sydney," 313–14; originally written in for the Finance Committee of Diocesan Standing Committee (5 November 1990).

107. There has been some speculation amongst scholars as to whether "congregation of faithful men" refers to a parish or something broader. Bray, for example, questions whether this would have been what Cranmer intentioned when drafting the Articles. See Bray, *Faith We Confess*, 107. We will maintain Robinson and Knox's position throughout this book that the "congregation" in Article XIX could/does refer to an assembly as would be consistent with a *prima facie* reading.

108. Robinson, "Doctrine of the Church," 109.

Activity

What, specifically, is involved in the activity of the people of God gathered? In other words, what happens at church? Robinson believed the answer to this question is bound to a proper understanding of the nature of the church. He wrote,

> The basis of corporate worship is to be found in the nature of the church, which in the New Testament is not an organisation or society, but an actual meeting or assembly of God's people. Ultimately, we all belong to the one united assembly of all God's elect which gathers round the throne of God in heaven, and participates without ceasing in the praise and thanksgiving which is offered to him, and hears the name of God "declared" by Christ as he stands as head over the assembly (Heb. 2:10–13; 12:22–24; Rev. 4 and 5). But here on earth our assembling together is, despite all our attempts at regularity, an intermittent and uncertain activity. Its basis is the promise of Christ to be present where two or three gather together in his name. We gather together "to meet Christ," just as the Israelites were assembled by Moses at Mount Sinai "to meet God" (Exod. 19:17).[109]

Robinson used the catchall term "worship" to describe the activity of the church. This terminology is based on descriptive passages in the NT of the corporate response to the presence of Christ. As Christ has promised to be present amongst the church (Matt 18:20), and the central activity of the church then is gathering in the presence of Christ, the best way to describe that activity is worship. In heaven, this is eternal and continuous. On earth, this is intermittent.

Christians turn to the Word of God as a guide for worship. The gathering in the presence of Christ might also be described as a "Word-centered" gathering, as it is in the Word that believers encounter Christ. Robinson believed, again in accord with Article XIX, that the Word must be central in the church. Robinson believed that the Prayer Book could "assist in achieving the true end of such worship of the church"[110] insomuch as it was written to lead the church in, and point people to, the Word of God. For this same reason Robinson firmly believed that the lectionary served as the "backbone of regular worship."[111] Ultimately, the people of God need to congregate around the Word of God for the purpose of meeting with the Lord Jesus.

---

109. Robinson, "Liturgical Patterns of Worship," 321 (repr.); originally delivered as a position paper at NEAC 1971.

110. Ibid., 323.

111. Ibid., 324.

Evangelism and Mission

Earlier we took notice of Robinson's comment that "the church has no face to the world."[112] Robinson argued that the church *qua* church is an inward-facing activity, equipping, encouraging, and exhorting Christians for godly living in the world. Christians, not the corporate gathering, have a face to the world. Robinson answered the question "Does the church have an evangelistic task?" as follows:

> The church has no such task or role. *Christians* do; and then *only* those Christians who in their particular callings are at work in these places. I cannot think of anything in the New Testament which suggests that the church (i.e. the assembly of believers), or even Christians as a visibly organized body, have a function of witness to or service *vis-à-vis* the world. Christians should think of themselves in the world, not as the church, but as God's people, set among the nations to show forth His excellencies by the character of their good works, and by any special ministry that may have been committed to each. But then their appearance is not that of a *church* or *congregation* but of a *dispersion*; they seem not a "kingdom of priests" but "strangers and pilgrims"; men see not their corporate "worship" but their individual "good works"; and their unity in such witness and service will be manifested only in "the day of visitation."[113]

Robinson's position was a matter of logic as much as anything else; those without the gospel do not normally come into the church, they exist outside of the gathering in the world. The church is the activity of those already in Christ. Outsiders encounter the gospel in the witness of Christians in the world. Robinson wrote, "The world sees only Christians, and sees them only when they are not, as a matter of fact, the church (i.e. are not assembled)."[114] As outsiders in the world receive the gospel message in faith, they are brought into the gathering, as they too come into Christ.

Robinson believed that any ascription of an evangelistic task to the church is an unbalanced understanding of God's economy for salvation in the world. He wrote, "The instrument of salvation in the New Testament is not 'the church' but 'the gospel' and, as to human agency, 'the apostle.' (Probably also 'the evangelist,' but we have little New Testament exposition of the role of the evangelist compared with the exposition of that of the

---

112. Robinson, "Doctrine of the Church," 109.

113. Robinson, "Church of God," 242. Robinson notes in a footnote to "see 1 Peter 1 and 2."

114. Ibid., 240.

apostle.)"[115] There are no texts in the NT that ascribe an evangelistic task to the church, only to Christians, and especially to those with the gifts of an apostle or evangelist.

Does the sharing of the gospel with the outside world only belong to those gifted as evangelists and apostles? No. Robinson described two sorts of gospel declaration to the world: that of the gifted (evangelists/apostles) and that of witnesses. The role of witness belongs to every Christian in the world, as they are identified with Christ and live a life accordingly. Robinson wrote,

> There is a significant difference between "witness" and "evangelism." To witness is to exhibit in the ordinary course of life the character of the God we serve and the fruit of the salvation he has brought us, and to give a reason for the hope within us when called upon to do so. This activity covers the whole scope of communal living including our conversation and the sharing of our interests and concerns with our neighbours. I recognize, of course, that some of this activity, especially when consciously motivated towards the salvation of our neighbours, is loosely called "evangelism" these days. But to "evangelize" in the NT sense implies a special gift of the ascended Christ, like that of the apostle, or prophet, or teacher.[116]

To distinguish between witness and evangelism is not to discount every Christian's role of testifying to the gospel, rather it is to say that there are some that will be more fruitful in this ministry because of the very particular gifts they have been given by God.

Pressing the issue further, Robinson argued that the regular gathering of believers is not the place for evangelistic appeal. He wrote,

> The church is not in itself—as the body of Christ, the household of God, or even as God's temple—the place where the gospel is preached to "those outside," and it would mistake its purpose to order its activities so as to aim at such a mission within it . . . we must assume that it is legitimate to use the basis of our liturgical worship as a platform from which to challenge those present to make good what the service, and those who take part in it, profess. In other words, we should assume that those present are "insiders," not "outsiders," and base our appeal on their profession, however tenuous. A "guest service" is therefore probably a

---

115. Robinson, "Diocese of Sydney," 315.
116. Robinson, "Church and Evangelism," 115.

> misnomer ... it must be the goal of the church—all its members and ministers—to seek to recover its "lost sheep."[117]

In other words, the membership of the church must be assumed to be Christian. If there are "lost sheep" in the midst of the congregation, it is enough to assume that the regular liturgy—with its gospel emphasis—will draw those back into the fold.

What then is the church's relationship to evangelism? Robinson concluded, "The church (in the New Testament sense of the gathering together of believers in any place in the name of the Lord Jesus) does not have direct responsibility for, or authority in, missionary work. Such responsibility and authority is given by the Holy Spirit to apostles or missionaries whom He calls, in the same way as He called prophets in the Old Testament dispensation."[118] However, although the church has no direct evangelistic responsibility, it partners in the work of evangelism in three ways: "(a) to pray the Lord of the harvest to send out labourers, (b) to recognise and attest to the authority of the Spirit in the call of a missionary, (c) to join in fellowship, through prayer and, if necessary, financial aid, with such as God sends forth (Phil. 4:15, 3 John 5–10)."[119] This support of the evangelistic mission of God recognizes the reality that those gifted apostles and evangelists are members of local churches.

Fundamental to a proper understanding of the church and evangelism is the recognition that the gospel creates the church. Robinson wrote, "I do not think the doctrine of the church has any direct implications for evangelism; at all events evangelism is the primary doctrine. The church stems from the evangel, not the evangel from the church."[120] The ministry of evangelism is what brings outsiders into the church. Therefore, the ministry of evangelism is before, and even over, the church.[121] The church is the end point of evangelism, but not its means or agent.

---

117. Robinson, "Diocese of Sydney," 314.

118. Robinson, "Authority of the Church," 305 (repr.); originally written for and read at the International Reformed Congress held at Cambridge, UK, August 1961.

119. Ibid., 305–6.

120. Robinson, "Doctrine of the Church," 109.

121. Robinson put it this way: "The ministry of God's word, especially through the apostle and the evangelist—stands *over* the church and not *under* it. Jesus did not commission the church to evangelize. He commissioned particular men whom he chose, and who, because they were so chosen and because they fulfilled their ministry, were recognized as apostles and evangelists. They might be themselves members of churches and act in fellowship with churches; but the sense of Christ's direction and lordship through his Spirit loomed larger than any relation to a church." Ibid., 112–13.

Robinson was insistent that the church is a creature of the Word. The Word (the gospel) goes forth into the world, through the people of God, especially those gifted for the task of evangelism, and brings people into the church. Robinson wrote of the constitution of the church, "The church is created and constituted by the Word of God. Men are drawn together by this Word, and together express their faith in confession, prayer and praise."[122] Elsewhere he wrote that "it is Jesus who convenes and constitutes it [the church]. . . . All whom Jesus Christ calls to Himself are members of His church or assembly, and they are 'the church' because Jesus *brings them together*."[123] Did Robinson contradict himself in saying on the one hand the church is "constituted by the Word of God," and on the other hand, "Jesus . . . constitutes it?" He did not believe so. Another way of saying this is, Jesus constitutes the church as he brings people together by his Word. Jesus is the subject, the Word is the instrument, and evangelists are the agents.

Authority

What did all this mean for the authority of the church and the exercise of authority within the church? Many contemporary ecclesiological models, including Episcopal and Presbyterian models, interpose external institutional authorities upon the local church. Within these models, denominational structures and figureheads have jurisdiction over parochial leadership. But how, if the church on earth is only local, do these authorities have any right to superintend multiple churches? More so, why should any local church participate in, and/or submit to, denominational structures and strategies?

Robinson understood denominations as servants to local church ministry. In his autobiographical comments he wrote, "We need to understand the roles of the episcopate as it came to be, of dioceses, councils, of national 'churches,' and of what we now call denominations. However imperfectly they may have functioned, their purpose has been to keep local churches on the rails, as it were."[124] Elsewhere he wrote, "If the overriding purpose of the Diocese is that 'the church' therein should be 'the church,' faithful to its foundation, growing in harmony into a holy temple for the Lord, becoming a house of prayer for all nations, and glorifying Christ as head, then the goals of the archbishop and the synod will be connected with ways and means of serving this purpose in a collective way."[125] The denominational structures,

---

122. Robinson, "Authority of the Church," 300.
123. Robinson, "Church of God," 232.
124. Robinson, "'Church' Revisited," 270.
125. Robinson, "Diocese of Sydney," 316.

then, are meant to guard, keep, and bolster the local church. These structures and figureheads are not intended to domineer parishes but to uphold them. In fact, Robinson did not believe denominations or national churches have authority, because they are not churches in the biblical sense.[126]

Exegetically, Robinson did not see any connection between the local churches in any organized fashion, nor does he see any coercive authority beyond the local church. He observed,

> There was no organizational link between Paul's churches, though there were natural affinities between churches in the same province (Col. 4:15–16; 1 Thess. 4:10). All were expected to submit to Paul's authority in matters of the faith—hence the role of Paul's letters and of the visits of Timothy—but this authority was spiritual and admonitory, not coercive (2 Cor. 2:5–10). No church had superiority over any other, though all acknowledged Jerusalem as the source of "spiritual blessings" (Rom. 15:27), and the collection for the saints there was a token of this acknowledgement.[127]

The leadership of the church in the New Testament was local. The only external authority binding on the local church was concerning matters of faith, for which the apostles were judiciaries and mediators because of the authority given to them by Christ.

Authority concerning matters of faith is representative of the highest authority in the church: the Word of God. Robinson understood the church itself to possess no inherent authority. He wrote, "The church has no authority. The church is subject to Christ's authority in everything. One cannot speak of the authority of a body in relation to its head. The obedience of the church is expressed by *submitting* to the Old Testament scriptures, to the gospel brought by its apostle, and to the 'pattern of teaching' handed on by the same apostle."[128] Elsewhere he wrote, "Every true church must, of course, stand in the gospel (1 Cor. 15:1–3) and the one essential mark of its

---

126. Reflecting on both the ecumenical cause and current ecclesiological models Robinson writes, "The present day quest for an ecumenical church is . . . vain. If all denominations in the world were persuaded to unite, the resultant body would not be a church in any biblical sense, no matter what formula of faith or what order it adhered to. Nor would such a body possess any authority of a spiritual kind. The same must be said with regard to national and denominational 'churches.' Such bodies are not churches in any New Testament sense of the word, and they cannot fulfill the functions or enjoy the prerogatives of an *ekklēsia* in matters of authority." Robinson, "Authority of the Church," 299.

127. Robinson, "Church," 228.

128. Robinson, "Authority of the Church," 300.

genuineness is its submission to the apostolic *kērygma*."[129] The Bible governs all matters for the church as the expression of Christ's authority.[130] Submission to the Bible was, for Robinson, submission to Christ. Christ reigns supreme over the church as its head and he exercises that role through his Word.

Though convinced that the local church is *the* church on earth, Robinson was not dismissive of denominational or diocesan structures or leadership. He himself spent the final twenty years of his ministry in episcopal leadership positions. However, his participation in these positions was qualified by how he understood them in relationship to the local church. Reflecting on the Diocese of Sydney and its relationship to parochial ministry, he wrote,

> The Diocese of Sydney is still bound to understand itself as in some sense "the church of God which is at Sydney," and to hold that its distinctive character (as compared with other bodies) is that, by historical derivation and in its present faith and order, it is at once catholic, apostolic, protestant and reformed; that, in support of this character, it is episcopal in ministerial government, scriptural and credal in authority, and liturgical in worship; and that, for the order and good government of its affairs, it is synodical, ensuring the participation of the laity in such ordering.[131]

He continues,

> The process of time has caused dioceses to develop which are no longer capable of assembling "*in* one place" (*epi to auto*) as did primitive churches, except in an occasional and representative (and therefore rather symbolic than actual) manner. The locus of regular functioning as the church has therefore moved to the individual congregations in parishes which make up the constituent parts of the diocese. While therefore the combined and corporate activity of parishes via clergy and representatives (e.g., through synod) is significant in relation to Sydney as a whole, in a number of ways, and while the episcopal ministry gives coherence as well as oversight to the whole (not least in maintaining the catholic and apostolic character referred to above) as well as an actual shared ministry with the presbytery

---

129. Ibid., 303.

130. With regard to the primacy of Scripture over the church Robinson writes, "A church cannot recognise a canon of scripture without committing itself to the claims which that scripture makes for its own character." Ibid., 300.

131. Robinson, "Diocese of Sydney," 312.

in each parish, the individual parish is inevitably the operative locus of the characteristic functioning of "the church."[132]

Robinson authored this reflection on the place of a diocese within ecclesiology later in his ministry, near the end of his tenure as archbishop of Sydney. The timing of the article is interesting because it is well after Robinson's ecclesiological convictions have been established, and it is during his tenure in an office that is in his theology extra-ecclesial. Robinson, therefore, trod carefully in his comments on the place of the diocese, with respect to the office he held. But did he rescind his ecclesiological conclusions in light of his office? No, Robinson was seeking to answer the question "For what purpose does the diocese exist?" He recognized, however, that prior to defining the purpose of the diocese, preliminary questions must be asked: "What is the church and what is its purpose?" Robinson wrote, "The locus of the church is . . . in the parish."[133] He believed it is easier to describe biblically what the church is, than what the church does.[134] Whatever the church is and whatever the church does, the diocese ultimately has the purpose of resourcing churches accordingly.[135]

CONCLUSIONS

What can be identified as the key elements of Robinson's developed ecclesiology? We turn to consider these elements as a summary of Robinson's ecclesiology and anticipate issues for evaluation in our next chapter.

Donald Robinson has constructed an ecclesiology that is steeped in the Cambridge exegetical tradition and shaped by a biblical-theological method. The resulting ecclesiology is one built upon linguistic observation, namely the semantic evaluation of the use of *ekklēsia* in the LXX and the New Testament, and upon exegetical reflection on key ecclesiological texts. This ecclesiology has not been developed in isolation, but rather in conversations with others who both wrote before Robinson and were his contemporaries. This has meant that while his ideas about the church may have been original to him (though how much is original cannot be ascertained),

---

132. Ibid., 313.
133. Ibid.
134. Ibid.

135. As cited earlier, Robinson wrote, "If the overriding purpose of the Diocese is that 'the church' therein should be 'the church,' faithful to its foundation, growing in harmony into a holy temple for the Lord, becoming a house of prayer for all nations, and glorifying Christ as head, then the foals of the Archbishop and the synod will be connected with ways and means of serving this purpose in a collective way." Ibid., 316.

they have not always been unique. What can be said is that his conclusions are situated in a minority strand of ecclesiological reflection, cutting across the grain of contemporary ideals especially with regard to the ecumenical movement of the twentieth century.

The starting point for Robinson's ecclesiology was the application of his biblical-theological method to the theme of "the new man," or "Adam at last." As he traced the soteriological activity of God throughout the Bible, he observed the central theme of God gathering a people to himself. This activity of God, seen in the actual activity of the people gathering together, directed Robinson's ecclesiology. *Ekklēsia* is not an identity of a people, as if coterminous with "people of God," rather it is an activity of the people.

After a semantic and exegetical study of *ekklēsia*, Robinson drew conclusions regarding the place, form and continuity of the church. These conclusions shaped all of his ecclesiology. Though he did not employ the traditional categories of visible and invisible, his conclusions can be summarized within those categories as follows: the visible church is earthly, multiform, and intermittent; the invisible church is heavenly, uniform, and continuous. The earthly gives expression to the heavenly, and each earthly expression is *the* church. His conclusion on the connection of the earthly and heavenly is one that is eschatological rather than philosophical in nature. In other words, Robinson believed that the ultimate expression of the earthly church(es) will be realized in the heavenly gathering at the eschaton. He did not subscribe to a platonic understanding of the church in which one is a mirror of the other, only finding perfect expression in the supernal reality. Rather, Robinson believed that both the earthly and the heavenly are *the* reality, the earthly giving very real expression to the heavenly. This will be examined and developed further in the evaluative chapter.

It is important to see the conclusions that Robinson reached based on his textual work before examining the application of his work to the ecclesiological conversation of his day. This is not to suggest that the ecclesiological issues of his day did not drive his work. They may have, but that will be examined later. We must first work towards an understanding of the conceptual framework of his thought, arrived at through his method, which will then be applied to his historical context.

The most pressing ecclesiological issue of Robinson's day related to the nature of the church was the matter of ecclesial unity. Based upon his textual analysis, Robinson concluded that efforts for ecumenical unity are futile because they pursue a goal that already exists: the church is already one. The church of Christ is one because it is in Christ and Christ cannot be divided. In heaven there is one church and on earth there are many churches. There is no unity to be sought on earth between the churches because on earth the church is multiform, not requiring a singular expression between the churches (as no such expression would be physically possible). Neither is there any unity to be sought in heaven, as there the church is uniform. What must be asked is if Robinson has been too restrictive in his understanding of the language of the New Testament authors. Is there more to be said of a two-sense usage of "church," one being local and the other universal? If so, is the universal always supernal, as Robinson suggests, or is there truly a universal reality on earth? Along with this question, is Robinson correct in assuming that there is no unity to be sought in the church and is this unity truly a fact as it stands? Or is the present church divided in some sense as the ecumenical movement continues to postulate?

Connected to these issues of unity and place, particularly with regard to the form of the church on earth, Robinson concluded that the church on earth does not exist in traditional institutional forms such as a denomination. While a denomination may be helpful for the church, that is the local gatherings, it is not itself a church and has no authority over the local church. In fact, there is no ecclesial authority beyond the local church as there is no church on earth apart from the local church. Within the local church, ultimate authority belongs to the Word of God. It must be asked of Robinson how his own views of the nature of the church coincide with his own tradition's self-understanding. Does he find agreement with the Anglican Church formularies? Have his convictions placed him outside of the sphere of traditional Anglicanism? Along with this, it should be also asked if his rejection of institutional authority is grounded in the biblical text or if it is merely characteristic of Australian antiauthoritarianism.

Concerning the purpose and identity of the church, Robinson believed the church to be an activity of the people of God, rather than coterminous with the people of God. This means that the church by nature is inwardly focused rather than outwardly focused. While not opposed to mission, the church does not itself have an evangelistic mission to the greater world. Instead, the church gathers around the Word of God for the purpose of worship. This gathering fuels mission as the people of God are challenged and equipped from God's Word, but the church itself does not accomplish this mission, its people do. While the "missional church" concept was not prevalent in Robinson's day, it has become a very common view in contemporary ecclesiological literature. It should be asked of Robinson's ecclesiology whether or not mission can be divorced from the church gathering, as the church is constituted of God's people and all of those people share a missional purpose. It also should be asked whether there is carry-over of the missional purpose of the gathering in the Old Testament (Exod 19) to the gathering of God's people in the New Testament and beyond. Or, is there a biblical-theological shift in the concepts of gathering/scattering in the Testaments?

Along with this issue of purpose of the church, it must be asked if there is indeed a clear conceptual divide between the identity of a people and the activity of the people. In other words, can we observe a real distinction between the people of God and the church in the Bible? This question ultimately has bearing on the issue of continuity. Does the church on earth cease to exist when it is not gathered? If so, do believers have any real sense of identity with the church (possibly in heaven?) when the earthly church is not gathered? If the church does not exist beyond the meeting, what consequence does this have for believers and contemporary ecclesiological institutions and systems?

6

Evaluation of Robinson's Ecclesiology

HAVING DESCRIBED AND ANALYZED Donald Robinson's ecclesiology, we turn now to evaluation. This evaluation will seek to ask questions of the ecclesiology's biblical, logical[1] and traditional value. We recognize that these categories are broad and undefined. This is intentional, wishing to highlight the general nature of the questions to be raised. It is important for our evaluation to be an engagement of Robinson and later Knox on their own terms. Robinson believed he was engaging the Bible with scholarly integrity, from within the Anglican tradition, and producing an ecclesiology that was coherent. We will therefore ask questions of how Robinson engaged the Bible, how his conclusions fit within his tradition, and if his conclusions hold together. We will engage the key propositions of his theology of the church in turn. Not every proposition will be engaged at the same level of scrutiny—many of them build upon others. These propositions are as follows:[2]

1. *Ekklēsia*. The church is almost always a gathering in the Bible, functioning as a verbal noun to describe an activity of the people of God rather than the people of God themselves.

2. *Place*. The church is where Christ is: on earth, where two or three are gathered in the name of Christ; and in heaven, where Christ is seated. Thus, there is a binary locale of the church, as it is both earthly and

---

1. "Logical" is being employed here and hereafter in the book in the common usage to express coherence and internal cogency.

2. These propositions are the product of the description of Robinson's ecclesiology in the previous chapter. These are my summaries of the key points he makes concerning the nature of the church. These are presented in an order I have chosen as the best logical sequencing. These propositions are mutually dependent.

heavenly. These are not two churches; rather the earthly gives expression to the heavenly.

3. *Form*. On earth the church is multiform, finding expression in the many local gatherings around the world. In heaven the church is uniform, meeting around the throne of Christ.

4. *Continuity*. On earth the church is an intermittent activity, meeting for a time and then scattering. In heaven the church is continuous, being constantly gathered in the presence of Christ.

5. *Unity*. The church is united in both heaven and on earth. There is an ontological connection of the church to Christ; because Christ is one, and the church is in Christ, then the church cannot be divided.

6. *Jew and Gentile*. The church is not coterminous with the people of God, but rather an activity of the people of God. Israel is preserved as an identity (ethnic?) in the church as a demonstration of God's wisdom of bringing together Jews and Gentiles. Therefore, the church is not the "new Israel."

7. *The Task of the Church*. The people of God gather around the Word of God to meet with God. The church as such does not possess an evangelistic task—Christians do.

8. *Authority*. The church possesses no inherent authority, nor does any external institutional structure beyond the local church (e.g., denomination). The sole authority in the church is the Word of God, for submission to the Bible is submission to Christ who reigns supreme over the church.

EVALUATION

1. *Ekklēsia*

The church is almost always a gathering in the Bible, functioning as a verbal noun to describe an activity of the people of God rather than the people of God themselves.

The foundational concept of Robinson's ecclesiology is "the church is a gathering." We observed that Robinson arrived at this conclusion in his semantic examination of *ekklēsia* in the canon accompanied by, or in agreement with, his reading of Hort and Campbell, amongst others. By stating that the church is an activity, a verbal noun of sorts, Robinson removed the possibility of construing the concept of church in any way that would depict an identity, with the exception of discerning those participating in the activity—those who gather.

Evaluation of Robinson's ecclesiology should begin with this linguistic study, as all of Robinson's theological conclusions about the nature of the church build upon this basic premise that the church is a gathering. Here our evaluative task will be to determine if Robinson's semantic study of *ekklēsia* produces conceptual isolation.[3] To some, defining conceptual parameters of church according to linguistic usage may seem too simplistic. Is a concept limited to the singular term usually employed to denote it, in this case "church"? Or, do we have a concept of church bigger than the word "church"? In the history of Christianity, the term has been used much more liberally to depict the entire population of Christians both in the world and throughout history. In our assessment we will examine Robinson's method as well as his conclusion, adhering to the criticisms raised by some of his respondents. If Robinson has isolated a concept it will have been because of a flawed or incomplete method, neglecting the correlation of the concept within a wider biblical and theological framework.

Robinson has been criticized because of the linguistic dependence of his argument. As such, his ecclesiology has been characterized as little more than a word-study,[4] and its theological depth has been called into question. However, while we have established that linguistic analysis was very much at the heart of Robinson's ecclesiology, we have also seen that this analysis fits within a larger framework of biblical theology. Nevertheless, we should investigate whether the critiques of an overdependence on linguistic analysis are valid. Has Robinson read too much into a word—*ekklēsia*—at the expense of conceptual clarity?

In 1961, James Barr's *Semantics of Biblical Language*[5] changed the trajectory of modern biblical hermeneutics, offering an exposé of common fallacies in contemporary interpretation. Amongst other pitfalls, Barr was critical of an "illegitimate totality of transfer." Barr identified this fallacy in the kind of linguistic work that sought a singular meaning for a word in an effort to assess a word's theological value. He did not believe that words should be understood with reference to the entirety of the canon, but rather based on their context, namely the sentence in which they occurred.[6] Barr wrote, "The idea of theology and philology belonging together is in general

---

3. The issue of conceptual isolation comes from Graham Cole's paper presented at Moore College in 1986 on Robinson's and Knox's ecclesiologies. Cole, "Doctrine of the Church," 3–17.

4. Jensen, *Sydney Anglicanism*, 85–86.

5. Barr, *Semantics of Biblical Language*.

6. Ibid., 218.

a pleasant and attractive one. But . . . easily it can produce a scientific failure; and many such failures can be traced to the philosophy of language which allows a theological argument to do duty for a linguistic one, or assumes that the linguistic facts will fit the patterns of theological relations."[7] Thus, the danger is importing a meaning of a word into a particular context so that the word carries more theological weight than what is to be understood by the word in its context.

But is Barr's critique one of assigning a definition to a word? It would not seem so. Barr is more critical of what he calls the "illegitimate totality transfer," in which the theological depth represented by a concept from its many uses in various contexts is imported into any/every usage of the word. He writes, "The attempt to relate the various relations and stocks of biblical language to a comprehensive and ultimate series of theological realities is an essentially idealist programme."[8] Thus, Barr is cautious about importing theological stock for words that is not indicated in any given context. Therefore, defining words is not necessarily problematic, as words have basic meanings that can be identified from a semantic range. Barr utilizes the example of *ekklēsia*.

> If we ask "What is the meaning of ἐκκλησία [*ekklēsia*] in the NT"?, the answer given may be an adding or a compounding of different statements about the ἐκκλησία [*ekklēsia*] made in various passages. Thus we might say (a) "the Church is the Body of Christ" (b) "the Church is the first instalment of the Kingdom of God" (c) "the Church is the Bride of Christ," and other such statements. The "meaning of ἐκκλησία [*ekklēsia*] in the NT" could then be legitimately stated to be the totality of these relations. This is one sense of "meaning." But when we take an individual sentence, such as "The Church is the Body of Christ," and ask what is the meaning of "the Church" in this sentence, we are asking something different. The semantic indication given by "the Church" is now something much less than "the NT conception of the Church." The realization of this is of primary importance in dealing with isolated or unusual cases; the obvious example is "my ἐκκλησία [*ekklēsia*]" in Matt. 16:18 (cf. 18:17).[9]

Barr's caution, then, is that the use of a concept not be confused with the concept itself. Everything that is to be said conceptually of something like "church" may not be meant in every usage of the word. Contextual exegesis

---

7. Ibid., 261.
8. Ibid., 259.
9. Ibid., 218.

must be done, and it must be done for concepts, but it must not be confused with linguistics.

It is at this point of an "illegitimate totality transfer" that Kevin Giles criticizes Robinson. In an appendix to his *What on Earth Is the Church?*, Giles challenges the semantic conclusions of Robinson (and Knox), along with those upon whose work they depended (Hort, Campbell). He systematically exposes what he sees as inconsistencies in the argument that *qāhāl* and *ekklēsia* must always refer to an assembly. Investigating the usage of *ēdâh* and *qāhāl* in the OT and their correlates in the LXX, *synagōgē* and *ekklēsia* (respectively), Giles describes how *ēdâh* is always rendered *synagōgē* but *qāhāl* is not always rendered *ekklēsia*. *Ēdâh* had the connotation of the totality of Israel and *qāhāl* often depicted the assembly of the nation. However, Giles believes that the universality of *ēdâh* became associated with *qāhāl*, as *qāhāl* sometimes was rendered *synagōgē* rather than *ekklēsia*. Building upon this line of argumentation, he argues that the *ekklēsia* in the New Testament represented the collective identity of the "Israel of God" as the "church of God." Giles writes,

> The possibility of added semantic development in the understanding of the word *ekklēsia* was provided by the fact that both Hebrew words, *qahal* and *edah*, as we noted above, could be translated by the one Greek word *sunagōgē*. Thus, although *ekklēsia* was never used to translate *edah*, some of the content of this almost technical Hebrew term for Israel, as God's elect covenant community, passed over to the Greek word *ekklēsia*, because in Hellenistic Judaism it was equated with *sunagōgē*.[10]

Giles seeks to express the development in understanding of the *ekklēsia* throughout the writing of the biblical canon, differentiating between the idea of abstract nouns and concrete nouns. That is, he believes it must be determined if a word is being used as an "abstract noun implying activity, or as a concrete noun—and thus alluding to the end product of this activity, a substantive entity."[11] Giles concedes that both *qāhāl* and *ekklēsia* are abstract nouns, but his argument details their development into being used as concrete nouns. Giles believes that what once was used to represent something happening—what we have identified as a verbal-noun in Robinson's analysis of *ekklēsia*—became something concrete to depict an identity or entity that extended beyond the actual happening of the gathering.

What Giles's argument does not take into account is that there are broader concepts that already function as concrete realities, allowing for

10. Ibid., 237.
11. Ibid., 232.

abstract nouns to refer to these concrete realities. There is potential for a both/and scenario when both concepts (*ēdâh* and *qāhāl*) are presented together. However, as the concepts can coexist, and at points refer to the same thing, there can remain differentiation between the two. For example, in this instance the broader concrete reality is the people of God represented by *ēdâh*. The *ēdâh* can exist and be referenced in a way that is distinguishable from the *qāhāl*. However, the *qāhāl* functioning as the abstract reality can never be separated from the *ēdâh*, because it is the people of the *ēdâh* (at least in part, depending on which gathering) that constitute the *qāhāl*.[12] When the *qāhāl* ceases the *ēdâh* remains. However, there is no *qāhāl* without the *ēdâh*. Thus, the *ēdâh* is the concrete reality with the *qāhāl* functioning as its abstract correlate.

In Giles's argument, then, the confusion lies in the points when the *ēdâh* and *qāhāl* function synonymously. He assumes that because there are times when the two appear to be the same reality, they must be coterminous. This is true for some properties, but not in total. Of this fallacy Barr wrote, "An object or event may be signified by word *a* or by word *b*. This does not mean that *a* means *b*. . . . The identity of the object to which different designations are given does not imply that these designations have the same semantic value. The mistake of supposing that it does we may for convenience call 'illegitimate identity transfer.'"[13] What must be realized is that because the *qāhāl* is the abstract of the concrete *ēdâh*, it will necessarily possess some similarities. What is said of the *qāhāl* may be said to be true of the *ēdâh*. However, the reverse is not true; what is said of the *ēdâh* may or may not be true of the *qāhāl*.

The distinction between the reality of an entity and an activity of that entity was precisely the concern of Graham Cole in his response to Robinson's (and Knox's) ecclesiology.[14] He believed that there was a necessary distinction to be made between the people of God, as the broader (concrete) category, and the (abstract) activity of that people, "church." Giles is on the right track of distinguishing the abstract from the concrete; however, he unnecessarily ends up concluding that the abstract became the concrete. He has failed to identify a conceptual clarity, parsing out the entity and the activity, and as a result his conclusion is a conceptual inflation. The *ekklēsia*

---

12. Cole is correct in noting, "*Ekklesia* may be subsumed under 'people,' but not vice versa. For the gathering is the people of God so gathered, whilst the people of God scattered, though still the people of God, are no longer strictly speaking the *ekklesia*." Cole, "Doctrine of the Church," 9.

13. Barr, *Semantics*, 217–18.

14. Cole, "Doctrine of the Church," 3–17.

is made to carry more weight than it is worth. We will investigate this further below.

Returning to Giles's critique of Robinson's method, we continue to investigate if there is legitimacy to the claim that Robinson's conclusions represented an "illegitimate totality transfer." Robinson certainly sought to understand the usage of words across the canon—and in using the term canon, we are implying Robinson's appreciation of biblical unity—but he did not presume that unity implied uniformity in linguistic meaning.[15] Robinson was well aware of the diversity of genres and authorship in the Biblical text, and therefore sought to understand the meaning and usage of words in their context. His singular definition of *ekklēsia* does not entail that he has been negligent of the context and development of word usage. Rather, Robinson recognized that in the instance of *ekklēsia*, almost every usage is of a gathering.[16] Indeed, Robinson preempted this critique in an autobiographical essay on his method, stating that he used a concordance rather than a lexicon to establish the semantic value of words.[17]

While Robinson seems to have been aware of the potential dangers of philological examination, has he been inconsistent in his evaluation of *ekklēsia*? Has he sought to supply a theological meaning encompassing every usage in the Bible? Or has he observed, in the context of each word (for Barr, the sentence in which the word is used), that the semantic range of *ekklēsia* (almost) always depicts a gathering? It may be that Robinson did not intend to give expression to the theological depth surrounding the *ekklēsia*, which must be explored in the many metaphors employed of the term/concept, but rather to establish the semantic boundaries of a fundamental meaning: a gathering. This serves then, not as a theological importation superimposed

---

15. The greatest distinction between Barr and Robinson would surely be their understanding of the unity of the biblical texts—Robinson holding a very high view of the unity of the biblical texts as a canon, whereas Barr did not believe the Bible should be read as a unit.

16. Robinson did not specify the exceptions, but he never spoke with certainty about the universal meaning and usage of *ekklēsia* as a "gathering." In spite of him leaving room for other renderings, it appears that he held this singular meaning. Knox would stress with certainty this singular meaning.

17. We have already cited this in an earlier section but it is worth quoting Robinson's comments here once again: "From Shipp I learned a little about how to assess the actual semantic value of words as they are used by individual writers and in particular contexts, without simply importing a dictionary meaning into them with a heavy hand.... I began, in my theological studies, to discover that many commentators and theologians tended to read more into the meanings of words than either context or usage warranted, and did not allow for subtle changes of meaning of words from one writer to another or even from one context to another in the same writer." Robinson, "'Church' Revisited," 261–62.

upon the word, but rather a defense mechanism to keep such imports out. By establishing a linguistic sense of *ekklēsia*, grounded in semantic investigation of the canon,[18] the integrity of the word/concept is preserved against the threat of theological inflation.

In 1986 Graham Cole argued that the ecclesiology Robinson (and Knox) had developed might be too narrow in its emphasis and therein in danger of conceptual isolation.[19] The solution to this danger is to locate the church in the broader category of "people of God."[20] Robinson conceded to this suggestion from Cole in his autobiographical fragment, and in fact had begun to develop his own thinking in this direction in 1962. Cole's caution against conceptual isolation was grounded in concern for a loss of Christian identity—amongst other broader theological concerns[21]—as many Christians find their identity synonymous with church. If the church is intermittent, only ever existing when gathered, then what is to be said of Christian identity? Robinson argued that Christians primarily identify with Christ and therefore meet based on that identification. The matter of concern is Christian ontology.

It seems that Cole *was* correct in identifying a danger in Robinson's ecclesiology, as Robinson acknowledged, and that a final necessary development in the linguistic work of Robinson is the establishment of conceptual clarity. While Robinson expressed that "church" and "people of God" are not synonymous, there is room for further clarification. There is a lack of continuity in the abstract and concrete if there is not a clarification of the people of God as the broader theological category and the church as the activity that people.

We now conclude with the initial question of the theological quality of Robinson's ecclesiology. Michael Jensen writes that the model

> is certainly a linguistic analysis of the usage of a particular word in the New Testament texts. Is this sufficient to provide for a proper *theological* description of the concept of the "church"? . . . What Scripture says about the concept of "church" is not merely confined to the way it uses the particularly [sic] word "church." That *ekklēsia* usually describes actual gatherings of people in the

---

18. Again, this work is best exhibited in the essay by Campbell, "Christian Use of the Word ΕΚΚΛΗΣΙΑ," 41–54.

19. Cole assumed that what Robinson and Knox developed in ecclesiology was a unit. However, Robinson and Knox did not argue the same position with regards to the distinction of the greater concept of "people of God" and the more specific "church."

20. Cole, "Doctrine of the Church," 9–11.

21. Cole also addresses the issue of christomonism. Ibid., 10.

New Testament is not in fact grounds to limit the theological concept to actual particular gatherings.[22]

But is Jensen correct? Even in secular usage the *ekklēsia* of the *dēmos* referred to the *actual* gathering of people. Why should we not expect that the meaning of words have conceptual bearing? Jensen *is* correct that a theological concept is not always bound to a singular word. The many metaphors for the church are demonstrative of the greater conceptual framework up and running in the Bible. But is he right in concluding that Robinson's ecclesiology is insufficiently theological because it is governed by the meaning of the representative term?

It is not difficult to demonstrate Robinson's awareness of the broader conceptual reality of the church beyond the actual language of "*ekklēsia*." This can be seen particularly in the autobiographical description of his ecclesiology, in which he expressed the dependence of a proper biblical theology of the church upon an understanding of God's soteriological activity in the canon.[23] This being said, Robinson's thought should be appraised according to his own self-understanding and his own disclosure of his method. Robinson understood himself as a biblical theologian, primarily seeking to observe thematic developments across the canon. Thus, Jensen's question of the theological sufficiency of Robinson's ecclesiology is valid insomuch as Robinson's ecclesiology did not move to engage the history of theology or many of the other theological systems. However, this should not detract from the deeply theological claims he made in his efforts to exegete biblical texts on the church and draw together theological threads from across the Bible. Finally, we note that Robinson set up a biblical-theological framework upon which a theology of the church could be built.

2. Place

The church is where Christ is; on earth, where two or three are gathered in the name of Christ, and in heaven, where Christ is seated. Thus, there is a binary locale of the church, as it is both earthly and heavenly. These are not two churches; rather the earthly gives expression to the heavenly.

Traditional Protestant ecclesiology has understood the church as twofold: the church militant and the church triumphant; or, the visible church and the invisible church. But as some have grappled with how these two

---

22. Jensen, *Sydney Anglicanism*, 85–86.
23. Robinson, "'Church' Revisited," 269.

notions of church correlate, there has developed a third category: general.[24] If the triumphant (invisible) church comprises all believers of all time, then there must be a relationship between the local churches globally within the notion of church militant (visible). Thus, the church militant (visible) is subdivided into two categories: local and general. "Local" church describes church at is most basic form, believers congregated in one locale. "General" church describes the sum total of all Christians in the world. This threefold conception of the church stems from a twofold division of realm (visible and invisible), but a threefold division of space (local, global, heavenly). The identification of the binary locale of the earthly church—local and global—arises from a theological conception of the church as something coterminous with the people of God. Where is the church?—wherever God's people are. The church, then, as we have seen in our earlier discussion, entails a conception of identity.

Robinson, however, disagreed with the common threefold locale of the church, seeking to address the issue of place from his foundational proposition of the church as a gathering. The church cannot be a global reality if it cannot gather, for a church is always a gathering. Robinson's theological move was to understand realm and space together, though he never articulated his position meticulously. In fact, he did not employ the language of visible and invisible. Instead, he referred only to the locations of the church as earthly/local and heavenly. He did not need the visible and invisible categories because of the close connection of his understanding of realm and space; the visible is the earthly church that is always local, and the invisible is the heavenly church. These churches are *bona fide* churches because Christ has promised his presence when Christians gather (Matt 18:20).

Robinson was convinced that the evidence of the New Testament supported his case. Denying the church as a global reality did not require him to dispute much conflicting evidence. The one passage that he identified as seemingly problematic was Acts 9:31,[25] which he explained contextually. He believed that the church (singular) across many regions was a reference to the church of Jerusalem that had been dispersed because of persecution, but which now enjoyed peace. The singular reference described the people who previously congregated.

---

24. See Graham Cole's discussion in "Doctrine of the Church," 3–4. He examines W. H. Griffith Thomas as an example. This third category has been the operating assumption of many, including the ecumenical movement.

25. Acts 9:31: "So the church throughout all Judea and Galilee and Samaria had peace and was being built up. And walking in the fear of the Lord and in the comfort of the Holy Spirit, it multiplied."

Kevin Giles argues strongly against Robinson's twofold locale of church, particularly because it rests on a narrow definition of *ekklēsia*. Giles believes that this understanding endorses a position that is more platonic than biblical.[26] Much of this will be addressed below in our discussion of continuity. But for now we ask: How are Christians present in the heavenly places here and now? Does this represent an over-realized eschatology? How it is that Robinson understood the earthly giving expression to the heavenly? Are these two separate gatherings?

Robinson believed that there was broader community identity, but that this identity resided in the Christian's self-understanding as presently being a congregant in the heavenly gathering. As mentioned above, the language of the present heavenly reality of the church, existing simultaneously with the earthly church—even being the same church—has brought to Robinson's ecclesiology the accusation of Platonism. This critique would appear to gain traction largely because Robinson never explored how this expression of the heavenly in the earthly worked. Indeed, his claims might be construed as platonic, as though the heavenly represents an ideal church.[27] But did Robinson really envision the heavenly church as the "ideal" in comparison to the earthly church? Was the heavenly the pure form of the earthly shadow?

A close reading of Robinson indicates that he believed the earthly to be a full expression of the heavenly gathering. Therefore, the heavenly does not represent an ideal to be achieved, but rather a greater gathering of the redeemed community and participation in Christ in a different sense. Robinson would have served his readers well had he anticipated this critique and offered further explanation of how the earthly and heavenly correlate. In particular, it seems that for Robinson the heavenly and the earthly gatherings are connected in an ontological sense. That is, the heavenly and the earthly both find their expression in the presence of Christ. The "in Christ" language is key to a proper understanding of the church. Therefore, Robinson might have explained the ontological connection as the earthly and the heavenly being the same church because they are fully in Christ's presence and those gathered are actually *in* Christ. Along with these ontological explanations a fuller development of the significance of Christ's presence as a constitutive element for the gathering, as well as the relationship of Christ's presence in the heavenly versus the earthly, would have also greatly helped his readers.[28]

26. Giles, *What on Earth Is the Church?*, 14.

27. For an understanding of what is meant by "platonic," see the Allegory of the Cave, in Plato's *Republic*, VII.513–20, 220–27.

28. As we will see later in our study, it was Knox who further identified the significance of the presence of Christ for the *ekklēsia* and elaborated upon the way in which

Robinson's pupil P. T. O'Brien pushed Robinson's conclusions further to seek clarity on the nature of place in ecclesiology. In his studies of the books of Colossians, Ephesians, and Hebrews, O'Brien described the heavenly and eschatological reality of the church.[29] The church is something that is, but also something that will be. It, like many other realities of the New Testament, is both already and not-yet. However, this still does not fully explain the relationship of the earthly and heavenly assemblies. O'Brien allows the tension to remain unexplained. He writes,

> The New Testament does not discuss the relationship between the local church and the heavenly gathering. The link is nowhere specifically spelled out. Certainly the former is neither *part* of the church of God nor *a* church of God, as the openings of several of Paul's letters make plain: so at 1 Cor. 1:2 the apostle writes to "*the church* of God which is at Corinth." Perhaps it is best to suggest that the local congregations or house-groups are earthly manifestations of that heavenly assembly gathered around God and Christ.[30]

O'Brien believes, as Robinson does, that the earthly and the heavenly are deeply connected. O'Brien suggests an explanation of how these gatherings are connected, and does so in a way that is compatible with Robinson.

What remains underdeveloped in Robinson's ecclesiology with regard to the place of the church? Is it satisfactory to leave a tension unexplained because the text of the New Testament seems to allow for such a tension? It seems best to recognize that there is a tension in the New Testament that may remain unresolved from a biblical-theological perspective. And yet, the identification of the eschatological character of the heavenly gathering may be useful in a biblical theology and it may be that there is some greater clarity to be achieved from such recognition. For instance, identifying the heavenly *and eschatological* character of the church may help resolve the seemingly platonic character of Robinson's thought. The eschatological nature of the church informs the tension created by thinking in terms of time and space. It would seem that the accusation of Platonism in Robinson's ecclesiology comes from an inability to reconcile the simultaneous present reality of the earthly and heavenly gatherings. The eschatological character of the heavenly gathering relocates the heavenly gathering in another time and place, but with very real present implications. Just as Christians are in a

---

Christ is present in both the heavenly and the earthly.

29. See O'Brien, *Colossians, Philemon*, 57–61; *Letter to the Ephesians*, 146–47; and *Letter to the Hebrews*, 111–12; 477–91.

30. O'Brien, "Church as a Heavenly and Eschatological Reality," 97.

very real sense saved, so too they look forward to the day when they will be saved. Just as the heavenly gathering is present before the throne of Christ and finding earthly expression now, so too those gathered on earth now look forward to the day when they will be in the physical presence of Christ.

But we might add that the ontological connection would also greatly aid in establishing how and why Robinson's ecclesiology does not concede to Platonism. Both the church on earth and the church in heaven are *the* church. It is the ontology of the church in both realms that establishes their authenticity. Robinson did make claims about the ontology of the church (though not using the language of ontology), but he was neither explicit nor thorough enough to expel platonic accusation. We will see in Knox's work that he made further attempts to establish this ontological connection between the earthly and the heavenly, but even in his work not enough to prevent accusation of Platonism from some quarters.

Several contemporary scholars (e.g., O'Brien, Peterson, Adams) have worked towards clarity regarding the seemingly platonic heaven-earth duality of the church in the book of Hebrews.[31] One of these scholars, Edward Adams, writes,

> The heaven-earth duality is not for our author an antithetical dualism: heaven and earth are not polarised. . . . The "heavenly" country is valued above the existing earth, but the distinction is hierarchical ("better") not oppositional. . . . The emphasis on (the higher) heaven in the epistle to the Hebrews is Christologically motivated: heaven is where Christ is now and where he carries out his high-priestly role.[32]

Rather than observing an ideal, or a distinction between the physical and the realm of ideas, Adams seeks to observe the qualitative difference established by the presence of Christ. Because Christ has moved between the realms—heavenly and earthly—there is a distinction of place and time as much as anything. What constitutes the greatest distinction is the perfection of the heavenly, not because it is the realm of ideas, but because this is where God is and this is where Christ carries out his high priestly role. David Peterson has clearly acknowledged this perfection of heaven and identified the participation in that perfection that Christians currently enjoy on earth. He writes, "*The relationship with God that believers may now enjoy, by virtue of Christ's finished work, involves as its implied end the transfer of believers to the heavenly city. . . .* The approach to God in his heavenly sanctuary, which is

---

31. Of course, for Robinson Hebrews 12 was foundational for his emphasis on the primacy of the heavenly gathering.

32. Adams, "Cosmology of Hebrews," 134.

a present possibility for Christians by faith, becomes the means of entering the actual presence of God in the age to come."[33] He continues, "Christians in their conversion have already, in a sense, reached their heavenly destination. However, the heavenly city is still the goal of the Christian's pilgrimage (13:14; cf. 4:1–11). The vision in 12:22–4 is of the ultimate, completed company of the people of God, membership of which is now enjoyed by faith."[34]

Contemporary scholars, such as we have seen in O'Brien and Peterson, have identified the already/not-yet tension present in regard to the heavenly church in the book of Hebrews and other New Testament writings. Robinson articulated the primacy of the heavenly existence but did not elaborate on the *eschatological* nature of this gathering. Clarity may be found in identifying "heaven" as a realm, having implications for both time and space. These implications may not be completely linear or material, as the future/eschatological/final has bearing on the present. Therefore, in a very real sense the heavenly church can be understood as a present reality to which believers have already come (e.g., Eph 2; Heb 12). The heavenly/eschatological reality is experienced now in the earthly gathering. This relationship may best be expressed as an ontological connection. The earthly finds its being in the heavenly. But this is not platonic dualism, as the earthly is the consequence of the heavenly, and the heavenly is the destination of the earthly. These realities are in some sense one and the same. The sameness is particularly identified when considered christologically, recognizing the presence of Christ as *the* constitutive element of the church.

3. Form

On earth the church is multiform, finding expression in the many local gatherings around the world. In heaven the church is uniform meeting around the throne of Christ.

We will not spend as much time examining Robinson's position on the form of the church, as this follows logically from his previous statement concerning the place of the church. But it is appropriate to explore further his thoughts concerning the earthly form of the church, especially his understanding of singular location of the earthly church—local.

We have seen the consequence of Robinson's identification of the *ekklēsia* as a gathering, as a multiform earthly church. On earth there are many gatherings in many locations, and therefore many expressions of the heavenly church each fully being *the* church. Robinson developed his case

33. Peterson, *Hebrews and Perfection*, 166 (emphasis original).
34. Ibid., 167.

through the New Testament's identification of a plurality of churches, even in a singular region (e.g., Galatia, Judea, Macedonia).[35] The recognition of a plurality of churches, including a plurality in a particular region, further supported Robinson's conclusion that the only *uniform* church is in heaven. A church must be able to gather, and logically separation of distance prohibits the opportunity for gathering. Therefore, the necessity and reality of a plurality of churches arose as the gospel was disseminated amongst the nations.

Kevin Giles has argued that Robinson's multiform understanding of church promotes individualism and neglects the community understanding of the New Testament.[36] Giles believes that a proper New Testament ecclesiology makes use of the word *ekklēsia*, but also looks beyond it to the greater sense of community that is often represented in other ecclesial images expressed in metaphors (e.g., the body of Christ, the temple, the bride, etc.).[37] The language of a singular church beyond the local church in the New Testament need not be conceived of exclusively as a heavenly reality; the church on earth may be understood as one. We have already identified a fundamental difference between the thought of Robinson and Giles. Giles believes that a proper ecclesiology encompasses all ideas of community in the New Testament. Robinson would not deny that community is the proper context for the doctrine of the church, but he believed that the church is a function of the community, not the community itself. We will investigate the ramifications of both Giles's and Robinson's ecclesiology for identity in the believing community in the next section on "continuity."

Essential to this discussion is the presence of Christ. Robinson believed that the church is only ever a gathering of believers *in the presence of Christ*. The uniformity of the heavenly gathering is without contest. But the presence of Christ on earth is less clear, for Christ's presence on earth is spiritual—in his Word and by his Spirit. Questions that naturally follow are "How is Christ present by his Spirit?" and "When is Christ present by his Spirit?" If Christ is with believers always to the end of the age (Matt 28:20), is this a promise for his constant presence? If so, can it be said that the church is always on earth? Is there a means by which Christ is present spiritually in a special way with his gathered people? These questions lead us into the next area of discussion of Robinson's ecclesiology: "continuity."

---

35. For example, 1 Cor 16:1; 2 Cor 8:1; Gal 1:2, 22; 1 Thess 2:14; etc.
36. Giles, *What on Earth Is the Church?*, 14.
37. This understanding demands that *ekklēsia* is but another metaphor.

4. Continuity

On earth the church is an intermittent activity, meeting for a time and then scattering. In heaven the church is continuous, being constantly gathered in the presence of Christ.

Of the challenges to Robinson's ecclesiology, the question of continuity presents the greatest practical problems. What happens to Christian identity when the church is not gathered? Is there no corporate identity when the *ekklēsia* is dispersed? If not, what does this mean for Christian living beyond the *ekklēsia*? If there is a continued identity, where is it to be found? Also, what is the guarantee of regular participation in community if the church ceases when it is not gathered? Is there any sense of belonging/membership to be found in the earthly church?

Here again, we return to Kevin Giles's critique of the "individualism" of Robinson's ecclesiology. Giles is concerned that much of the communal responsibility and identity present in the New Testament is lost in Robinson's position. He appears to think the New Testament demands that every notion of community belongs to the church. Therefore, his critique of Robinson relies on an all-or-nothing scenario in which a community identity cannot be located elsewhere beyond the church. Every image or reference to community must refer to the church.

We recall our earlier examination of Giles's understanding of concrete versus abstract realities.[38] It is helpful to see that there is a defined concreteness to the concept of church as Giles has suggested, but this is only to be said insomuch as there is a range of metaphors that are used of the concept church to describe the reality. Thus, Barr is correct in observing that a term in a specific biblical text should not be understood to encapsulate all that is represented conceptually by the term elsewhere, what he calls an "illegitimate identity transfer."[39] The church conceptually, as the gathered people of God, is the sum total of all the metaphors employed surrounding the term church in the canon. In order to be included in a biblical ecclesiology, the reality each metaphor represents needs to be predicated of the assembly, rather than simply the people of God understood corporately. Thus, the church in a particular context is the body of Christ. But in a broader theological conception, the church is not only the body of Christ, but also the bride of Christ, and so forth. We may therefore state that the term *ekklēsia* is always an abstract noun, depicting an activity, but there is concreteness to this reality insomuch as there are metaphors used to describe this reality.

---

38. Section 1 above.
39. Barr, *Semantics*, 217–18.

However, this abstract reality is always the correlate to the concrete reality of the people of God, for which there are also many metaphors to describe the fullness of the concept.

Paul Minear's *Images of the Church in the New Testament* presents a similar thesis. He identifies as many as ninety-six community analogies in the New Testament, all representing the church. As we have seen in this study, the corporate reality—in fact, the *concrete* corporate reality—is the people of God. Thus, there is a necessary reassignment of the corporate metaphors, distinguishing between those that depict the abstract concept of church and those that depict the concrete concept of the people of God. He mistakenly identifies the people of God as an image of the church, rather than the concrete reality, with *ekklēsia* as the abstract correlate. This is in part because he believes that we cannot distinguish between metaphor and reality because metaphors in the ancient world were so often tied to the community's understanding of reality.[40] In view of how the people of God are understood in biblical theology, with the distinguishable activity of the people gathering, it seems that Minear's thesis is incorrect.[41] There is need for a fresh reappraisal of Minear's work, with a view to discerning which images indeed belong to the church and which belong to the people of God.

We have seen that Graham Cole approached Robinson's ecclesiology from a different angle. He too shared concerns over continuity in Robinson's position. However, he did not envision that all notions of Christian community needed to be bound up in the church. Rather, he advocated conceptual clarity to be achieved by distinguishing between the church and the people of God. The "people of God" identifies the broader redeemed community in a way that does not over-inflate the concept of the church beyond exegetical allowances. Here also is found a helpful guard against the potential for "ghettoism or social introversion,"[42] addressing any critique of individualism by maintaining a community identity—the people of God—while preserving the notion of church as a function of that community.

Robinson's understanding of continuity might well be understood to faithfully represent the biblical texts depicting the *ekklēsia*. But it demands further development, as he would agree.[43] The church in heaven is continuous. The church on earth is intermittent. But when the church on earth scatters, there is a broader identity for the Christian as a member of the

---

40. Ibid., 14–27.
41. Graham Cole seems to agree; see "Doctrine of the Church," 9.
42. Ibid., 13.
43. Robinson agreed with Cole's correction/clarification in his autobiographical essay. Robinson, "Church Revisited," 269.

people of God, the redeemed community purchased by Jesus's blood. So, we might ask: What is the nature of the correction/clarification required of Robinson's position on continuity? How is it that the Christian should constantly identify with the heavenly and not extend that to the earthly? What does it mean for one to continue while the other ceases? Robinson did not provide detailed answers to these questions. What could be developed in his thought is the ontological nature of the Christian identity and its relationship to the Christian self-understanding. Christians are primarily identified with Christ. Their participation in the heavenly gathering owes itself to their participation in Christ. They have been raised with him to be where he is (Eph 2). Once again we recognize the need to identify the eschatological reality of the believer's participation in the heavenly church, alongside the ontological reality of their position in Christ.

5. Unity

The church is united. There is an ontological connection of the church to Christ; because Christ is one, and the church is in Christ, then the church cannot be divided.

Robinson's understanding of the unity of the church developed in the face of the mid-century ecumenical push epitomized by the World Council of Churches. Robinson was very open about the influence of the WCC on his need to "go public" with his ecclesiology, and as such the tone of his comments on unity were often polemical. Robinson argued for the existing unity of the church from the church's ontological location in Christ; because the church belongs to Christ, as his body, the church must be united. Christ cannot be divided. Robinson understood Jesus' prayer for unity in John 17 to be fulfilled with the advent of the Holy Spirit at Pentecost. This argument was bolstered by Robinson's exegetical conclusions from Ephesians 4—a passage stating that unity is something to be maintained, which implies existing unity. Thus, his conclusions were both logical deductions (Christ's body cannot be divided) and exegetical analyses (e.g., John 17; Acts 1, 2; Eph 4).

With the "century of the church" largely focusing on ecumenism, Robinson's comments arguing for the *present* unity of the church cut across the grain of the vast majority of the ecclesiological discussion. The difference between Robinson's theology and that of ecumenists is the location of the church. Robinson's argument for the place of the church was built upon his fundamental premise that the church is only ever a gathering, thereby restricting the conversation of the earthly church to the local congregation.

Ecumenists, on the other hand, recognized a broader earthly entity in the universal church on earth. Therefore, when considering the church's unity, ecumenists believed that this unity must be experienced (achieved?) on a global scale. Therefore, the starting point for the ecumenical movement is a presupposition of current disunity, whereas for Robinson, the unity of the church is presupposed as a fundamental property of the church's nature.

Robinson developed his case in view of the creeds. His argument was that all Christians confess faith in the "one, holy, catholic, and apostolic" church. The difficulty of grasping this unity comes when the church is understood to be broader than the local gathering. For what constitutes true unity within a broader conception of the church? Institutional amalgamation? Table fellowship? If so, where does this table fellowship occur? Is it in a hypothetical (or actual) scenario when members of other denominations visit and are welcomed at a church that is associated with a different denomination? Robinson argued that true unity is expressed at the local level, when and where Christians gather regularly. This local unity ultimately finds its basis in the uniform church of heaven.

If the church is united, one should explore why the churches are implored to "maintain the unity of the Spirit in the bond of peace" (Eph 4:3). Does this presuppose the possibility of disunity? And what would be the cause of disunity? Perhaps this is akin to other Pauline ethical charges to "live according to who/what you are" (e.g., Eph 5:8). Robinson did not explore these issues in his writings. We cannot ask many more questions here of the location of the church than we have already addressed. Therefore, we must engage Robinson on the level of his own conclusions. If the church on earth is only ever local, then we should explore how the unity of the church is to be maintained. Is it simply a given? If so, why is there the exhortation to maintain unity? And what would threaten to undo that unity? We might speculate that it is something like the false doctrine that Jude warns about (Jude 17–23). If so, this could explain why Paul in Ephesians 4, after contending for the maintenance of unity, discusses the teaching ministries for the building up of the body. Still, does this mean there remains the threat of disunity that could be the result of poor teaching and/or a lack of understanding? Maybe it is best understood that the Agent maintaining unity in the church is the Holy Spirit (Eph 4:3), not believers. After all, those that defect from the church are those who do not possess the Spirit (Jude 19).

A further issue to address in Robinson's ecclesiology is the nature of unity within the Christian life. Are Christians called to unite with other Christians generally? If so, can this be distinguished from ecclesial unity? If so, how? Robinson did address unity amongst Christians, and even amongst congregations, but he was careful not to confuse that which belongs to the

Christian life (e.g., general fellowship) with that which belongs to the gathered people of God. But is there such a clear distinction between the Christian life and church? Again, it seems that the key to distinguishing the two is found in the clarification suggested by Cole of separating the people and the activity of the people. Christian unity must be sought in the Christian life because Christians belong to the redeemed community and share fellowship with the same God through the same Savior. Can it not be said that this unity in the Christian life is a consequence of fellowship in the heavenly assembly? If so, is the difference between pursuing unity in the Christian life and in the *ekklēsia* over-emphasizing a trivial distinction? It could be if the issue is divorced from Robinson's context. We remember that Robinson was resisting the move of some within the ecumenical movement to draw together congregations into an ecclesial unit. He resisted this move, as he feared this institutionalization would promote what he understood to be an over-inflation of the doctrine of the church.

But surely Robinson's position on the institutional church conflicted with his Anglican heritage. It is true that the Thirty-Nine Articles primarily envision the church as a local entity. Articles XIX,[44] XX,[45] XXIII,[46] XXIV,[47]

---

44. Article XIX: "The visible Church of Christ is a congregation of faithful men, in the which the pure Word of God is preached, and the Sacraments be duly ministered according to Christ's ordinance in all those things that of necessity are requisite to the same.

"As the Church of Jerusalem, Alexandria, and Antioch have erred: so also the Church of Rome hath erred, not only in their living and manner of Ceremonies, but also in matters of Faith."

45. Article XX: "The Church hath power to decree Rites or Ceremonies, and authority in Controversies of Faith: And yet it is not lawful for the Church to ordain anything contrary to God's Word written, neither may it so expound one place of Scripture, that it be repugnant to another. Wherefore, although the Church be a witness and a keeper of holy Writ, yet, as it ought not to decree any thing against the same, so besides the same ought it not to enforce any thing to be believed for necessity of Salvation."

46. Article XXIII: "It is not lawful for any man to take upon him the office of publick preaching, or ministering the Sacraments in the Congregation, before he be lawfully called, and sent to execute the same. And those we ought to judge lawfully called and sent, which be chosen and called to this work by men who have publick authority given unto them in the Congregation, to call and send Ministers into the Lord's vineyard."

47. Article XXIV: "It is a thing plainly repugnant to the Word of God, and the custom of the Primitive Church, to have publick Prayer in the Church, or to minister the Sacraments in a tongue not understood of the people."

XXVI,[48] and XXXV[49] in particular seem to identify the church as a local gathering. This is clear in Article XIX—*the* Article on the nature of the church—which states, "The visible Church of Christ is a congregation of faithful men. . . . " But there also is an identification of a national church in

---

48. Article XXVI: "Although in the visible Church the evil be ever mingled with the good, and sometimes the evil have chief authority in the Ministration of the Word and Sacraments, yet forasmuch as they do not the same in their own name, but in Christ's, and do minister by his commission and authority, we may use their Ministry, both in hearing the Word of God, and in the receiving of the Sacraments. Neither is the effect of Christ's ordinance taken away by their wickedness, nor the grace of God's gifts diminished from such as by faith and rightly do receive the Sacraments ministered unto them; which be effectual, because of Christ's institution and promise, although they be ministered by evil men.

"Nevertheless it appertaineth to the discipline of the Church, that inquiry be made of evil Ministers, and that they be accused by those that have knowledge of their offences; and finally being found guilty, by just judgement be deposed."

49. Article XXXV: "The second Book of Homilies, the several titles whereof we have joined under this Article, doth contain a godly and wholesome Doctrine, and necessary for these times, as doth the former Book of Homilies, which were set forth in the time of Edward the Sixth; and therefore we judge them to be read in Churches by the Ministers, diligently and distinctly, that they may be understanded of the people . . . [the Article continues to list the Homilies]"

Articles XXXIII(?),[50] XXXIV,[51] XXXVI,[52] and XXXVII.[53] This dual understanding of the local and national (denominational) church is most clear in Article XXXIV, which states, "Every particular or national Church hath authority to ordain, change, and abolish, ceremonies or rites of the Church ordained only by man's authority, so that all things be done to edifying." Did Robinson then stand in disagreement with his Anglican tradition? It seems

50. Article XXXIII: "That person which by open denunciation of the Church is rightly cut off from the unity of the Church, and excommunicated, ought to be taken of the whole multitude of the faithful, as an Heathen and Publican, until he be openly reconciled by penance, and received into the Church by a Judge that hath authority thereunto."

51. Article XXXIV: "It is not necessary that Traditions and Ceremonies be in all places one, and utterly like; for at all times they have been divers, and may be changed according to the diversities of countries, times, and men's manners, so that nothing be ordained against God's Word. Whosoever through his private judgement, willingly and purposely, doth openly break the traditions and ceremonies of the Church, which be not repugnant to the Word of God, and be ordained and approved by common authority, ought to be rebuked openly, (that others may fear to do the like,) as he that offendeth against the common order of the Church, and hurteth the authority of the Magistrate, and woundeth the consciences of the weak brethren.

"Every particular or national Church hath authority to ordain, change, and abolish, ceremonies or rites of the Church ordained only by man's authority, so that all things be done to edifying."

52. Article XXXVI: "The Book of Consecration of Archbishops and Bishops, and Ordering of Priests and Deacons, lately set forth in the time of Edward the Sixth, and confirmed at the same time by authority of Parliament, doth contain all things necessary to such Consecration and Ordering: neither hath it any thing, that of itself is superstitious or ungodly. And therefore whosoever are consecrated or ordered according to the Rites of that Book, since the second year of the forenamed King Edward unto this time, or hereafter shall be consecrated or ordered according to the same Rites; we decree all such to be rightly, orderly, and lawfully consecrated or ordered."

53. Article XXXVII: "The Queen's Majesty hath the chief power in this Realm of England, and other her Dominions, unto whom the chief Government of all Estates of this Realm, whether they be Ecclesiastical or Civil, in all causes doth appertain, and is not, nor ought to be, subject to any foreign Jurisdiction.

"Where we attribute to the Queen's Majesty the chief government, by which Titles we understand the minds of some slanderous folks to be offended; we give not to our Princes the ministering either of God's Word, or of the Sacraments, the which thing the Injunctions also lately set forth by Elizabeth our Queen doth most plainly testify; but only that prerogative, which we see to have been given always to all godly Princes in holy Scriptures by God himself; that is, that they should rule all estates and degrees committed to their charge by God, whether they be Ecclesiastical or Temporal, and restrain with the civil sword the stubborn and evildoers.

"The Bishop of Rome hath no jurisdiction in this Realm of England.

"The Laws of the Realm may punish Christian men with death, for heinous and grievous offences.

"It is lawful for Christian men, at the commandment of the Magistrate, to wear weapons, and serve in the wars."

that Robinson disagreed with the institutional language of the church, but not necessarily the purpose of the institution. He believed titles like the Anglican Church of Australia were misnomers. Such institutions are service structures representative of networks of churches, but should not be called a church or the church. However, Robinson did not reject his tradition or even its notion of what/where the church is, rather he preferred to think about it under different terms. For instance, denominations need not be dismissed; they simply should not be considered "the church." The purpose of upholding a national church in the Anglican tradition appears, from the Articles, to be a concern for the preservation of truth. The institution regulated church affairs insomuch as required to maintain doctrine. Robinson would not contest the usefulness of the institution in these matters.

Robinson's concern was that denominations not become an end in themselves, but rather remain as servants to the churches. With regard to unity, denominations unite churches by serving as vehicles for cooperation and edification. But this unity between churches was not creating a greater church (e.g., an amalgamation of churches); the churches remain churches independently without becoming "the church" collectively.

But Robinson's rejection of naming the institution the church was never too hostile; he himself went on to serve as a bishop and then as archbishop in Sydney. In fact, in principle he embraced much of what the Articles promote for the "church" as a larger institutional entity, such as governance over church leaders and the guarding of doctrine and practice. Therefore, his understanding of the church fits within Anglicanism, but presents a nuanced understanding of traditional Anglican language. Some may question whether Robinson embraced his own theological conclusions. If the denomination and the episcopacy are extra-ecclesial, then how could Robinson work within such structures? Did he abandon his conclusions in order to embrace traditional Anglicanism? Robinson continued to understand the local church as *the* church on earth, with the episcopacy and denomination serving local churches, until the end of his ministry as archbishop. But how his authority as archbishop actually came to bear on churches, even with his own theological nuancing of the episcopacy as a service structure to the local church, may not have been congruent with his theological conviction. He still maintained an influential overarching responsibility for local churches in the Diocese of Sydney. Was it that he felt compelled to fulfill the expectations of the role as they had long been established? Did he fulfill this role with as much theological nuance as he was "allowed" within the confines of the functional polity set before him? Or did he dismiss his theology, or at least ignore it, pragmatically? It is difficult to assess how Robinson's role fit within his ecclesiology, for his ministry spanned many years. It also is difficult because Robinson did not articulate a full-fledged polity for episcopal churches. Robinson's discussion of the episcopacy primarily involved discussion of the nature of authority in the church. It is probable that Robinson understood his role of bishop to be a helpful position within the fellowship of churches, expressing care for and maintenance of the health of parochial ministries.

6. Jew and Gentile

The church is not coterminous with the people of God, but rather an activity of the people of God. Israel is preserved as an identity (ethnic?) in the church as a demonstration of God's wisdom of bringing together Jews and Gentiles. Therefore, the church is not the "new Israel."

Robinson's conclusions regarding the continuing distinction between Israel and the church were grounded in his biblical-theological method. Where his ecclesiology has been accused of not being theological, Robinson's work on the "new man" demonstrates theological rigor. The church cannot be the new Israel because there is a new work that God has done that upholds the Jew and Gentile distinction, all the while incorporating them into one "new man." Thus, Robinson oriented his ecclesiology according to soteriological concerns. He arrived at a position that is neither covenantal (supercessionist), nor dispensational; rather, a position that is in between. He argued for a promise and fulfillment scheme that identified the Christian community within the covenantal relationship God had established with Israel, yet he did not see the new covenant abolishing the identity of the Israelites or their place within the soteriological purposes of God. He believed that preservation of the Israelite identity, in distinction from the Gentile converts, was fundamental to understanding the redemptive plan of God. Central to this understanding of the church in relationship to Israel is the distinction between the church and the people of God.

Perhaps, here as earlier, further clarification is required in order to make sense of Robinson's conclusions. In particular, what distinctions exist between the old covenant and new covenant people of God, especially regarding the ways in which they relate to God and what place and function the church holds under each covenant? A proper grasp of these distinctions would require an exhaustive study in soteriology. We detailed Robinson's conclusions regarding the distinctions between Jew and Gentile, and the continuity and discontinuity of the church under the new covenant with Israel and the church of the old covenant. Clarifying Robinson's work and building upon it, we might suggest the following brief conclusions.

First, there is continuity in the people of God between the old and new covenants. In other words, there is only *one* people of God. The distinction between the old and new covenant people is first and foremost a shift in the means of relating. How do the people of God relate to the God to whom they belong? The old covenant required the people to keep the Mosaic law and included inbuilt sacrificial provisions for the people. The new covenant relationship is through the Son of God, his faithfulness and his sacrificial provision.

Second, there is a shift in the ethnic constitution of the people of God between the old and new covenants, more as a result of a paradigm shift than as a change of permissions or purpose. All peoples of all nations have always been called into relationship with God, but under the old covenant the means of relating to God came via a particular ethnic people (i.e., the Hebrews), represented in the nation of that people—Israel. Under the new covenant, the means of relating to God continues through a particular people, but especially through the person Jesus, Israel *par excellence*. As the Son of God is raised, all peoples are drawn to him. The old covenant granted provision to a particular ethnicity to be extended to all, whereas the new covenant grants provision to all people without exception.

Third, there is a shift in the location of the church. This shift came with the move away from the church being the congregation of the nation of Israel, to the congregations of all who profess faith in Christ. Robinson identified a key moment in the narrative of Acts (8:1) in which the church first comprised converted Jews, but subsequently shifts to a diaspora model in which the believing Jews are driven out amongst the nations. Unlike the curse of scattering under the old covenant, the scattering in Acts *achieved* mission. With the scattering of proselytes amongst the nations, the gospel spread to the nations and Gentiles were converted. Instead of the sum total of the people of God constituting the church on earth, as the nation of Israel once did gathering in one place, the new covenant relocated the total gathering from a physical reality to a heavenly reality. The church in its most universal sense is gathered before Christ in heaven.

The continuity between the old and new covenants can be seen most clearly in the soteriological conduit. That is, under both the old and new covenants it is through Israel that God's renown extends to nations. Under the old covenant the nation was to testify to God's goodness amongst the nations through their law keeping and close fellowship with God in the law-mediated relationship. Under the new covenant, Israel is still the vehicle for God's renown. First, this goal of reaching the nations is achieved in and through Christ, Israel *par excellence*. Second, the apostles were Israelites, and were the first missionaries carrying the gospel to the nations. Third, in the rejection of Israel as a nation a way was opened to the Gentiles (Rom 11).

Robinson's main argument that the church is not the new Israel was grounded in his soteriology. God always intended for Israel to reach the nations and bring people into relationship with himself. However, God's aim in establishing a redeemed people—the people of God—was not to build the nation of Israel. His aim was to demonstrate he is the God of all peoples. In redeeming a people unto himself, God was bringing people under the new covenant into himself—into the person of his Son. God brought peace for all peoples, both with himself and with humanity, in and through his Son. This work of redemption achieved a "new man" or new humanity, a redeemed people.

7. The Task of the Church

The people of God gather around the Word of God to meet with God. The church as such does not possess an evangelistic task, Christians do.

Robinson's understanding of the church as an activity of the people of God had implications for his understanding of the task of the church. The earthly church is intermittent and primarily made up of believers, not unbelievers. As such, the gathering fulfills a role in the life of the *believing* community. Evangelism and mission belong to the people of God rather than the church, as it is the people who encounter the unbelieving world outside of the congregation.

Robinson believed that the primary function of the church, as the people of God gathered before God, was to hear from God in his Word. This conviction was driven by his biblical theology of the church, with the prototype of the new covenant gathering being the gathered people at Sinai/Horeb. The early gathering and the subsequent festal gatherings served the primary purpose of the people hearing from their God. Likewise, the new covenant gatherings had the same purpose. Further support for this conviction can be found in Article XIX of the Thirty-Nine Articles and in "An Homily of the Right Use of the Church or Temple of God, and of the Reverence Due unto the Same."[54] Few would contest this strong emphasis on the Word in the congregation, as it is the Word that builds the body—though many may find this conviction overly simplistic. Should worship/liturgy, fellowship, or some other element be given primacy? Robinson believed that the Word of God provided the basis for worship, fellowship and all other church activities.

54. "Homily," 164–65.

More controversial of his conclusions is what the church is *not* intentioned to do, namely evangelism. A common tenet for most ecclesiologies is an external purpose of mission. But Robinson argued that the church has no face to the world. Instead, Christians do. Francis Foulkes offered a rejoinder[55] to an article in *Interchange*[56] in which Robinson articulated a theological rationale for not ascribing an evangelistic task to the church. In the rejoinder, Foulkes challenged Robinson's narrow understanding of the church as a gathering (and that of Paul Barnett after him), contending for a broader usage encompassing the entire Christian population. He also challenged Robinson's distinction between God giving particular evangelists and the responsibility of all Christians to be witnesses, seeing this as a matter of splitting hairs. He wrote, "The tasks of 'witness' and 'evangelism' need not be seen as distinct but belonging together, and the second as well as the first as work in which every Christian is privileged to share."[57] He concluded, "The word 'church' does not seem to me to be limited as it is in this [Robinson's] article. It has a wider use; and even if it could be proved linguistically and from usage that it was not thus limited, we would still have the wider and fuller concept of 'the people of God' which is relevant when consideration is given to evangelism."[58] It appears that Foulkes believed that Robinson's conclusions devalued evangelism, and therein advanced a diminished view of the good news that every Christian possesses. There is a sense that Foulkes' criticism is legitimate if the church is understood as a synonym for the people of God. But in a response to Foulkes' rejoinder, Robinson made it clear that the fundamental difference of opinion is what the church is.[59] It is precisely because Robinson did not equate the church with the whole Christian society, that he was able to make his point without devaluing evangelism.

But do Robinson's conclusions downplay the proclamation of the gospel? Robinson's exegetical conclusion that the gospel goes forward via gifted evangelists, with a general obligation for witness belonging to all Christians, is not a diminished view of evangelism. His conclusions relocate the onus of evangelism from the corporation to the individual, as it is not the corporation that encounters those in the world, but the individual. Perhaps Robinson could have been clearer on the relationship between gifted evangelists and general witnesses. It appears that he places the obligation

---

55. Foulkes, "Church and Evangelism," 26–33.
56. Robinson, "Doctrine of the Church," 110.
57. Foulkes, "Church and Evangelism," 31.
58. Ibid., 33.
59. Robinson, "Church and Evangelism," 114.

of gospel proclamation on all believers, but with recognition that some will be especially gifted for the task. This may be likened to the sense that all parents teach their children, but some are especially gifted teachers and take teaching as a vocation. The major thrust of Robinson's argument is not to restrict the activity of evangelism, but to relocate it away from the activity of the gathered people of God into the lives of the people of God who gather.

Another area needing further explanation following Robinson's conclusions is precisely how evangelism occurs and where. We have seen that he has emphasized the witness to "outsiders" where they are to be found, outside of the gathering. But does this mean that there is to be no proclamation to the congregation? Robinson argued that the congregation should be assumed to be believers and should be treated as such, trusting that the regular preaching of the gospel will call home the "lost sheep." But is this right? Is there not an expectation in the New Testament that unbelievers will be present within the congregation regularly? If unbelievers were expected, then it would seem appropriate that there should be a regular gospel appeal of sorts.

These issues are addressed in the First Epistle to the Corinthians, especially ch. 14, in which Paul exhorts the Corinthians to make sense of things in the congregation for the *idiōtēs*.[60] Paul assumes that there will be unbelievers or outsiders who will enter the congregation from time to time. It seems that Robinson advocated a focus on the believing congregants, figuring the unbeliever as an anomaly. But this does not settle the role of the evangelist *within* the congregation. If God has given gifted evangelists for the church (Eph 4:11), then there surely must be a place for expressing this gift within the church. Did Robinson resist evangelism *in* the gathering, or the assignment of evangelism *to* the gathering? Robinson seemed to stress that evangelism belongs outside of the congregation. This area of his thought could use more attention, especially the question of whether some gatherings can serve the purpose of evangelism (e.g., Acts 2) or have evangelistic emphases.[61] It is probable that Robinson believed that the regular proclamation of the Word would deliver the gospel to both insider and outsider, both in need of the

---

60. Many render *idiōtēs* as "outsider" (ESV) or "inquirers" (NIV). Lexically this is perhaps best understood as an "unlearned" or "a plain person" (Mounce). Here it receives the "outsider" gloss because of the context including *apistos*, "unbelieving." When put in apposition to *idiōtēs* it can serve a clarifying and/or expansive function, as in 1 Cor 14:23.

61. In short answer, we can assume that Robinson would gladly accept the idea of gatherings for evangelistic purpose, but he may not call these "church." With reference to Acts 2, Robinson would likely see this instance as a group of people gathered to hear the Word from which the church was created. The distinction between this gathering and a church is that those gathered were not yet in Christ and therefore were not meeting in his name.

gospel truth. But what remains unsettled is how the particular gift of evangelism finds its expression in the church. Perhaps this gift is one that is given *for* the church, but happens *before* the church temporally, in order to grow the church (quantitatively) by reaching those outside to bring them inside.

8. Authority

The church possesses no inherent authority, nor does any external institutional structure beyond the local church (e.g., denomination). The sole authority in the church is the Word of God, for submission to the Bible is submission to Christ who reigns supreme over the church.

Building once again upon the primary recognition of the church as a gathering, Robinson established that authority in the church is limited to the Word of God. No external institution has inherent authority over the local church. Within the local church itself the Word of God is the sole authority. Denominational structures serve the local church, existing for the purpose of bolstering parochial ministry.

Robinson's conclusion both embraces and rejects his Anglican heritage. In one sense, he echoes the Articles' declaration of the ultimate authority of the Word in Articles XX, XXI, and XXXIV. The Word reigns supreme. But in another sense Robinson's conclusion stands against the Articles where they identify a "church" that extends beyond the local congregation to a national church, and declare that this "church" has authority in matters of practice (Article XXXIV).

It was in his disagreement with the national church that Robinson was accused of promoting an isolated or individualistic view of the church.[62] If the earthly church is only ever local and the denomination has no authority over the local church, then how should local churches avoid isolation? We noted earlier that Robinson arrived at bold conclusions, and yet he himself served as a bishop and archbishop. Did his practice find agreement with his theology? Leaving aside an evaluation of how his ministry matched his theology, we can recall his comments late in his ministry that placed the denomination in the life of the church. The denomination, particularly at the diocesan level, provided helpful accountability and stability for local churches in matters of faith and practice.

For all of his theological articulation of the nature of the church, Robinson did not move on to specify a polity that promoted the practice of his theological conclusions. He made general comments about things such as the usefulness of denominations, but never clearly set forth how churches

---

62. See Giles, *What on Earth Is the Church?*, 14.

should consider their relationship with denominational structures. We do not here wish to develop polity from Robinson's ecclesiology, but we should ask how his ecclesiology might fit within a traditional episcopal framework. Perhaps local churches might participate in an opt-in fashion, in which they willingly allow denominational structures to govern them. These matters are of particular concern when denominations are responsible for funding properties and pensions. There must be discernment, from a theological foundation, of how churches will partner within the denomination for kingdom ministry, receiving resources (and refusing them?), and how authority will be exercised within this partnership. Robinson was an advocate of denominations resourcing local churches and serving as a conduit for churches to serve others. But to what extent do denominational leaders have authority in or over the local church? Did Robinson see his role as a bishop over the churches, under the churches, or beside the churches?

CONCLUSION

We set out in this evaluation to appraise the biblical, logical and traditional value of Donald Robinson's ecclesiology. Having examined the eight core propositions of his theology of the nature of the church, we can draw the following conclusions.

First, biblically, Robinson has demonstrated a method of detailed linguistic studies within a biblical-theological framework. His method has been to search out the developments of themes in the biblical canon. This amounted to conclusions that appeared fresh in the realm of ecclesiological studies, primarily in the removal of a "third" location of church, the general/universal church on earth. While some may disagree with Robinson's assessment of the biblical data, his method nonetheless was rigorous engagement of the biblical text. Therefore, we can conclude that Robinson's ecclesiology was intentionally biblical.

Second, logically Robinson developed his ecclesiology according to his method of biblical theology. His primary premise was that the church is a gathering, demonstrated through the unfolding story of the Bible. The integrity of his argument is seen in the maintenance of his original thesis throughout each of the subsequent propositions. It would be fair to ask whether his subsequent propositions were driven by this original conclusion, or if they were arrived at by genuine independent examination of the biblical texts. We have already stated that Robinson sought to develop each proposition according to his biblical-theological method, and therefore his ecclesiology might be deemed properly biblical. We may conclude that

Robinson's conclusions were coherent and did not deviate from his primary thesis. The only accusation of incoherency in Robinson is not in his theology, but rather in praxis. Did he effectively implement his own theology? We have argued that he found great opportunity in his episcopal ministry to carry out support of parochial ministry, but total integrity of his praxis with regard to his theology remains to be examined.[63]

Third, Robinson located his ecclesiology within the Anglican tradition. However, fidelity to the Bible over and against tradition was his greatest concern.[64] As such, Robinson expressed the agreement that he found between what he observed in the Bible and the Anglican tradition. But there were also points of disagreement, such as the conception of a national church. We remember that Robinson staunchly defended the Anglican heritage that he knew and loved, in both his episcopal ministry and his contributions to the Australian Anglican Prayer Book.[65] We therefore conclude that Robinson's ecclesiology was intended, and largely succeeds, as an Anglican ecclesiology, while demanding a nuancing of that tradition. In particular, Robinson was not comfortable with a conception of an earthly church beyond the local congregation or an institution that sought to express authority over the local church under the claim of being a greater ecclesial entity. The nuance he offered was to observe the usefulness of denominations, but not as ecclesial entities, rather as service structures for the only church(es) on earth, the local church.

The areas needing greatest further development in Robinson's thought are threefold. First, there must be further conceptual clarity of the distinction between the people of God and the church. Second, Robinson's theology should be brought into serious engagement with the modern missional church conversation.[66] How does Robinson's ecclesiology inform the contemporary push to allocate mission to the church? Could the distinction between people and activity aid this conversation? Third, Robinson's ecclesiology establishes what on the surface seems to be a congregational model of church. What does his theology of the nature of the church mean for the polity of the church? Can his theology find congruence with episcopal polity?

---

63. We have not examined Robinson's praxis here any further, as our subject is his doctrine.

64. Oddly, we can say that this concern is actually verification of his Anglicanism, as this is the concern of Article VI.

65. He never challenged or undermined his own theological tradition. The identification of the incongruence of his ecclesiology with the Thirty-Nine Articles' national church is by observation, rather than his direct comments.

66. Some resources for this conversation include: Hill, *Salt, Light, and a City*; DeYoung and Gilbert, *What Is the Mission of the Church?*; Hirsch, *Forgotten Ways*; Ashford, *Theology and Practice of Mission*; Driscoll and Breshears, *Vintage Church*.

SECTION III

David Broughton Knox

7

The Ecclesiology of D. Broughton Knox

THIS CHAPTER SEEKS TO present the ecclesiology of D. Broughton Knox in both an analytic and descriptive manner, seeking—where this is possible—some degree of conceptual unity from a series of disparate works spread over a teaching and research career of more than forty years. In order to fairly and accurately present his thought, and to hear his own words before evaluating them, this chapter will make use of longer quotes where necessary. The aim of this chapter is to draw ecclesiological threads together from the many pieces of Knox's work throughout his ministry. Evaluation of his ecclesiology will follow in chapter 8.

The presentation of Knox's ecclesiology will progress in much the same way as the presentation of Robinson's contribution. Indeed, there will inevitably be some overlap and repetition between these two accounts. First, we will consider briefly those elements in his background that may have contributed to the development of his ecclesiology; second, we will assay Knox's theological method; third, we will examine key areas in his ecclesiology related to the nature of the church; finally, we will draw conclusions from the analysis and anticipate issues for evaluation in the next chapter.

DAVID BROUGHTON KNOX[1]

David Broughton Knox[2] was born on December 26, 1916, in Adelaide, South Australia, to David James (D. J.) Knox and Doris Emily Broughton Knox. D. J. Knox was an Anglican minister and soon after Broughton's birth took a parish in the greater Sydney area where Broughton would be raised. Knox's entire upbringing, even after university—when he served as a catechist in his father's parish—took place in the context of evangelical ministry; Knox was imbued with a commitment to gospel work from a young age.

Knox began his tertiary education at the University of Sydney, where he studied classics, receiving second-class honors in Greek. Later, he travelled to England and began study at St John's College, Highbury (later the London College of Divinity) under Dr. T. W. Gilbert, where he graduated an associate with first-class honors and with a second-class bachelor of divinity (University of London). After a few years in a curacy at St-Andrew-the-Less in Cambridge, Knox began reading in the Theological Tripos at Cambridge. This study was interrupted by World War II, during which Knox enlisted in the Royal Navy Reserve. Following the war, he returned to lecture at Moore Theological College for four years, while reading for a master of theology from London University in biblical and historical theology. In 1951 he returned to England to complete a doctorate in Reformation theology at St. Catherine's College, Oxford.[3] During his doctoral studies he served as tutor and lecturer in New Testament at Wycliffe Hall and assistant curate at St Aldate's parish church.

After completing his doctoral studies, Knox returned to Sydney to lecture at Moore College. Following on from T. C. Hammond's retirement as principal of the college in 1954, Marcus Loane was appointed principal and Knox was asked to serve as vice-principal. In 1959 Loane was consecrated as an assistant bishop in the Diocese of Sydney, and Knox became principal with Donald Robinson as vice-principal.[4] He remained principal of the college until February 1985. After retiring as principal, he continued lecturing at Moore until 1988, at which time he founded George Whitefield College

---

1. There are several biographies of Knox in existence. The most thorough is Cameron, *Enigmatic Life*. Several shorter biographies include: Robinson, "David Broughton Knox: An Appreciation"; Robinson, "David Broughton Knox: What We Owe Him"; Loane, "David Broughton Knox"; Thompson, "Knox, David Broughton."

2. Hereafter, "Knox" or "Broughton."

3. Knox, *Doctrine of Faith*.

4. Knox was not the first choice of the college for principal, but rather R. A. Cole. However, Cole declined the invitation, and Knox was appointed. See Cameron, *Enigmatic Life*, 160.

(GWC) in Cape Town, South Africa. In 1992 he retired from GWC and from public ministry. Knox died on January 15, 1994.

The majority of Knox's ministry involved theological education. Alan Cole has described Knox's approach to theological education as follows: "[Knox] maintained that the task was to train people theologically to the highest possible level and he felt that many of these other things, like the training of pastors and so on, would better be left until they were in the parishes."[5] Knox's approach to theological education was more academic than practical, insomuch as he valued biblical and theological knowledge over pragmatic skills. But this did not mean that his pedagogy was simply wooden. In an appraisal of Knox's theological contribution, Donald Robinson reflected thus:

> DBK's great work has been his own theological teaching. He has a powerful and original mind and the enviable gift of a teacher—the ability to create an appetite for theology in his students. Though widely read and well informed, with a good sense of history and public affairs, DBK has little interest in scholarship for its own sake. He has relentlessly pursued the quest for the heart of theology, which for him is nothing other than the knowledge of God. He has found that heart in the nature of God as he has revealed himself to us through holy scripture. The correlative truth is faith as trust and worship. Theological study can therefore never be a mere academic pursuit; it is integral with personal obedience and growth in grace. But error is the enemy of truth and must be exposed at every attempt to parade in whatever guise.[6]

Knox's theological ministry was one that was dedicated to the highest level of training, but more with a view towards the church than the academy.

Beyond his work at Moore College, and never divorced from that work, Knox was involved in several other ministries, including contributing to and editing the *Australian Church Record*, serving as a member of the Faith and Order Commission of the World Council of Churches (WCC), a member of Synod and Standing Committee of the Sydney Diocese, and a member of General Synod. These extracurricular activities provided the impetus for Knox's engagement with issues pertaining to the nature of the church, as it was in these venues that many ecclesiological questions and issues came to the surface. As we have seen, in the 1940s and 1950s controversy was brewing over a new constitution for the Anglican Church in Australia (at that

---

5. Ibid., 161.
6. Robinson, "David Broughton Knox: An Appreciation," xi–xii.

time the Church of England in Australia). Knox disapproved of many of the constitutional revisions, particularly with what he identified as apparent weaknesses with regard to ecclesiology. He voiced his opinion about these weaknesses in his editorials in the *Australian Church Record*.[7] There were many responses to his editorials published in the *Record*, which generated some heated debate. Alongside these national conversations there was also the global ecumenical movement, most centrally represented in the WCC. We have already noted that Archbishop Mowll asked Knox to be an official representative at the WCC, for which Knox served as a delegate in 1952 (Lund) and 1954 (Evanston). The WCC was concerned with the questions of the nature of the church, especially the oneness and catholicity of the church. It was in the context of these extracurricular ministries, coupled with lecturing at Moore College, that Knox developed his ecclesiology.

Significantly, Knox did not produce many theological works of an academic nature.[8] Many have discussed the reasons for such a low output during the course of his lifetime. Donald Robinson reflected that the "increasing demands of the College, and his participation in a variety of concerns outside it, probably prevented DBK from engaging as effectively as he might have done in a much wider theological debate. Yet he really has very little interest in such debate."[9] Thus, the reasons for Knox's minimal engagement with the academy are twofold: (1) demands of his ministry; (2) a lack of concern for such work. However, it may best be understood in the *synthesis* of these two reasons: Knox's ministry focused on the work he was most concerned with—that of training would-be ministers in theology. His concern was decidedly *not* the academic guild of theologians. His writing ministry was directed towards ministers and parishioners in the churches, primarily those in close proximity to Moore College. The bulk of his theological essays were published in a local peer-reviewed journal—*Reformed Theological Review*—and much of the remainder of his work was delivered in chapel or academic conferences at the college.

Knox's primary theological focus was the doctrine of God; however, undoubtedly his greatest theological legacy is his ecclesiology.[10] The advancement of this legacy is somewhat peculiar, given that he never pro-

---

7. A reference to these works can be found in our ch. 3, n17.

8. There are three academic monographs produced by Knox: *Doctrine of Faith in the Reign of Henry VIII*; *Everlasting God*; and *Thirty-Nine Articles* (reprinted in *D. Broughton Knox: Selected Works*).

Knox also produced several other monographs that focused on Christian living, though not void of theological depth: *Sent by Jesus* and *Not by Bread Alone*.

9. Robinson, "David Broughton Knox: An Appreciation," xvii.

10. Ibid., xi.

duced an ecclesiological monograph. In fact, Knox's ecclesiology only exists in fragmentary form in essays, sermon notes, and occasional academic or popular articles; only in the last decade have these pieces been collected into three volumes of selected works, and even then, only one volume focuses on his ecclesiology.[11] This book is the first attempt to produce a serious synthesis of Knox's ecclesiology. However, his ecclesiological influence can be seen today in Sydney, across Australia, and in many other places around the world.[12] Students disseminated Knox's ecclesiology through the practice of the principles learned in the classroom applied to local church ministry.

To date, an account of the legacy of Knox's ecclesiology has largely been piecemeal and often polemically charged. Several writers have formally engaged and challenged his ecclesiology, often viewed as the "Knox-Robinson" ecclesiology, blending his insights with those of Donald Robinson and rarely distinguishing the two contributions.[13] Here we will aim to set forth a synthesis of *Knox's* thought, representing the sparse material and ideas in a clear presentation of his ecclesiology. We will turn to evaluation of his thought and engagement of those that have offered rejoinders in another chapter. Before we examine his thought, we first turn to assay Knox's theological method.

METHODOLOGY

It is difficult to discern Knox's theological method for his ecclesiology, as we do not possess an autobiographical account of Knox's method in ecclesiology, as we do for Robinson. It is especially difficult to discern the background and sources on which he based his conclusions. Questions remain: Was he working alone? Did he read widely in ecclesiology? How did his training as a historical and systematic theologian impact his ecclesiology? What we know of his theological method can only be discerned through his theological writings and accounted for by those who knew him—namely a few articles that were produced for a *Festschrift* and others produced after his death remembering his theological legacy.

---

11. *D. Broughton Knox: Selected Works*, 3 vols.

12. This is not evidenced so much in published ecclesiological material, as it is in the practice of those who trained at Moore College under Knox and went on to serve around the globe. However, the work of renown Sydney Anglican scholars who trained under Knox, such as P. T. O'Brien, have also demonstrated Knox's impact and extended the reach of his influence in their writing.

13. See, e.g.: Giles, *What On Earth*; Porter, *Sydney Anglicans*.

Knox was a systematic theologian. As we have stated, his doctoral research was in Reformation theology.[14] We have already mentioned that Knox read widely, but gave little indication of those with whom he was in conversation in his works. Peter Jensen explained: "Since Broughton believed that God speaks uniquely and sufficiently in Holy Scripture, the exposition of the Bible occupied the central role in his method. . . . Because he believed this so firmly, he broke with a tradition of systematic theology in which doctrine consists of commenting on the views of others whether historical or contemporary."[15] Knox's preoccupation was the text of the Bible. His method for theology was ascertaining what the Scriptures taught about particular issues. Ecclesiology was no exception. Rather than beginning with the teaching of traditions or scholars, Knox searched the Scriptures. This is not to say that he was unacquainted with the theological field, or even that he was negligent of it in his discourse. Quite the opposite; Knox drew from others when appropriate for clarity and support of his conclusions, or to demonstrate a departure from the teaching of Scripture in others. In fact, many of his ecclesiological essays engaged the Thirty-Nine Articles, demonstrating that he was a man who belonged to and identified himself within a very specific theological tradition.

When Knox began his teaching and writing ministry he was an understudy to T. C. Hammond. Hammond was the principal of Moore College and taught doctrine. Hammond's method for teaching was to examine a systematic theology textbook—E. J. Bicknell's engagement of the Thirty-Nine Articles.[16] However, Knox embraced a different approach. He included a theological textbook, T. C. Hammond's *In Understanding Be Men*, but this was only discussed as a supplement. Peter Jensen recalls, "For Knox, Hammond's book was a mere adjunct to his lectures. The real text-book was Scripture itself. Broughton was far from ignorant of historical theology; but he left no doubt that he was grappling with Scripture, not with the writings of others, no matter how sharp or how learned."[17] Knox's teaching method was to lead students through the Bible to see how theology arises from the text. Other theologians were not insignificant in his approach, but Knox wanted to train his pupils to be students of the Bible, more than students of history and contemporary scholarship.

While remembered for his doctrine of Scripture and of the church, these were not Knox's primary doctrinal concerns. His focus was the

---

14. Published as *Doctrine of Faith in the Reign of Henry VIII* (London: Clarke, 1961).
15. Jensen, "Broughton Knox," 23.
16. Bicknell, *Theological Introduction to the Thirty-Nine Articles*; see ch. 2 above.
17. Jensen, "Broughton Knox," 23.

doctrine of God.[18] He valued Scripture as the locus of revelation of the character and activity of the Triune God. He valued the church because that is the place where believers are drawn in fellowship with one another to *commune* with the Triune God, around the *Word* of God. This is highly relevant to a consideration of his method. Every doctrine he considered was examined to the end of knowing God.

Although Knox was a systematic theologian, his method is perhaps best described as biblical theology. Marcus Loane reflected, "[Knox] was primarily concerned to develop a Biblical Theology; his teaching was rooted in the textual study of the New Testament as practised in Cambridge."[19] Peter Jensen adds further clarity:

> In the Knox theology everything had to be tested by scripture, and the business of systematic theology was to be biblical. . . . He had no aim to introduce studies of modern theology, and even historical theology was a mere hand-maid to the chief business. . . . All studies in the curriculum fed into the central study—the knowledge of God and of his ways as revealed in scripture; all served this central focus.[20]

This method may well be called biblical theology. However, biblical theology can limit its scope to thematic development in the metanarrative of the canon. This narrower biblical theology is more akin to the method of Robinson. Knox, however, moved beyond the parameters of biblical theology to examine how these thematic developments interacted with the broader scope of Christian doctrine, and how these doctrines have been understood in the history of Christianity. This is the task of systematic theology. But for Knox, this systematic always involved the foundation of biblical theology.

Knox's ecclesiology must be seen in the context of his overarching approach to systematic theology. As we examine his ecclesiology further, we will see that Knox began with the Bible. He examined carefully how language was employed (i.e., *ekklēsia*) and how the use of this language reflected themes across the Old and New Testaments. But he also related these thematic observations to other Christian doctrines (e.g., God), and referred to how these have been understood in Christian history (e.g., Ignatius, Thirty-Nine Articles, the ecumenical movement). The starting point was the Bible and this served as the anchor for Knox. However, Knox never pretended to be independent of history. He operated from within the Anglican

---

18. Ibid.
19. Loane, "David Broughton Knox," 9.
20. Jensen, "Broughton Knox," 26.

tradition, but sought fidelity to the text *before* tradition, seeking a heuristic rather than historical reading of the Bible.[21]

It is evident that Knox engaged in broad theological reflection with other scholars, but his interlocutors were not detailed in much of his theological work. Footnoting and other sorts of bibliographical referencing are scarce in his theological writings, to the frustration and sometimes misunderstanding of those who engaged his work. Commenting on an article that Knox wrote, his biographer Marcia Cameron writes,

> "Limited Atonement" indicates a high level of understanding of contemporary debate in a particular area of theology, as well as a sound grasp of classical theology, so he was either reading contemporary theological work or discussing it with fellow theologians, or both. Despite this, the lack of references gives the impression that he preferred to think independently. While this might appear to indicate that he approached the Scriptures with a clear, fresh and unbiased mind, this was impossible for a man of his training and background. He was, after all, a Reformed theologian.[22]

These comments of Cameron are very insightful with respect to Knox's work, though her doubts concerning the originality of his thinking, based on his training, are unreasonable.[23] Marcus Loane, archbishop of Sydney during most of Knox's tenure as principal of Moore College, wrote, "It is not too much to say that no other contemporary Australian Churchman has had a more original mind or has shown a more penetrating insight into questions of pure Theology, and that insight was derived from his understanding of the supreme revelation of truth in the Bible."[24] The probable

---

21. Knox does not openly challenge Anglican ecclesiology in his writings; in fact, he finds great support for his conclusions in the Thirty-Nine Articles. But it must be clear that he does not justify his biblical conclusions in Anglicanism, he justifies his Anglicanism in the Bible. Of course, there is no neutral reading of any text and Knox certainly read the Bible as an Anglican. But the point here is that he did not try to fit what he saw in the Bible into an Anglican box. This will become more evident as we encounter his ecclesiological propositions.

22. Cameron, *Enigmatic Life*, 149.

23. There is no good reason to assume that Knox was unable to work in the original languages and have detailed engagement of the Scriptures. Knox was known to be a man who read the Bible in its original language as often as possible, especially the New Testament. He received significant training in Greek during his undergraduate studies, and furthered this training when he set out to read for the Tripos at Cambridge. Therefore, it should not be assumed that his expertise as a Reformed theologian negated his abilities to work in the Scriptures.

24. Loane, "David Broughton Knox," 10.

explanation for Knox's lack of theological interchange is that explicit methodological convictions shaped his style: detailing theological interchange was not significant for what he was trying to achieve in leading others to be students of Scripture more so than students of history.[25]

Knox read widely in theology throughout his academic ministry. In the D. B. Knox archives in the Moore College library there are copies of the library borrowing slips from Knox's studies in the UK, demonstrating the breadth of his reading during his formal theological education. Later, while working at the college he twice took sabbatical leave, in 1968 and 1980, to read in England.[26] He also engaged in theological discussion at Moore College and actively engaged in wider theological conversation through his participation in General Synod and the World Council of Churches. Thus, Knox's reading often served the purpose of sharpening his theological positions for engagement in live theological disputes of his time.

It is significant that Knox had a very close working relationship with Donald Robinson. This relationship was widely known by their friends and colleagues, and has contributed to the identification of their ecclesiologies—rightly or wrongly—being joined under the label "Knox-Robinson ecclesiology." We will consider this later as we seek to identify a model, to the extent that this is possible, discerning elements of congruence and contrast. But for now we must observe that Knox was probably greatly dependent upon Robinson, especially for linguistic conclusions. Nevertheless, it is also very probable that this was a reciprocal relationship. As we will see later, Knox advanced Robinson's linguistic conclusions by drawing out greater theological principles from the linguistic work and situating them in broader systematic categories. It may be said that the theological conclusions Robinson arrived at may well have been derived from Knox's theological analysis.

We can conclude that the lack of disclosure concerning interlocutors in Knox's work is best understood like his own lack of academic output: Knox was not interested in intellectual disputation and the academy for their own sakes. His agenda was not to be an academic. Fundamentally, for Knox, theology provided the opportunity to know God and to instruct men and women on the knowledge of God.

---

25. A further explanation could be that his lack of citation is congruous with the format of his time. Propositions were not expected to be so carefully supported as they are in the modern academic arena.

26. Loane, "David Broughton Knox," 9.

ECCLESIOLOGY

We now move to analyze the central matter of concern in this chapter, the ecclesiology of D. B. Knox. His ecclesiology has here been organized according to major themes in his work. A preliminary summary of these themes is as follows: The *ekklēsia* is a gathering, and the Christian *ekklēsia* the gathering of believers around Christ. However, the *ekklēsia* is primarily a heavenly reality, gathered around Christ where he is. The heavenly finds physical expression of its spiritual reality in the local assembly, which is a full representation of the heavenly church and is gathered by the Holy Spirit. The local assembly gathers for the purpose of fellowship, as it gathers to encounter Christ. This encounter is spiritual as believers encounter the Spirit of Christ in each other. The distinguishing mark of Christian fellowship is the Word of God. The word gives shape and substance to the gathering, and has authority over the congregation. As the congregation is the only legitimate church on earth, there is no institutional authority naturally set over the local church. However, the local church may choose to fellowship with other churches in an institutional framework.

Ekklēsia and Exegesis

Knox's starting point in ecclesiology was his observation of conceptual development within the canon of Scripture. In particular, he observed that in the Bible God repeatedly draws a people unto himself to gather in his presence. He focused mainly on these thematic movements and developments in Scripture, employing linguistic and grammatical analysis to test and prove his data. Here we will examine both Knox's biblical-theological conclusions and his linguistic findings that supported those conclusions.

It is difficult to discern whether the conceptual or the linguistic studies of *ekklēsia* came first chronologically for Knox.[27] The conclusions from each study complement one another; it cannot be discerned if findings from one study colored the other. For instance, because the linguistic study of *ekklēsia* leads to a rendering of "gathering," does this then affect the examination of

27. The distinction here between conceptual and linguistic is as follows. The conceptual study is of the representative idea associated with "church," whereas the linguistic study is of the word "church" and its uses specifically. We will see that Knox's conceptual understanding was closely tied to his linguistic understanding. For others, the conceptual understanding would embody broader figurative language in the Bible, understood to be referential to the concept "church." Knox did not deny these figures, but allowed his study to be governed by the narrower study of "church" (*ekklēsia*). This is a fundamental difference between Knox and Giles, as we saw with Robinson and Giles as well. See the Evaluation of Robinson's ecclesiology, section 1.

how *ekklēsia* is used and developed thematically? Although the overlap cannot be firmly established, the logic is that one would inform the other and this not to a detrimental end. The subject of both studies, whether linguistic or thematic, is singular: *ekklēsia*. The conclusions therefore ought to be complementary so as to prove their legitimacy. Mutually exclusive findings concerning the same subject cannot remain. In other words, the method is recursive—a movement from large scale observation to detailed analysis and back again.

Linguistically, Knox examined the usage of *ekklēsia* in both the New Testament and in the LXX. However, he did not go to great lengths to demonstrate how he arrived at his linguistic conclusions. This suggests that Knox most likely saw himself building upon the work of others that he believed was adequate for justifying this exclusive rendering of *ekklēsia*.[28] One could speculate about other influences, but most likely his source was Donald Robinson. He and Robinson had a close working relationship at Moore College, even having offices on the same hall, and it is probable that Knox depended on Robinson and his research for his linguistic conclusions.

Early in his career (1950) Knox examined the usage of *ekklēsia*, employing the then popular method of root analysis.[29] He wrote,

> The root meaning of the Greek word "church" is "called out" ἐκκλησία, *ekklesia*. The emphasis falls on God's activity. The church is not an agglomeration of men and women who have been chosen to associate themselves together for religious purposes, but it is an assembly of sinners, called out and redeemed by God, and constituted into his church, the body of Christ, by the sovereign power of regeneration through the Holy Spirit. The word focuses the attention on God who calls, and thus it is eminently applicable to the people of God in the Old Testament.[30]

Although Knox's linguistic method would later be refined, and he would move away from overemphasizing etymology, it is significant to see how, early on, Knox was trying to think about both the meaning of words and the conceptual implications of studying their origins.

---

28. Because Knox often did not supply interlocutors for his thought development, his sources cannot be stated with certainty.

29. This method was popular during the rise of the biblical theology movement, which would later come under great scrutiny from scholars such as James Barr. Knox in places seems to be influenced by K. L. Schmidt's article on ἐκκλησία in TDNT, however that article was not published in English until 15 years after Knox began writing on the church. His work is therefore most likely reflective of his work under the philologists at the University of Sydney.

30. Knox, "People of God," 10 (repr.).

Later, Knox moved to examining the semantic range of a word identified by usage in context. He examined the New Testament and the LXX, as well as the Hebrew Old Testament, to identify how *ekklēsia* functioned. He wrote,

> In the New Testament the word "church" always means "a gathering" or "an assembly." Acts 19 shows it was not a technical ecclesiastical word, for in verse 32 St Luke used it of the gathering of the mob in the amphitheatre in Ephesus, and in verse 39 of the regular political assembly of the citizens. In the Old Testament the two Hebrew equivalents of the Greek ἐκκλησία, *ekklesia* are applied to the Old Testament people of God, especially when that people is conceived of as assembling or gathering; for example when gathered around Mount Sinai for the giving of the law, or later on Mount Zion where all Israel were required to assemble three times a year. The usual English equivalents of the Hebrew are "congregation" and "assembly," but Stephen in Acts 7 used the word "church" (ἐκκλησία, *ekklesia*) of this Old Testament congregation of God. In the New Testament the Christian church is the fulfillment of the Old Testament assembly. Jesus Christ is its constituent. Just as in Exodus 19:4, 5 God said to have gathered his people around himself at Mount Sinai, and as later they regularly gathered at his command around his dwelling place on Mount Zion, so Christ gathers his people around himself as their shepherd. He gathers them through the preaching of the gospel: "The Lord added to their number day by day those that were being saved" (Acts 2:47). It is Christ who builds his church (Matt. 16:18). He calls into one flock around him his sheep, whether near or far off (John 10:16, Acts 2:39).[31]

Knox made his case simple and clear. He withheld technical aspects that may have accompanied his investigation, and instead demonstrated how *ekklēsia* was understood in various contexts in the canon. For Knox it was clear that *ekklēsia* is a gathering of people, regardless of whether it refers, on the one hand, to a political assembly or, on the other, of the gathered people of God. He treated this rendering as an established fact that could be noted in passing as he moved on to develop more substantial issues in ecclesiology.[32]

---

31. Knox, *Thirty-Nine Articles*, 140–41 (repr.).

32. Knox is consistent to supply "gathering" (or "assembly") as the rendering of *ekklēsia*, however he only details reasoning for this in three written works. Of these three, only one (*Thirty-Nine Articles* quoted above in the text) provides much detail.

It should be noted that Knox found support for his usage of *ekklēsia* in the church fathers. In particular, he cited Origen, *Contra Celsum*, 3:29–30, to demonstrate *ekklēsia*

The fundamental passage of Scripture in Knox's ecclesiology was Matthew 16:18, which served as the key to unlocking much of how the canon understands *ekklēsia*.[33] In the Old Testament the constitutive event of the church was the Lord covenanting with his people at Mt. Sinai. In that episode the Lord asked Moses to *gather* the people before him on the mountain. Deuteronomy 4:10 referred to this as the "day of the church."[34] Knox believed that this gathering before Mt. Sinai, the "mountainous rock," was the prototype for the gathering that Christ was establishing.[35]

Knox saw a direct correlation of the language used by Jesus in Matthew 16 with the language of "the day of the church." He believed that this extended beyond simple similarities of vocabulary, of which "rock" and "church" are prominent. But the grammar of Matthew 16 also serves as an indication that the Sinai gathering is in view. Knox believed that this correlation had previously gone unnoticed because there has been a mistranslation of the preposition *epi*. He wrote,

> It is interesting to note the grammar of the Greek in Jesus' sentence "On this rock I will build my church." "On" is a mistranslation; it should be "before" or "in front of." The proposition translated "on" in Matthew 16:18 is ἐπι, *epi*. The meaning differs according to the case of the noun that follows. Earlier in his Gospel, Matthew had used the same three words "build on this rock," in chapter 7. Jesus said that the obedient hearer is like a wise man who built his house on the rock. The preposition ἐπι, *epi* here governs the accusative, indication that the action of building is directed onto the rock. The materials are brought and the house is built on the rock. The same grammatical construction is used of the foolish man. He builds his house "onto" the sand. Again ἐπι, *epi* is used with the accusative. However, in Matthew 16:18, although the same verb "build," the same noun "rock" and the same preposition ἐπι, *epi* are used, the case of the noun is different. Ἐπι, *epi* is followed by the dative; that is the church is not built "on" the rock, but "at" the rock, or "in front of" the rock. The Greek does not mean "build on the rock." There is no motion towards the rock in the way the preposition

---

used of an actual gathering. See Knox, "De-Mythologizing the Church," 26–27.

33. Knox wrote, "The most important passage in Scripture about the church, as well as the most controversial, is Jesus' words to Peter, "You are Peter and on this rock I will build my church" (Matt 16:18). Knox, "Church, the Churches," 85 (repr.).

34. This is the title ascribed to the event in the LXX, which is not contained in the BHS. LXX—ἡμέραν, ἣν ἔστητε ἐναντίον κυρίου τοῦ θεοῦ ὑμῶν ἐν Χωρηβ τῇ ἡμέρᾳ τῆς ἐκκλησίας, ὅτε εἶπεν κύριος πρός με Ἐκκλησίασον πρός με τὸν λαόν.

35. Knox, "Church, the Churches," 85–88.

ἐπι, *epi* is constructed. It is in front of the rock, that is, in front of Christ ("that rock was Christ," 1 Cor 10:4) that he builds his church.³⁶

The correlation that this better rendering of *epi* afforded was that, like God gathering his people before/in front of Sinai (and his presence at Sinai) in the Old Testament, Jesus is drawing people to/before himself, the rock, in the New Testament.³⁷

This grammatical correction is significant when one considers, "Who or what is the 'rock' in this passage?" Jesus addresses Peter on the back of Peter's confession that Jesus is the Christ (Matt 16:16), saying, "Blessed are you, Simon Bar-Jonah! For flesh and blood has not revealed this to you, but my Father who is in heaven. And I tell you, you are Peter [*Petros*], and on this rock [*petra*] I will build my church, and the gates of hell shall not prevail against it" (Matt 16:17b–18). The traditional Roman Catholic understanding is that Jesus' renaming of Simon as *Petros* establishes him as the *petra*. But Knox understood it otherwise. He observed that the Old Testament often used "rock" [*petra*] as a personal name for God. For instance, "Who is God except Yahweh, and who is a rock except our God?" (Ps 18:31).³⁸ Therefore, in declaring Jesus' divinity ("the messiah, the son of the living God"), Peter was identifying Jesus with the God, or "rock," of the Old Testament. Of this connection Knox wrote,

> "Peter" (πέτρος, *petros*) was the name that Jesus had given Simon at the beginning of his association with Jesus. Peter means "a stone," that is, a fragment from the rock mass. The meaning of Peter's surname now became clear. He was first to acknowledge

---

36. Ibid., 87.

37. Knox commented further elsewhere on the usage of *epi* in Matthew 16, Knox wrote, "The Greek in Matthew is ἐπι, *epi* with the dative and the natural translation of this construction is 'at this rock' or 'before this rock.' With verbs of motion such as 'build' ἐπι, *epi* takes, naturally, the accusative, as in the parable of the man who builds his house on the rock, narrated by Matthew earlier in his Gospel. Ἐπι, *epi* in this case, is followed with the accusative but in Matthew 16:18 the dative suggests that the translation should be 'at this rock' or 'in front of this rock' as in the Pentateuch references (in the Septuagint of Exodus 17 ἐπι, *epi* is with the genitive)." Knox, "De-Mythologizing the Church," 25.

38. Knox, "The Church, the Churches and the Denominations," 85. Other references to OT passages include Deut 32:4; Isa 44:8; Ps 28:1; Isa 24:4, 30:29; 2 Sam 22:2, etc.

It should be noted that Knox's argumentation for this point changed/developed during his ministry. Here he argues heavily for Jesus' divinity. In an earlier article he identifies Jesus as the "rock of Horeb," demonstrating that New Testament authors understood Jesus in this way (see 1 Cor 10:4). These should not be seen as exclusive lines of argument as both are true and both make reference to the same event and reality. See Knox, "De-Mythologizing the Church," 24–25.

Jesus as the rock . . . the first to be a member of the church of Jesus Christ, the first to be gathered by Jesus into his gathering—his church—to be "in him," part of his body, a branch of him who is the vine, a stone from him who is the rock.[39]

The rock is Jesus himself. Jesus is gathering his people before himself in an assembly, or church.[40] Presumably, one could question the accuracy of this semantic nuance; however, this distinction of definition finds ample support in the most reputable lexicons.[41]

Where then—according to Knox—does Peter fit into this biblical-theological understanding of what Jesus is saying in Matthew 16? If Peter is not the rock, but Jesus is, then what is to be made of Peter? Knox believed that Peter was being contrasted with Moses. He wrote,

> At the rock Moses and Aaron failed in faith. . . . Moses and Aaron shared the fate of all the people who formed this first church of God; their carcasses fell in the wilderness through a failure of faith. But in contrast to Moses and Aaron, Peter believed; his faith was not human faith but was divinely given and therefore was firm. As a consequence, he was representative of all Christ's church which Christ had begun to build with Peter. Death would not prevail as it had against the church of the wilderness because the faith of Christ's church was God given; it was written on the heart by the Spirit of God.[42]

Knox contended, therefore, that Peter is the representative Christ-follower, the first constituent believer in Jesus' church. His faith served as a representation of the faith that would constitute the church, the faith that would not be overcome by Hades. This faith is spiritual, given in the new covenant by the Spirit of God. Knox moved away from simple semantic nuancing to observations concerning the broader biblical-theological theme of faith. Faith is central to the notion of covenant, and Knox drew attention to a major shift in the establishment and maintenance of God's assembly, from human effort to divine sustenance.

---

39. Knox, "The Church, the Churches and the Denominations," 86.

40. Of this language, Knox wrote, "The verb 'assemble' and the noun 'assembly' could of course be translated 'church.' In the Septuagint the words are ἐκκλησια, *ekklesia* and ἐξ ἐκκλησιαζο, *ex ekklesiazo* though the noun in this case is 'synagogue,' the synonym for ἐκκλησια, *ekklesia*. Jesus declares his intention of forming his church in terms drawn from the formation of the Old Testament church of God in the wilderness." Knox, "De-Mythologizing the Church," 24.

41. See BDAG, "πέτρα," 809.

42. Knox, "De-Mythologizing the Church," 25.

Moving from this linguistic analysis of Matthew 16, Knox examined how his conclusions were developed later in the New Testament. If the Old Testament type of *ekklēsia* at Sinai is fulfilled in what Christ is building himself, what does this mean for Christians? Knox found the answer in Hebrews 12. He wrote,

> The epistle to the Hebrews makes it clear that the assembly or church, which Christ is building now, is a heavenly assembly. In Hebrews 12:18–24 the writer contrasts the assembly of which his readers are members with the Old Testament assembly of the people of God. That earlier assembly was gathered round God on Mount Sinai, but the present assembly into which Christian believers have been gathered is around the heavenly Zion, the city of the living God. This assembly is described as "the church of the firstborn who are enrolled in heaven." It is being gathered round Christ where he now is. Our membership of this assembly or church is a present reality. We have already come to the heavenly Zion and already are members of this "church of the firstborn who are enrolled in heaven." We are already "seated with him in the heavenly places" (Eph 2:6; cf. Col 3:1–4).[43]

Knox observed that the essential constituent element of both the Old and New Testament churches was the presence of God—that the people of God are gathered before God himself. In the Old Testament, God was present on the mountain before the people. However, now Christ has ascended to the heavens. This does not mean that there is no gathering in the absence of Christ. In fact, there is a better gathering, as Christians are gathered spiritually before the throne of Christ in heaven. Thus, the *ekklēsia* is primarily a heavenly reality. Many questions follow on from this conclusion, including how human beings experience this gathering existentially on earth and in time, and what the implications of this ethereal gathering are in the material world. Some of these implications will be explored as we see Knox's ecclesiology unfold.

The conclusions that Knox formulated about the *ekklēsia*—namely, that the *ekklēsia* is a gathering and that it is primarily a heavenly reality—informed all other facets of his ecclesiology.

Church: When and Where?

The church is a creaturely entity that exists in time and space. But the questions arise, in *what* time and in *what* space? When and where does

---

43. Knox, *Thirty-Nine Articles*, 141.

the church occur? For Knox, the church is primarily a heavenly reality—a gathering around Christ who is presently in heaven. This is to say that the church is a spiritual entity that finds physical expression in the local church on earth.

The Heavenly Gathering

The crux of Knox's ecclesiology was the priority he gave to the church as a heavenly reality. In a volume published by Judd and Cable in 1987, *Sydney Anglicans: A History of the Diocese*, several pages were devoted to Sydney Anglican Ecclesiology, namely the brand taught under Knox (and Robinson) at Moore College.[44] Judd and Cable emphasized a shift of thought in Knox's work towards the prominence of the local church. In an unpublished response to this section of the book, Knox gave a gracious rejoinder. He believed that Judd and Cable had misunderstood the heart of his ecclesiology. The apparent prominence of the local church in his ecclesiology came only as a consequence of his emphasis on the heavenly gathering.[45]

For Knox, the church is always a gathering in the presence of Christ. The believers who gather physically experience Christ's presence with one another (Matt 18:20). However, this presence and this gathering is primarily a *spiritual* reality. Christ is building his church, and Christ is in heaven. Therefore, the gathering that Christ is establishing in his presence must be, in an essential sense, *in* heaven. Knox wrote,

> Since Christ is now in heaven, it is there that the New Testament thinks of him as building his church, because the church of Christ is the assembly which he calls into being around himself. This heavenly church or assembly round Christ is a present, not merely a future reality, and we are to think of ourselves as already members of it, assembled with him in heaven. It is this church to which Jesus referred in Matthew 16:18 and which he is now building; it is this church or assembly which he loved and gave himself up for (Eph. 5:25). This is the church affirmed in the Nicene Creed (endorsed in Article 8), "I believe one catholick and apostolick church." Its principle of unity is the fact that Christ has assembled it around himself. It is logically impossible for him to assemble two churches; for Christ is to be primarily thought of as in one place only, that is, in heaven, if we

---

44. Judd and Cable, *Sydney Anglicans*, 289–91.
45. Knox, "What the Church Is."

are to use biblical imagery, which is the only imagery available in a matter which transcends experience.[46]

Knox regarded the heavenly existence of the church to be paramount when considering its nature. The church is a gathering of believers around Christ and Christ is seated in heaven; thus church is a singular and heavenly reality. In other words, the church is inherently unified. But what is the relationship of this singular gathering to the many churches represented on earth? Does the inherent unity of the heavenly congregation apply to the earthly congregations? *Should* it? That is, does the multiplicity of earthly congregations, and diverse theology within those bodies, express a present disunity? And how is catholicity to be understood on earth?

Knox believed that the heavenly reality of the church was not a new idea; he understood it not only as the biblical view of the church, but also the view that best represented the historical Christian teaching on the church's catholicity. He wrote, "This heavenly church is 'the catholic church.' This is how the adjective 'catholic' is applied when it first appears in Christian literature. 'Where Jesus is, there is the catholic church' (Ignatius *ad Smyrn.* 8). Jesus is in heaven."[47] Later, in his most mature piece of ecclesiological writing, he reflected,

> It will be seen that this doctrine of the church is the same as the traditional protestant doctrine of the universal, invisible church of Christ, but it gives it its biblical basis and completes it by making it clear that it is the church of Christ, that is the gathering of Christ—for the word "church" always means gathering—round Christ where he is in heaven, where we also are according to the teaching to the of the New Testament.[48]

This understanding challenges the commonly accepted notion that the universal church is an earthly reality, with Knox insisting that while there is a wider group of Christians called the "church," this agglomeration only exists in heaven. Therefore, unity expressed catholically must also be a heavenly reality.

The heavenly gathering comprises every Christian. Entrance into this gathering occurs at conversion. Knox wrote, "All Christians are members of the heavenly church from the moment that they recognize Jesus for who he is, and in faith, pray to him as Lord. They are in heaven, in spirit."[49] Member-

---

46. Knox, *Thirty-Nine Articles*, 142.
47. Knox, "The Church, the Churches and the Denominations," 93.
48. Knox, "What the Church Is."
49. Knox, "The Church, the Churches and the Denominations," 88.

ship in the church is a spiritual state, initiated by the Holy Spirit. The Spirit is the active agent in believers' lives maintaining the activity of gathering in the form of the local church. The local church thereby expresses the spiritual reality of the catholic, heavenly gathering. Thus we can deduce from Knox that membership in the catholic church is not determined institutionally, but rather congregationally, as it is the congregation that gives expression to the heavenly church, not an institution.

The Local Gathering

Further considering Knox's understanding of the local church, it can be seen that the local church is essential to the nature of the church. While the *ekklēsia* is primarily a spiritual reality in heaven, the Spirit draws believers into local gatherings to give expression to the heavenly. Knox wrote,

> Being in Christ's presence, through his Spirit present in them, naturally draws Christians into each other's company. They meet together in his name, and Christ is there in each. Thus the local church forms spontaneously as an expression, in the sphere of time and space, of the eternal reality of fellowship with God which each has, and who is in each. Christians are never exhorted in the New Testament to become members of the church, for that is synonymous with being Christ's. But they are exhorted to give expression to their membership by being present in the local church, or gathering, of Christ round himself.[50]

Knox believed that the local gathering was imperative for believers for both obedience (Heb 10:25), and for fellowship with Christ in the company of others (Matt 18:20).

Though meeting in the local church was an imperative, Christians have not often understood it this way. Knox believed, "Human slothfulness may turn them [believers] away from this essential expression of their personal fellowship with God and with one another in Christ, a reality which is metaphorically expressed as being in the church or the gathering of the firstborn enrolled in heaven."[51] Hence, the New Testament writers and the church fathers needed to exhort believers to continue to gather together. Knox wrote,

> As a consequence of membership of Christ's church there is a duty on Christians to assemble in local gatherings. Interestingly

50. Ibid., 89.
51. Ibid.

> enough this duty was not so obvious to the early Christians that they did not need to be exhorted not to forsake the assembling of themselves together (Heb 10:25). And the letters of Ignatius of Antioch are notorious for their constant iteration of the duty of Christians to assemble together rather than each to worship God on his own. These exhortations confirm that the word "church" refers to the heavenly assembly which Christ is gathering. For every New Testament Christian was vividly conscious, as he awaited his Lord from heaven, of belonging to his church. The fact that they nevertheless required exhortation to assemble together suggests that their concept of the assembly of Christ, of which they all knew themselves to be members, did not of necessity suggest membership of a local gathering. It may well be that the phrase in the Creed "the communion of saints," that is, "the fellowship of Christians," refers to the visible fellowship expressed in local churches or assemblies, just as the preceding clause refers to the heavenly gathering or church of Christ, which is the regulative antecedent of the local fellowship.[52]

Gathering in the local church is non-negotiable in the Christian life. Knox believed this was an essential expression of the heavenly church. He was also convinced that it is the Holy Spirit who leads Christians to this activity. (Indeed, the NT exhortation to congregate might even seem odd in light of the operative presence of the Spirit.)

Knox's identification of the "communion of saints" functioning as an antecedent to the "holy catholic church" is persuasive in view of his ecclesiology, and expresses his interest in aligning his ecclesiological conclusions with the historic Christian beliefs. Or rather, he may not be seeking alignment with the Apostles' Creed, but demonstrating that his position is *the* position of the creed, and indeed both biblical and historic Christianity. One should question, why did the authors of the creed distinguish between the holy catholic church and the communion of saints? What is meant here by communion of saints? Knox concluded that the creed used these two clauses to summarize the nature of the church, with the catholic church functioning as the antecedent to the earthly church. This is the conclusion that Knox himself arrived at theologically.

Knox wrote assertively of the fullness of the local church. In other words, the local church is not in any way deficient; it is the full expression of *the* church.[53] The local church reflects the heavenly gathering and is promised the presence of Christ, which is *the* defining element of the church

---

52. Knox, *Thirty-Nine Articles*, 142.
53. Knox, "Biblical Concept of Fellowship," 82 (repr.).

(Matt 18:20). Knox's concern in expressing this truth was to establish that there is no ecclesial reality to be sought on earth *beyond* the local church. Christ is present wherever two or three are gathered. These gatherings are *the* church. There is no set number that equates to the fullness of ecclesial expression (e.g., every believer on earth). This is not to say that the experience of God in the local church is perfect. Knox wrote, "Yet though our fellowship with God is true and precious, it is not yet full. We see only as it were in a dull mirror, and we look forward to seeing face to face (1 Cor 13:12), to seeing Jesus as he is (1 John 3:2), of knowing as fully as he knows us (1 Cor 13:12)."[54] There is a goal towards which the local church is heading; fellowship with the Triune God will not be enjoyed in the fullest sense until the eschaton. But if the church is the fullness of the heavenly church, how is it that the fullness of the heavenly is not experienced in the earthly? Does not the anticipation of fullness of the heavenly express a lack in the earthly? We will consider these issues further when we examine the creedal properties of the church.

Realm: Time and Space

Fundamental to Knox's understanding of the relationship of the heavenly and the local is the dynamic of the local church's metaphorical expression of the heavenly church. He provocatively entitled one of his most substantial articles on ecclesiology "Demythologizing the Church."[55] In it he tried to navigate the metaphorical usage of *ekklēsia* in Scripture. He wrote,

> In de-mythologizing the church, that is to say translating the concept of the metaphorical use of space/motion terms with regard to a heavenly reality, we conclude that the word "church" refers to a reality which believers have with God in Christ and with one another at the present moment; a fellowship which

54. Ibid.

55. Knox appropriates the language of Rudolph Bultmann, who sought to interpret what he described as the "mythological" concepts of the Bible in existential terms. Knox is likely borrowing the concept of "demythologizing" as a means of speaking to his task of discerning metaphors and their proper conceptual correlates. However, in contrast to Bultmann, Knox does not try to dismiss, or ignore, the reality of the transcendental and immaterial/spiritual. Rather, he distinguishes metaphors, such as the body of Christ, from the reality to which they point, the church. Knox's understanding of the primacy of the heavenly reality of the *ekklēsia* bears witness that he did not endorse the theology of Bultmann. That being said, Knox does demonstrate a desire to express the existential reality of the transcendental reality of the church, that is the local church as the expression of the heavenly church. For Bultmann's position, see Bultmann, *Kerygma and Myth*; Bultmann, *Jesus Christ and Mythology*.

> will, of course, be manifestly deepened at the Parousia. In understanding the New Testament use of the concept we most studiously avoid the way the word "church" has come to be used in modern usage where it is used of something which never assembles and indeed cannot assemble. Church, however, in the Greek of the New Testament times always refers to an actual assembling, either a physical one on the earth's surface or a spiritual reality in the presence of God.[56]

Knox was concerned that modern idiom ascribed more to the church than was indicated by the New Testament. The popular notion of the church was something universal that existed on earth. Knox argued that this notion was inconceivable as a universal (global) church could not and would not ever gather, and gathering is *the* definitive activity of the church.

Developing his thought in contrast to the inaccurate idiom of his day, Knox explained that the church must be understood with regards to time and space. The church is something that happens *in* time. It is constant in the heavenly realms as believers are presently seated, spiritually, in the heavenly places where Christ is (Eph 2:6). On earth, the church happens intermittently. It gathers regularly, giving expression to the heavenly gathering, but it does not remain assembled. This distinction of time in Knox's thought can generate potential confusion. One activity is constant and one is intermittent, yet both are speaking of the same ultimate reality, and both are experienced by the believer. How is this so? How can one (the heavenly) occasionally find expression in the other (the earthly), and yet continue without expression when the other disbands? It is likely that Knox understands the heavenly and spiritual reality of believers to be a positional experience of Christians on earth. When these Christians gather they give expression to the standing that they have spiritually in Christ.[57]

Likewise, both gatherings happen in space. They require presence, though this presence is not necessarily physical by both parties. The heavenly gathering is presently a spiritual reality, with all believers present in spirit before Christ where he is seated physically. This spiritual presence is often referred to in Scripture as believers' status of being "in Christ." On earth, believers gather physically to give expression to their spiritual presence before Christ in heaven. In the midst of that physical gathering, Christ promises his spiritual presence. Like time, Knox's understanding of space may initially cause some confusion. How is it that there is "presence"

---

56. Knox, "De-Mythologizing the Church," 30.

57. There is room for an excursus here on the relationship of time to this conversation. How is time experienced in the heavenly gathering? We will address these issues more in the evaluative chapter.

spiritually if spiritual implies immaterial? Does not space require matter? Again, the explanation of Knox's thought requires the recognition of the positional reality that believers have "in Christ" in the heavenly places, where he is physically.[58]

Knox understood there to be a reciprocal relationship in which believers are present spiritually in the heavenly places where Christ is present physically, and believers are present physically in the earthly gatherings where Christ is present spiritually.

The following table illustrates Knox's understanding of presence:

	Earthly Gathering (Visible)	*Heavenly Gathering (Invisible)*
Believers (New Testament and beyond)	Physical	Spiritual
Jesus Christ	Spiritual	Physical

Knox developed this understanding of presence from the movements he observed in the canon of Scripture. He wrote,

> The Old Testament assembly or church was a physical gathering of all the people of God, in the presence of God. In the New Testament, as so frequently with Old Testament concepts, the idea is spiritualized. Jesus builds his church as he said, but it is a spiritual gathering around himself in the spiritual world of heaven. Thus the writer of Hebrews in chapter 12, contrasting the position of the Christian with the Old Testament Israelite, says that Christians have not come to a physical mountain, Mount Sinai, but have come to a heavenly Mount Zion, where Jesus is. They are all there together in a group, or "church," which the writer calls the church of the first born, that is to say, the church or gathering of God's true people, for in the Old Testament all the firstborn were God's, being dedicated to him at birth.[59]

Knox recognized that the perfect tense verb "have come" (*proselēlythate*) represents a place where believers stand presently. Christians are not still awaiting their presence at, or enrollment in, the heavenly assembly, they

---

58. Just as there is room for an excursus on time, there is also an opportunity for an excursus on space. What is space in the heavenly places? Is this found in another dimension? If so, is this immaterial, and does it therein require a redefinition of terms? Can it be immaterial if Christ has ascended to that place bodily?

59. Knox, "The Church," in *Church and Ministry*, 19–20.

"have come" to that assembly.[60] This presence is a spiritual presence in the spiritual place, yet Christ is in this spiritual place physically.[61]

Knox elaborated on the spatial language used with *ekklēsia*. He wrote, "In the New Testament, 'church' belongs to those space motion terms drawn from the Old Testament which are used to describe our present spiritual relationship to God through the gospel.... Christians are said to have been 'brought near to God.'"[62] The word *ekklēsia* implies action, a verbal noun, describing an entity that is in motion. The church is the *gathered* people of God. Knox further explained,

> The word "church" belongs to this group of spatial terms which describe our relationship to God in terms of movement and space. "Church" or "gathering" means coming together and being together, and the church of God or church of Christ means being brought together and being together in the presence of God and of Christ. We are already citizens of the heavenly family. We are already in Christ; already in heaven, though still on earth waiting for the redemption of our bodies.[63]

This concept of "church" might be viewed as something of an enigma, as a spiritual presence is difficult to comprehend in a material world. Knox, however, was not concerned that his position make sense to the material mind, but rather that it best represented the teaching of Scripture.[64]

Does this spiritual quality compromise the reality of the heavenly gathering, as the earthly believer cannot materially experience it? Knox answered emphatically in the negative. He believed that the earthly gives expression of the heavenly. He observed that the development of the idea within the canon moved away from reference to a physical reality in the Old Testament to a spiritual reality in the New Testament. He wrote, "Under the old covenant the concepts are physical in their expression, but under the new covenant the same concepts are spiritual though equally real."[65] He elaborated further:

---

60. Knox believed that the present position of believers in the heavenly church was reiterated in other verses such as Gal 4:26 and Phil 3:20. Knox, *Sent by Jesus*, 19.

61. This physical presence of Christ is justified in the bodily resurrection and ascension of Christ. This body was material, yet transfigured. See John 20 in which Jesus' body is touched by humans, and yet he can move through walls.

62. Knox, "The Church," in *Church and Ministry*, 20.

63. Knox, "De-Mythologizing the Church," 29.

64. Knox recognized that our discussion of church often exceeds our experience. Thus, he depended on the language of Scripture to describe that which transcends our frame of reference. See Knox, *Thirty-Nine Articles*, 142.

65. Knox, "De-Mythologizing the Church," 23.

> In the Hebrews passage [Heb 12:18–24] the physical gives place to the spiritual. Terms which denote physical entities are now used to denote spiritual realities. In particular the people of God are now the church of the first-born enrolled in heaven.[66]

> The source of confusion of the modern discussions about the nature of the church is derived from a failure to recognize that the church in the New Testament is primarily a heavenly and not an earthly concept. It is not of this world but belongs to the world of the spiritual reality. It is one of the many New Testament concepts which are based on the Old Testament but which have transmuted the physical and spatial aspects of the Old Testament prototype into spiritual relationship.[67]

Thus the ultimate reality, upon the ascension of Christ, is the spiritual gathering of believers that Christ is building in heaven. Knox was not concerned about explaining the physics of such a reality, but rather faithfully representing the biblical realities.

How then are we to understand the relationship of the singular heavenly gathering and the many earthly gatherings? Are these distinct? Knox addressed these questions as follows: "The heavenly and earthly are not two fellowships, or two gatherings, one unseen, the other local and visible, but they are the same fellowship both heavenly in God's presence and at the same time local and physical because we live in a physical environment."[68] The reality of the spiritual is expressed in the physical. In fact, believers know and experience the spiritual in the physical, though the spiritual extends beyond the physical. The existence of the heavenly and the earthly are one in the same. It is perhaps best to understand Knox's beliefs concerning the nature of the church in terms of realms. The heavenly exists in the spiritual realm while the earthly exists in the physical realm. These gatherings are not distinct in their essence, but distinct in their realm of existence. In considering the two, the heavenly has preeminence.

The understanding of the preeminence of the heavenly gathering provides Knox's explanation to the ancient question of false members of the church.[69] Knox addressed the matter by applying the reasoning of the Thirty-Nine Articles. He wrote,

---

66. Ibid., 26.
67. Ibid.
68. Knox, "The Church," in *Church and Ministry*, 21.

69. This question dates back to Donatism and is the question that originally gave rise to the notion of the visible and invisible church. Augustine, *Writings*.

> Article 19 is concerned with the church in its visible aspect—the visible congregation. But the opening clause of Article 26 which also speaks of the "visible church" implies a contrast with the church in its invisible aspect around the throne of God, where the evil is not mingled with the good. The word "church" appears to be used of the "invisible" church in Article 27, which states that "they that received baptism rightly are grafted into the church." The reference here appears to be to the heavenly "invisible church," the mystical body of Christ; for all without exception who outwardly receive baptism are admitted to the visible church. But right reception (Latin *recte*), that is with a believing heart, is the requisite for being engrafted into Christ and into the assembly gathered around him in heaven.[70]

Thus, the invisible church comprises all who truly belong to Christ, as it is a spiritual reality. The physical gathering of the earthly church does not require authentic spiritual transformation, and thus unbelievers can "belong" without truly belonging to Christ and therein his heavenly church.

One might ask, which comes first—the heavenly or the earthly gathering? Does the earthly church only occur as a consequence of the heavenly church? Is the heavenly simply a sum total of all the earthly? Knox answered these questions as follows:

> The church of Christ, primarily a spiritual entity, must express itself in local, physical geographical assemblies or gatherings. The local gathering is not the consequence of the heavenly but is the heavenly expressing itself in the world of time and space of which we are members at present. It is as much a mistake to regard the local gatherings as being the consequence of the larger concept of the church as it is to think of the larger concept as made up of adding together, as it were, all the local gatherings. The local gathering is the complete church of Christ, even if it only consists of two persons gathered in Christ's name, for

---

70. Knox, *Thirty-Nine Articles*, 145. Here, Knox is clear to state that the Thirty-Nine Articles definitely have the invisible church in view, even though Article 19 only explicitly mentions the visible church. He wrote, "The concept of the invisible church was uniformly held by the reformers and was affirmed as early as the Bishop's Book of 1537 and the Thirteen Articles 1538. It would be very unlikely, and in fact is not the case, that the Thirty-Nine Articles repudiated the concept of the invisible or mystical church of Christ, or fell into the mistake which Hooker castigated when he wrote: 'For lack of diligent observing the difference between the church of God mystical and visible, the oversights are neither few nor light that have been committed'" (Knox cited Hooker *Laws of Ecclesiastical Polity*, III). Ibid.

he is there with them. They are his church, the expression of Christian fellowship.[71]

For Knox, then, the notion of church is not quantitatively but qualitatively referenced. "The church" is not a specific, determinate roster of believing participants, but rather believers in communion in the presence of Christ. There is no set number of believers to quantify *the* church; it is wherever a quorum is gathered—at least two or three. Most important to note about this emphasis on quality is Knox's removal of the association of church with an identity, and instead associating the church with an activity. Thus, the people of God gather in the church, but the gathering is not necessarily the people of God.

Ecclesial Unity and the Confessional Reality of the Church

Since the local churches are expressive of the heavenly gathering, how do we account for the multiplicity of churches? And what is to be said of their relationship? We will explore the purpose of the church further in a section below, but for now we must begin to see the purpose of fellowship. Knox wrote,

> The heavenly church is visible in its expression, the local congregation, and in the visibility of the Christian character of its members. . . . There will be fellowship in Christ within the congregation, created by the indwelling Spirit of God in the hearts and lives of all, and there will be fellowship between congregations, through the impulse and leading of the same Spirit.[72]

Local churches will naturally find fellowship with others, just as Christians will naturally find fellowship with one another. The impetus for this fellowship is the Spirit of God. So, there is a place for denominations and other networks of churches.

Throughout history the profession amongst all Christians has been that the church is "One, Holy, Catholic, and Apostolic."[73] But how does Knox apply these attributes to the church? He believed that much of what has been said of the church historically is a confessional reality. That is, the attributes of the church in the Nicene Creed (and the Apostles' Creed) are attributes of faith, belonging to the heavenly church (which is also an object of faith). This does not mean that they are unreal, but rather that they may

71. Knox, "De-Mythologizing the Church," 30–31.
72. Knox, "The Church, the Churches and the Denominations," 94.
73. Nicene Creed.

be either unseen, or awaiting full revelation at the eschaton. In short, like the heavenly church being an object of faith, so too are the attributes of the creed. Knox wrote of the properties of the heavenly church,

> This gathering or church is holy, because it is God's; it has been called out by God for himself. It may also be called holy because its members are holy, not only in status but also in character (1 John 3:2). It is catholic because the gospel is no longer confined to the literal seed of Abraham, but rather Christ is gathering into his church "out of every nation and of all tribes and peoples and tongues." It is apostolic because it is founded on the apostles, that is to say, Christ's commissioned missionaries who founded the church by preaching the gospel of Christ. It is the heavenly church which is apostolic (*Rev.* 21:14) as well as catholic, holy and indivisibly one.[74]

The properties of the church, confessed in the creed, belong to the heavenly gathering, as it is only in the heavenly gathering that these are all actualized. This is not a lack of fulfilled potential in the earthly gathering; rather the only church with potential for the creedal properties is the heavenly gathering. Once again, it should be asked of Knox's ecclesiology whether this reservation of creedal properties for the heavenly church allows for genuine "full expression" of the heavenly church in the earthly church. If the earthly church is lacking these creedal properties that can *only* be possessed by the heavenly church, how then is the earthly the full expression of the heavenly? Does not the lack of catholicity of the earthly church demonstrate that these properties have been diminished? It will be worth drawing attention to this tension when we turn to the evaluation of Knox's contribution, probing more deeply into what Knox meant by the earthly church being the "full" expression of the heavenly.

If the church on earth does not extend beyond the local congregation, then what should be said of church unity? Is there a unity to be sought amongst churches on earth? Many attempted to address this question during the twentieth century, particularly those affiliated with the World Council of Churches.[75] As we have seen, the WCC held the strong belief that the

---

74. Knox, *Sent by Jesus*, 57.

75. Following after the World Council of Churches, Vatican II also discussed the potential for church unity. Of Vatican II and the ecumenical movement (WCC), Knox wrote, "One of the difficulties is that Vatican II and the Ecumenical Movement have both made the mistake of identifying the church with those outward visible structures which were created to serve the fellowship. The church is the fellowship which God has with us and which we have with one another. Since you cannot have fellowship unless you meet, the fellowship is a church or gathering, a gathering thought of primarily as

church is presently divided and ecumenism should be sought as a remedy. Knox, a WCC delegate, reflected on his differing views on the nature of the church:

> The local churches come into being as their members are joined to Christ. These local churches will never be visibly one assembly until the second coming. Then, when Christ will be manifested, the church (that is, all believers) will be seen united around him (Col. 3:4). St Paul in 2 Thessalonians 2:1 speaks of this quite correctly as our "gathering together" around him in the air. But just as at the present time Christ's Lordship is not yet manifest as it will be but remains an object of faith, so his gathering or church is not yet manifest but remains an object of faith, not only in its characteristic of unity, but in all its characteristics as his church, so that quite properly the Creed affirms "I *believe* in one . . . church."[76]

Here Knox detailed the ramifications of the confessional reality with regards to ecclesial unity. Like all other attributes that the creed ascribes to the church, unity itself remains an object of faith. Key for understanding Knox's position is the identification of the precise language of the above statement. He distinguished between an object of faith and an object of sight. His declaration that church unity will never be *visibly* one assembly is a matter of fact; nowhere on earth is there the potential of physically gathering all Christians into one assembly. This is fundamental in Knox's ecclesiology. Earthly gatherings are physical; and if it cannot represent itself physically, it is not a church. The heavenly gathering, on the other hand, is spiritual, and therefore it is an object of faith; it remains unseen. True unity of all believers in an assembly only occurs spiritually at the eschaton (2 Thess 2:1).

The unity and catholicity of the church go hand in hand. Knox believed that his understanding of the catholicity of the church was nothing novel; it dated back to the church fathers. A favorite reference for Knox was the epistle of Ignatius of Antioch to the Smyrnaeans (ca. AD 110).[77]

---

with Christ around God's throne, and at the same time in physical gatherings. We who are members of Christ's church should lift our thoughts to where Christ is, and remember that the purpose of Christ's gathering us in his presence is for fellowship with him and with one another by our hearing his voice which comes to us in the preaching of the gospel within that fellowship." Knox, "The Church," in *Church and Ministry*, 21–22.

76. Knox, *Thirty-Nine Articles*, 143–44.

77. Knox references Ignatius *Ad Smyrn.* 8 at least three times throughout his writings: ibid., 142–43; Knox, "The Church, the Churches and the Denominations," 93; Knox, "What the Church Is."

> It is worth noting that Ignatius, who was the first to use the term "the catholic church," seems to apply it to the gathering of Christians around Jesus in heaven. "Where Jesus is, there is the catholic church" (*ad Smyrn.*, 8). From the way Ignatius is arguing it would appear that it is the heavenly assembly ("where Jesus is") which Ignatius designated as catholic or universal, for he contrasts it with its counterpart, namely its local manifestation in the assembly of Christians around their minister. It is not a spiritualized presence of Jesus to which Ignatius is referring, as this would defeat his argument, which is that just as the catholic church is gathered around Jesus (in heaven), so the Christians should gather around their bishop (in their own locality).[78]

Knox detects in Ignatius' writing the clear understanding that the catholic church exists in heaven where Christ is. As Christ is in heaven and he is the object of Christian faith, so too believers' spiritual presence is with him there. Thus, the catholic church also remains an object of faith.[79]

For Knox, both the unity and catholicity of the church were bound to the presence of Christ. Christ is the focal point of the church, the person around whom and for whom the people of God gather. Christ is not only the focal point, but the *cause* of the church; he himself is gathering people unto himself, as he himself is building the church (Matt 16:18). Therefore, Christ guarantees the unity of the church. He is in one place and therefore he is only gathering one church. There is no potential for division or disunity. Knox wrote,

> The unity of the church springs from the unity of the relationship with Christ, which all believers have. They are all gathered in Christ's church in his presence round him in heaven. That is, they each experience the immediate presence of Christ which comes from being with him face to face through his Spirit present to their spirits. They talk with him, obey him, they are his friends, love him and love all his. The unity of the visible church consists of accepting into full membership of the congregation all true believers who happen to be in the congregation at the

---

78. Knox, *Thirty-Nine Articles*, 143.

79. Knox elsewhere clarified about the catholic church and the usage of the singular versus the plural of *ekklēsia*: "'Where is the gathering of the church of Christ?' It is, of course, not difficult to point to the local gatherings as when St Paul refers to the churches of Galatia or 'to all the churches'; but when the word is used in the singular referring to a larger concept than a local group, as sometimes in the New Testament, where is this single gathering or church thought to be? The answer is that it is a gathering around Christ. 'Where Christ is, there is the catholic church.'" Knox, "De-Mythologizing the Church," 27.

meeting of the congregation. It is Christ's church; he has gathered all its members. Every one who is Christ's and has been gathered by him is as true a member of that congregation or church ... Thus the unity of the heavenly church is expressed in the unity of the visible church by the complete acceptance into full fellowship of all who call upon the name of the Lord.[80]

The unity of the church emanates from the believers' spiritual presence around Christ in heaven. This is a singular gathering that gives expression in many local (earthly) congregations, and of which each is the full expression. The unity of the heavenly is guaranteed by the singular presence of Christ. This unity spills over into the local congregation through the spiritual presence of Christ in the lives of all believers who are gathered. Thus, the reciprocal presence we have already seen earlier in Knox has bearing on issues pertaining to the unity of the church. The unity of the church is a reality, not a goal, as the heavenly church is united around Christ and his Spirit unites the earthly church in Christ.[81]

Knox's conclusions regarding the unity of the church have considerable implications for the ecumenical movement by the WCC. Knox believed that local church unity is the only earthly unity to be sought, as the local church is the only earthly ecclesial reality. Ultimately, from Knox's perspective, the mistake of the WCC was the confusion of the heavenly and earthly church. That is, the WCC ascribed properties of the heavenly church to the earthly church, namely catholicity. But the earthly church is incapable of catholicity, as a catholic gathering cannot and does not occur. Thus, seeking unity amongst catholicity is a pointless task. Catholicity only exists in heaven; therefore, catholic unity is only seen and realized in heaven. As the church is only local on earth, the unity of the church is expressed in the local congregation.

It is clear that Knox saw Christ as the guarantor of ecclesial unity. However, equally clear is his conviction that the means by which Christ affects this unity is by the Spirit.[82] The doctrine of the Spirit was critical as a presup-

80. Knox, "The Church, the Churches and the Denominations," 94.

81. Knox believed that unity of the church was achieved at Pentecost when the Spirit descended upon the believers, and afterwards indwelt all believers henceforth. Knox wrote, "This prayer of Jesus [for unity (John 17)] was answered on the day of Pentecost, when God's Spirit was given to the disciples and to all who believed in Jesus through their word. The Spirit of God unites Christians into a unity. The Spirit of God indwells each Christian heart. God is in them and they are in God, just as Jesus had prayed. No more real unity can be imagined. This unity has already been given to us and can never be dissolved, but we ought to give expression to it by our relationship to each other." Knox, "Christian Unity," in *Church and Ministry*, 35.

82. Knox wrote, "The Spirit is the principle which unifies the Christian group into

position for his doctrine of the church. The Spirit's work is particularly seen in the light of the biblical metaphor of the church as the "body of Christ." Knox understood that Christ is building his church, his body, of which he is the head. But in Christ's body, it is the Holy Spirit who draws people into this body, animates the body, and unifies it.[83] Knox wrote,

> We Christians are a body, created by the Holy Spirit who indwells each one of us. He indwells each part of the body and so brings it into a unity. The body metaphor is a perfect description of the Christian fellowship . . . Christ is in each person in his Spirit. The one Spirit indwells each member and each acts in response to his guidance. The analogy between our physical body indwelt by our being and Christ's spiritual body indwelt by him is complete.[84]

For Knox, there is a very close nexus between Jesus and his Spirit in ecclesiology, as is appropriate in orthodox Trinitarian theology. The presence of Christ in the life of believers is the presence of his Holy Spirit.[85] Furthermore, inherent within the body metaphor is an interaction amongst the parts of the body. The body metaphor highlights the *raison d'etre* of the church as fellowship.

Fellowship

The primacy of the purpose of fellowship within the church extends beyond ecclesiology in Knox's theology. Fellowship is a broader category in which ecclesiology is situated. We noted earlier that the doctrine of God set the agenda for his theology. It is this doctrine that led him to value the concept of fellowship. He noted the fellowship that the Trinity has within itself, and looked to that relationship being the grounds for all other relationships. The

---

a body, "for in one Spirit we have all been baptized into one body and have drunk one Spirit." Knox, "Body of Christ," 38.

83. Ibid., 37–39.

84. Knox, "Biblical Concept of Fellowship," 67.

85. Demonstrating the nexus of Christology and Pneumatology, Knox wrote, "Christ is the life of the body, that is, of Christians in fellowship. Jesus is the life of every individual, 'Christ lives in me' (Gal 2:20) and he is the life of the group 'Christ who is our life' (Col 3:4). There is a close parallel here to the notion of the Spirit. Just as life is in every part of our natural body, so Christ is in every part of his body. Since Christ is in each individual Christian, the Christian's body is also Christ's body and at the same time part of Christ's body." Knox, "Body of Christ," 39.

purpose of fellowship for humanity—fellowship both with other human beings and with the Godhead—extends to the purpose of the church.[86]

Fellowship Defined

Knox defined fellowship as "friends sharing a common activity or a common possession. It's not just friendship. It's friendship sharing something."[87] Friendship is something that humans seek and experience with one another. Knox wrote, "It is a relationship between persons who appreciate, have affection towards, and wish to advance the welfare of each other."[88] Fellowship, then, is an extension of friendship. Knox explained, "It is friendship expressed in joint endeavor, friends doing things together. It makes friendship even more enjoyable. It is the happiest human experience. Friendship implies possessing one another but fellowship implies possessing something else in addition. It is friends sharing a common possession leading to a common activity on the basis of that sharing."[89] Fellowship, then, can happen among all people, Christian or not. However, the definitive mark of Christian fellowship is the possession that Christians share: the Holy Spirit, God himself.[90]

Christian fellowship extends beyond mere human relationships to humans having fellowship with God himself. Knox continued,

> Our truest fellowship is the sharing of Christ. The fellowship of our Lord Jesus Christ is parallel to and indeed the same as the fellowship of the Spirit. In both it is the fellowship we have through sharing the one Lord, sharing the one Spirit, for the Lord is the Spirit. But because the common possession in which we share is a person, it is not only sharing a possession but sharing a relationship. Our fellowship unites us all into one, with God the Father, Son and Holy Spirit and one with one another in Christ. We all should participate in mutual friendship and fellowship. God with us and we with God and with one another. To be conscious of this fellowship means being conscious of our

---

86. Indeed, there are systematic links between ecclesiology and other doctrines, such as the restoration of fellowship (soteriology), which was fractured at the Fall (anthropology), with the Triune God who enjoys perfect fellowship in himself (doctrine of God) and with humanity (reconciliation a part of soteriology, Christology and pneumatology).

87. Knox, "Acts 2:42," 52.

88. Knox, "Biblical Concept of Fellowship," 57.

89. Ibid., 57–58.

90. Ibid.

> relationship with God and with one another in God. The means to this is remembering Jesus, dwelling in him, setting our minds on things above where he is. All these phrases mean the same thing—namely being consciously in his presence.[91]

Christians, then, have fellowship with one another in the possession of the Holy Spirit. And with this possession of the Spirit, Christians also possess Jesus Christ and participate in him. Through this fellowship in the Son, through the Spirit, Christians have access to the Father. Thus the fellowship of the Christian is with other Christians and with the Triune God himself.

The basis of Christian fellowship is the sacrifice of Jesus the Christ. This sacrifice enables horizontal reconciliation with other Christians, as well as vertical reconciliation with God. Knox explained, "We were reconciled to God in one body when we were crucified with Christ and shared his sacrifice, and the words 'body and blood' look back towards the cross on which all fellowship is based and also to the present reality that Christ is in us and we are in one another in Christ. The church is a fellowship of the body and blood of Christ."[92] Thus Christian fellowship is a mediated activity, grounded in the soteriological work of Christ.

The mediation of Christ grants Christians constant access to the presence of the Trinity. Knox wrote,

> Christians are also always in God's company, in Christ's company, and in the Spirit's company. As Jesus promised, "If a man love me, he will keep my word; and the Father will love him, and we will come and make our home with him" (John 14:23). This promise is fulfilled by the Spirit's presence. The Christian is always in the presence of God as his friend. Christ prayed, "As you, Father, are in me and I in you, that they also may be in us" (John 17:21). This prayer was fulfilled at Pentecost. That is why Christians have fellowship with the Father and the Son through the Spirit, in the works of God and in the world; they are always in the company of the Trinity, and they share in forwarding his work. They are led by the Spirit of God to fulfill the work of God, to believe and obey the Lord Jesus Christ, for they work the works of God when they believe on the one whom he has sent (John 6:28–29).[93]

The presence of God is constant in the lives of Christians through the indwelling of the Holy Spirit. But if Christians are always in the presence of

---

91. Ibid., 70.
92. Knox, "Body of Christ," 41.
93. Knox, "Biblical Concept of Fellowship," 63–64.

the Trinity spiritually, why might they gather for the sake of experiencing this presence (Matt 18:20)? Is there an existential reality that is reserved for the corporate gathering? The presence of Christ, by his Spirit, finds its expression most naturally in the presence of other Christians. Thus, Christians gather together on earth to experience not only the joy of each other's company, but the presence of the Spirit of God in the lives of other believers.

Fellowship in the Trinity

As we have already noted in passing, for Knox the concept of fellowship in the Christian life and in the church is established upon the eternal relationship of the members of the Triune Godhead. He wrote,

> Fellowship is the basic human experience and it springs directly from the image of God in which men and women have been created. God is ultimately reality and God is Trinity, three persons in one. The Son is in the Father and the Father is in the Son and the Spirit is both. Ultimate reality, God, is persons in relationship, [sic] Thus there is no experience more ultimate than personal relationship, nor more blissful, for this is how God's being is, and God is ultimate blissfulness.[94]

Fellowship is perfectly expressed in the Trinity. Thus, the basis for fellowship is located ontologically in the Trinity, and the goodness of fellowship is grounded in the perfection of God.

Though perfection of fellowship is complete within the Trinity, it is being perfected amongst human beings. Of the perfect fellowship in the Godhead, Knox wrote, "In all God's works in the world, the one God is undivided. This is a most important theological dictum. What the Father does, the Son does, the Spirit does; what the Son does, the Father does, the Spirit does. The fellowship is complete."[95] The Father, Son, and Spirit are perfectly one. But of the state of human fellowship, Knox wrote,

> Perfection of the image [of God] was fatally marred through the Fall, but was restored and reached its perfection in Christ who is the true image and likeness of God, of whom God was speaking when he said, "Let us make man in our own image and in our likeness." Those in Christ are, by the Spirit, being transformed

---

94. Ibid., 59.
95. Ibid., 63.

into the same image as they turn to Christ and dwell in his presence (2 Cor 3:16–18).[96]

Once again, the significance of the mediated nature of Christian relationships is highlighted. Christians are being perfected in their fellowship by the Spirit, and indeed the grounding of that fellowship is their position in Christ. Christ has brought reconciliation between God and humans, and through the Spirit is working reconciliation amongst humans.

Fellowship in the Congregation

Christian fellowship is experienced more frequently and is a broader concept than the *ekklēsia*, as it occurs beyond the gathering; however, it is not less than the *ekklēsia*. The local church is essential to the Christian experience of fellowship, both with other Christians and with the Trinity. Knox believed that the church is essentially fellowship. He expressed both the vertical and horizontal aspects of fellowship in what he called "fellowship in God." Indispensable to this fellowship in God is the Word of God.[97] The Word of God is the substance around which the church has fellowship. It is also through the proclamation of the Word of God that Christians are called into faith. Thus the church is a creature of the Word.

The fellowship that Christians enjoy in the local church is a manifestation of the greater spiritual reality to which all Christians belong—that is, being in Christ; and is an anticipation of the full realization of that spiritual reality at the eschaton. Knox explained,

> Church is fellowship and it reflects the fellowship of heaven; for heaven is fellowship. The vision of Revelation 21:3 sums up God's purposes for his people: "God shall dwell with them and they shall be his people and God himself shall be with them and be their God and he shall wipe away every tear from their eyes and death shall be no more." We already begin to experience this fellowship with God and with one another through our own faith in Christ. As St John says, "our fellowship is with the Father and with his Son Jesus Christ" (1 John 1:3). Real life is meeting and heaven is people.[98]

---

96. Ibid., 59–60.

97. Knox wrote, "The Christian church is nothing else than fellowship in God, and this fellowship is deepened and maintained by the teaching of the word of God by the minister. Without this teaching there can be no fellowship, that is, no church." Knox, "Priority of Preaching," 241.

98. Knox, "Heaven Is People," 250.

True Christian fellowship involves participation in the Christ-mediated relationship that believers enjoy together, and this happens in the gathering of the local church. This is a present foretaste of the fellowship that Christians will enjoy eternally with other Christians in the one gathering of believers from all ages and nations around the throne of Christ that is to come at the Parousia.

The language of Rev 21:3 is covenant language, identifying the relational promises of God to his people. Does Knox rightly understand the covenant faithfulness of God to his people? It appears that the realization of God's presence and his identification with his people happens primarily at the eschaton. If this is realized in some sense now, then there is further need for clarification of whether or not this presence is bound to the people's participation in the congregation. If so, can it be said that Knox believes that God's presence amongst the gathered believers is in and through his people? If so, this would further add emphasis to the significance of gathering in Christian life.

Fellowship in the Denomination and Beyond

As we have seen, Knox's view is that on earth there is no ecclesial reality beyond the local church—but there *is* a broader experience of Christian fellowship between churches that extends beyond the local gathering. The most common expression of this fellowship between congregations is in a denomination, in which churches unite in common conviction and cause. Knox believed that fellowship is required for health in both the Christian life and the life of the church. He wrote,

> Both Christians and congregations need fellowship to grow in Christ-likeness. The denomination expresses fellowship beyond the congregation. Members and ministers of congregations need to know and consciously remember that they are part of the larger heavenly church of Christ, and to experience that wider fellowship. This is the contribution that denominations make to the spiritual growth and joy of the Christian and the congregation.[99]

Reflecting further, Knox stressed the interdependency of Christians and churches:

> Congregations should be in fellowship with one another. They should not act independently of other congregations.

---

99. Knox, "The Church, the Churches and the Denominations," 95–96.

> Independency is not a Christian concept. It is contrary to God's nature, and to our nature as he has created it. Independency is a contradiction of Christian fellowship. Congregations should not act without respect to other congregations. Denominational structures assist the interdependence of congregations. These links are a natural creation of the fellowship of the Spirit of God. The denomination and its officers have a ministry which is common to all Christians, that is to help, advise, encourage and exhort the congregation and its members.[100]

Knox emphasized the value of denominations in a manner that on first glance appears disproportionate to his understanding of the nature of the church. This feature of his work is surprising, as congregational independence would at least appear to be the most reasonable conclusion to his theology. But his understanding of fellowship constrains him from permitting this separation. He argues that independency is not a Christian concept, but he does not corroborate this claim with reference to Scripture. Could it be argued that the congregation is the place where Christians express their interdependence? Need there be an expression of interdependence beyond the local gathering? Knox believed so, but did not specify where he found this in the Bible. Perhaps he had in mind the interdependence of congregations in the New Testament, especially for missionary tasks and doctrine (e.g., Acts 15, Rom 15).

Greater clarity in Knox's view of denominations is achieved when it is understood in relation to the broader conceptual framework that he outlined. Denominations belong in the conceptual category of fellowship, not ecclesiology. He wrote,

> The doctrine of the church has no place within it for denominations. These are like missionary societies, being expressions of Christian fellowship, and the ministries of their office bearers are helping ministries to facilitate those whom Christ has built into his church to express their fellowship with Christ the better, both in their local church and as his witnesses and servants in the world.[101]

Knox believed that denominations are helpful for congregations, but was careful to stress that the local church is *the* church on earth. No larger group of churches, no matter what extent of fellowship they share, is a church, since a church implies gathering. Knox wrote,

---

100. Ibid., 98.
101. Knox "What the Church Is."

> Denominations are called "churches," and this nomenclature misleads many into thinking that they are part of the one holy catholic apostolic church. But the denomination is not a church, inasmuch as the denomination never gathers. Gathering is the only meaning of the word "church" in the Old and New Testaments. . . . The denomination is an organizational structure to facilitate the fellowship of the church with Christians in other churches. To call the denomination a church is strictly inaccurate, and in furtherance of clarity of thought ought to be dropped, and the word "denomination" always substituted.[102]

Knox preferred to think of denominations as parachurch organizations, existing alongside local churches to aid in fellowship.[103]

Denominations function as service structures for the local church, with the purpose of helping other churches to join in fellowship. The purpose of this fellowship is to facilitate a range of ministries such as mission and theological education that a local church could not carry out alone in the same capacity. However, it is crucial for the denomination not to overstep its bounds. It is not designed to *surpass* congregations, but rather to *support* local congregations.[104] The displacement of the authority of the local church for the sake of denominational dominance is an error that has subverted much local church viability. The end of these organizations has been misunderstood; the *telos* is not the institution, but the congregation.[105] The denomination is not the church, but a support agency for it. Even so, we should ask of Knox whether churches have freedom to align with a denomination, and in aligning, how much concession is given to denominational authority over the church? Is there a voluntary submission to the institution? If so, is this biblical? If the church is only the local church, how can any

---

102. Knox, "The Church, the Churches and the Denominations," 96.

103. Ibid., 95.

104. For more on the danger of denominations and the necessary correctives, see Knox, "De-Mythologizing the Church" 31.

105. In one instance, Knox cautioned against misplaced allegiance due to misunderstanding the end. Knox wrote, "Perhaps the most serious danger which the denominational groupings of Christian congregations presents is that such groupings provide a focal point for loyalty. For many members, especially for the more carnal members, the denomination replaces the true centre of loyalty which a Christian assembly should have, namely Christ who gathers his assembly together. Thus nowadays we witness Christians assembling, both locally and on a world-wide scale, on the ground of their denominational allegiance, and the issue is confused by the fact that invariably the denominations is called 'the church,' as though Christ who assembles his church were also the one who is assembling the denominational gathering." Knox, *Sent by Jesus*, 61.

institution govern it? We will return to the notion of authority in the church later. For now, we move to consider the task of the church.

The Task of the Church

If fellowship is central to the purpose of the church, how is this fellowship achieved? What does this fellowship entail? Is there any further purpose for which the church exists beyond fellowship? Here we now explore the task of the church. In accordance with Knox's ecclesiology, this will be examined first in view of the heavenly gathering, and second in view of the local church.

The chief task of the church in its truest form—the heavenly gathering—is to declare the excellences of God. Knox reflected on this purpose as it is seen in several crucial New Testament passages (Eph 3:8, 10; Rev 14:1–3),

> The mission of the church is to manifest and make plain the character of God to the denizens of heaven and this is in accordance with the New Testament concept that the church is essentially a heavenly entity. It is an assembly of the redeemed gathered round God in heaven (*Heb.* 12:22, 23). As Christ adds to this assembly of saints more and more converts from every tribe, nation and language, God's gracious character and extraordinary wisdom are made evident. He is seen to be a God who justifies the ungodly, yet not in the corrupt way of a venal human judge, but in a way through which he remains absolutely and completely just and righteous. The world does not recognize the nobility of the work of God in transforming sinners into Christlike persons, nor his power in overthrowing the strongholds of Satan. This work of God proceeds unnoticed by the secular historian. But the angels of heaven see it and glorify God for it.[106]

The heavenly church is the display case of the glory of God's soteriological purposes and activity. For the church is the product of God's soteriological work: the gathering of the people he has delivered and called unto himself. But this purpose is entirely ethereal. For terrestrially bound human beings, this seems to declare a purpose that is achieved completely in an unseen realm. How does this correlate with the earthly church? Does it share the same purpose of declaration to the "denizens of heaven?"

The local church expresses the heavenly gathering, constituted of believers who are spiritually gathered in heaven, and therefore shares a similar purpose.[107] In simple and explicit terms, Knox wrote, "These local assem-

---

106. Ibid., 18–19.

107. Knox wrote, "Christians, God's little ones, are in heaven even while living on

blies have no function except to be true expressions of the heavenly church. Their members should express those characteristics and engage in those actions which make the heavenly church glorious and which redound to God's praise."[108] The grounding for the local assembly is always in the heavenly gathering. Christians are to remain focused on their spiritual presence before Christ, and are to embody this spiritual presence in the company of one another. This embodiment, the act of gathering, is both an active and a passive action.

Passively, Christians gather together as the indwelling Holy Spirit leads them. Knox believed, "The real reason [Christians attend church] is that the Spirit of God in each of them has drawn them into each other's company, to meet with Christ in each other, in accordance with his promise to be present with them. The Spirit has drawn them that they might experience the fellowship of the Spirit whom they all share."[109] The Holy Spirit is the guarantor of the gathering of Christians, both in the creation and maintenance of the *ekklēsia*. Indeed, if so-called Christians are averse to gathering with other believers, Knox believed that there is good reason to question if they possess the Spirit of Christ.[110]

Actively, Christians pursue fellowship in the congregation and do so with a view towards others rather than themselves. Knox explained, "The principle for behaviour in church is the divine principle of service. This involves gathering in each other's company to build each other up in the holy faith. Christians in church are to encourage one another in attitudes and actions of love and good works, strengthening one another in the hope of the coming of the Lord (Heb. 10:25)."[111] Elsewhere Knox remarked, "Like all fellowship it requires as a *sine qua non* 'other-person-centredness,' that is, being genuinely interested in the other person as a person and, in particular, as a Christian person."[112] Thus, the active participation requires a kind of selflessness, or a self in service to others, for this is the authentic demeanor of Christian relationship. This demeanor is grounded in the character of God himself, who within his Triune perfection expresses selfless love for each Person.

---

earth. Their spirits are always beholding the face of their Father in heaven. Their heavenly existence is their real existence and the heavenly assembly of which they are part is the real assembly, *ecclēsia* or church, of which the local assemblies are the earthly and transitory counterparts or expressions." Ibid., 19.

108. Ibid.
109. Knox, "Biblical Concept of Fellowship," 74.
110. Ibid., 76.
111. Knox, *Sent by Jesus*, 19–20.
112. Knox, "Biblical Concept of Fellowship," 80.

How does this declaration of the character of God to the denizens of heaven coincide with fellowship? The connection must lie in the fellowship being expressive of God's character, namely God's inherent fellowship within the Trinity and the extension of that fellowship to humanity. Knox does not articulate this correlation, but it may be deduced from his conclusions. It may be that Knox sees the soteriological work required to gather the fellowship, along with the reconciliation expressed in the fellowship, as characteristic of God's great attributes. Thus the gathered people of God are declarative of God's great character, as the gathering only exists because of his great character (e.g., mercy, love, covenant faithfulness; see Exod 34:6).

What occurs in the *ekklēsia* to facilitate genuine fellowship? We recall Knox's description of Christian fellowship as believers sharing a common possession, namely the Spirit of God.[113] But how is that common possession experienced? Put simply, Christians gather to hear the Word of God. Knox wrote, "Christian fellowship is evoked on the word of God, and response to that word. For God is in his word, indeed God is his word, and the Spirit of God, God himself, is in us as we respond to him. John wrote his letter in order to promote this fellowship (1 John 1:3–4)."[114] The Apostle John makes explicit in his epistle that the Word of God is given for fellowship with one another, and the fellowship that is shared by believers is fellowship with God. Therefore, the possession of the Spirit is expressed as Christians encounter the Word of God together.

Knox believed that all of the activities of the gathering should be Word-activities. He explained,

> "We come to church to hear the word. This is the only reason." Frank. This is correct, but to hear the word of God is to hear God. For hearing the word of God is hearing God speaking to us (Matt. 22:31). This is a better way of putting it, as the former way impersonalizes the word of God and so makes the purpose of coming to church focus on ourselves and the spiritual benefit to us. God speaks to us through one another so we come to church to meet with God (God is his word) through his ministry to us through our fellow Christians. When God speaks to us we respond with adoration, praise, thanks, petition. Thus we have fellowship with God and with one another in God. Jesus has promised to be these and this is the way he is these. This is worship, as every action of the Christian should be worship.[115]

---

113. Ibid., 57–58.

114. Ibid., 74.

115. Knox, "Sermon Notes," 99. Knox elaborated, "When I say 'God is his word' I mean it in the same way as when I say 'I am my word,' for another person only knows

For Knox, every activity of the congregation is to be grounded in the word of God. The word of God is the substance of the fellowship. This word is vital as it is *the* means by which God addresses his people, and therefore *the* means for Christians to encounter God himself.

Knox found corroboration for the word-centeredness of the gathering in his Anglican tradition. In the Thirty-Nine Articles, Article XIX expounds upon the nature of the church, the defining characteristics of the word of God preached, and the word of God visibly displayed in the sacraments.[116] Knox remarked of Article XIX,

> Article 19 gives the marks by which a Christian assembly may be distinguished from assemblies called for other purposes. It defines it in terms of its constitutive principle—the word of God. It states that those who form the assembly have already received this word of God into their hearts. It is a congregation of believers. The Article further states that the activity in which the assembly engages is the ministry of the word of God. Faith is the highest form of worship, i.e., honouring of a God whose character is love, and faith springs from hearing the word of God. Nor can there be nobler acts of praise and adoration than proclaiming the gracious acts and promises of God. Ministering the word of God to one another is the primary activity of Christian assembly (Heb 10:25; cf. Eph 5:19, Col 3:16).[117]

In Knox's ecclesiology, the Word of God gives shape and substance to the fellowship, that is, it maintains the purpose for which the gathering gathers.

Incidentally, it is significant to notice that although Knox identified worship as the activity of the congregation, he did not set this in opposition to the rest of the Christian life. Knox was adamant that the purpose of the church was not just for worship, as worship spans beyond the time of gathering with others. He reasoned,

> Why come to church? The universal answer amongst evangelicals is "to worship God," and we call the service a "worship service." But this is quite out of line with the New Testament. In the New Testament, worship is a moment by moment, daily activity. What we do is our worship of God, for we do everything,

---

me through my speaking to him and my facial expressions, which are physical words and my actions when the meaning of these are known to him." Ibid.

116. Knox borrowed from Augustine the notion of the word expressed visibly. Knox believed that the ministries of preaching and of the sacraments are one and the same ministry, as both were kerygmatic—one being verbal, the other dramatic. Knox, *Thirty-Nine Articles*, 144.

117. Ibid.

without exception, for him, for his glory, that is, to show forth his character (Rom 12:1; 1 Cor 10:31). So it cannot be to worship God that we come to church, for we are doing that every moment of the day. Such language betrays an inadequate concept of our daily life. The reason for coming to church cannot primarily be in order that we might pray, for normally we pray privately, entering into our room and closing the door, as Jesus told us to. Nor can it primarily be to hear God's word, for we read and meditate on it at home, where these days we also listen to tapes of the world's best preachers and expositors.[118]

If not for worship and if not for other activities that constitute what many would refer to as a "worship service" (e.g., prayer, reading the Bible, sermons), then why church? Knox firmly held that the purpose for going to church is fellowship.[119] Worship extends beyond the church so the purpose or unique vocation of the church cannot simply be found in the idea of worship. It isn't a case of "worship" *versus* "fellowship," but worship *in* fellowship. In other words, the *unique* purpose of church is fellowship, as fellowship implies togetherness. This fellowship is both with other believers and with God in his spiritual presence in the lives of other believers.

Is Knox dismissive of worship in the gathering? No—the gathering serves as a venue and a catalyst for worship. In other words, Knox seemed to believe that worship was a component of the gathering, but not the main purpose. Fellowship around the Word of God will lead believers to reflect on truths of God's character and will engender worship. But is this not the task that Knox expressed in the church's declarative purposes amongst the denizens of heaven? Is not the church in existence for expressing the glory of God? Knox did not explore this issue further. It is likely that he believed that fellowship was the purpose for believers, and that worship was the product of this fellowship amongst the heavenly beings. In the lives of believers, too, this worship is a product of their gathering, both in the gathering itself and beyond it.

---

118. Knox, "Biblical Concept of Fellowship," 75–76.

119. We could ask: Does not fellowship, like worship, extend beyond the time of the gathering? What then makes worship less central in the gathering than fellowship? Knox did not explore these questions, but it is likely that he believed that worship is something that is both individual and corporate. Worship happens in the totality of life, whereas fellowship requires the company of others. We should add, as it has already been explained, fellowship in the corporate gathering is a unique opportunity to give expression to the heavenly church. One could say that worship does not require the corporate gathering to properly express worship, just as all of life is an expression of worship, so too God is worshipped by many beyond the gathering, both animate and inanimate, physical and spiritual, human and angelic.

Knox believed that fellowship is an end in itself.[120] People are not gathering to have fellowship with an aim towards something greater. Fellowship itself is the aim. Knox claimed that "going to church is an expression of fellowship. It is a microcosm of the fellowship Christians have with Christ and with one another, in the presence of Christ in heaven at the present moment, around God's throne and the throne of the Lamb."[121] The uniqueness of the expression of fellowship in the church is the promised presence of Christ. Christians gather together "seeking Christ's face for he is in each of us and we meet him in one another."[122] Though Christians experience this fellowship in a very real and meaningful way in the local church, the fullness of the fellowship is yet to come at the Parousia.[123] We might again question here the lack of fullness of the church on earth, as we have elsewhere, but it might be answered simply that Knox has in mind the already/not-yet tension that is demanded by a biblical eschatology.[124]

Authority

We now move to consider the final subsection of Knox's ecclesiology: authority. If the task of the church is to gather around the Word with the purpose of fellowship, then this Word must have authority in and over the congregation. Indeed, for Knox, the Word of God is the best representation of God amongst the people. Knox held a very high view of Scripture, as we have already seen, even preparing to insist God is his Word. Thus, the Word of God must have authority over the people of God, especially as they gather in the presence of God.

Knox understood authority to be something expressed in the Word-activities of the gathering. The most prominent of these activities are the preaching and teaching of God's Word. The pastor of the congregation is ultimately responsible to see that the Word is at the center of the gathering, governing the church. Knox wrote,

> Christ rules our consciences through his word and the pastor who rules the flock of God must teach the word, and apply it to the conscience. This is his only instrument for ruling in the name of Christ. It is not possible to be pastor without being a

---

120. Knox, "Heaven Is People," 248.
121. Knox, "Biblical Concept of Fellowship," 79–80.
122. Ibid., 76–77.
123. Ibid., 82.
124. See 1 Cor 13:12

teacher, and that is why the scripture insists that those who are admitted to the office of pastor must be "apt to teach."[125]

Within the local church there is governance, namely through the pastor, but this is only ever a derivative authority. The extent to which the pastor has authority is the extent to which he conveys the Word of God.

There is no institutional authority over the local church as there is no earthly ecclesial reality beyond the local church. Knox's ecclesiology appears to support an autonomous local church, under the Word of God.[126] But he also recognized local churches often find themselves in fellowship with other churches, and in this fellowship natural patterns and structures develop, such as denominations.[127] The establishment of these structures must keep the reality of the church in view. Knox wrote,

> The conclusion is that the ecclesiastical institution has no responsibility in the life of the congregation, for the congregation is responsible for his own life. But the ecclesiastical institution, since it exists, has the opportunity for helping. Opportunity and ability to help always creates obligation to help, but this does not in itself confer responsibility, with its concomitant authority. The ecclesiastical institution and its office bearers are helpers of the congregation which means that it must confine itself to exhortation, encouragement, advice, but it must exclude all sanctions, even spiritual sanctions. For that would be an exercise of authority and the institution has no authority, for it has no responsibility for the life of congregation (church) or for the ministry exercised within it.[128]

Institutions have great potential and value as service structures, but they must always only be seen as such—service structures. As there is no earthly church beyond the local congregation, there should be no institution seeking any semblance of ecclesial authority, especially with exercise over local churches. Once again we return to the question of freedom of the congregation to affiliate with an institution. If it is "natural" or commonplace for congregations to find fellowship in institutions, do congregations opt-in to submission to institutional authority? For example, must an Anglican

---

125. Knox, "The Spirit, the Church and the Denomination," 33.

126. For justification of this notion, Knox observed Paul's example of leadership (e.g., 1 Cor 5:3–4 and 2 Cor 1:24). See Knox, "Biblical Concept of Fellowship," 83.

127. Knox wrote, "Fellowship in the present life not only requires propinquity with a word and a response, but because of our human nature and the way we do things, it forms patterns." Knox, "De-Mythologizing the Church," 31.

128. Knox, "Notes on Authority in the Church," 101–2.

congregation obey its bishop? If there is no church beyond the church, is there ever an appropriate external authority?

Knox could be accused of advocating independence, even exemplifying (what might be construed as) a typically Australian antiauthoritarian disposition. But Knox's argument was not based so much on his cultural ethos, as it was his biblical and theological conclusions on the nature of the church. The church is primarily a heavenly reality, a gathering, and the earthly expression of that reality is the local church, where believers gather. Denominations *per se* do not gather. Thus, in matters of the church authority must be thought of in the confines of the church, which by his conclusion is only the local church. He wrote,

> The ecclesiastical institution only arose centuries after the beginning of the gospel. It cannot be traced to the New Testament, even in embryo, and for centuries there was nothing corresponding to it at all. It cannot therefore have any responsibility for the life of the congregation. Its only function can be to help the congregation discharge its responsibility for its own life. This help must remain help; it must be free from strings, i.e., from sanctions. For help, with strings or sanctions, ceases to be pure help and takes on the character of pressure—the exercise of authority.[129]

The resistance to institutionalism, then, is a resistance to a false ecclesiology. If the denomination is given greater authority than warranted biblically, it may endanger the vitality of the local church.

Knox developed some of his conceptions with respect to denominational structures. He believed the gravest danger is that of making a denomination the end rather than the means. He wrote,

> The danger is that instead of the denominational structures serving the fellowship it comes about that the fellowship is made to serve the structures, and this destroys the fellowship. Structures, too, may become top heavy or out of date, and so injure the fellowship instead of assisting it. They may become authoritarian and centralistic, and so injure the exercising of those ministries which the Spirit of Christ gives directly to each of his members. The test of any church structure is whether it assists the fellowship of the Spirit and aids the Spirit-given ministries of the members.[130]

---

129. Ibid., 102.
130. Knox, "The Spirit, the Church and the Denomination," 34.

Once again, we see that Knox was concerned for the primacy of the local church. Denominations can be very helpful in serving local church fellowships, but they only remain helpful when they keep the local church fellowship as the end, not the institutional structures and allegiance thereto.

Knox was not against denominations, however. He believed that denominations are essential, as the notion of an absolutely independent church is false. He wrote, "Denominations are essential to the full flower of Christian fellowship. An independent congregation of Christ is a contradiction of terms. Inter-dependence, not independence is the principle of which the world has been created, for interdependence is the principle within the Trinity itself, who is ultimate reality."[131] It might not always be clear how such a sentiment fits with his other observations. But once again we see Knox return to the theological starting point for his ecclesiology, the doctrine of God. This doctrine prevents Knox from allowing his ecclesiological findings to be pressed too far, in this case to independence. Thus, while local churches are by nature autonomous—self-contained, full expressions of the church—there is a healthy interdependence that is necessary. Denominations are helpful service structures that demonstrate and facilitate this interdependence.[132] It is also helpful to draw attention, once again, to the fact that in Knox's theology, ecclesiology is a less inclusive concept than fellowship. That is, ecclesiology is situated within the broader purview of fellowship as a piece of the whole.

CONCLUSIONS

What are the distinctive elements of Knox's ecclesiology? We turn now to consider these elements as a summary of Knox's ecclesiology and to raise questions that will guide our evaluation in the next chapter.

The ecclesiology of D. B. Knox was developed through his own style of systematic theology that highly esteemed the Bible. We might call his method biblical theology, as it was an investigation of thematic elements developed throughout the Bible; however, this would not do justice to the

---

131. Knox, "Biblical Concept of Fellowship," 83.

132. Knox listed five ways the ecclesial institution can aid local churches without exercising usurped authority: (1) In ordination and selection of ministers; (2) In providing an impartial tribunal for disputes; (3) In providing a corporation to own the property used by the congregation; (4) In providing a forum for the discussion and resolution of matters of mutual interest between congregations; (5) In providing a ministry of encouragement, exhortation advice and instruction, as long as no sanction beyond the word of God on the conscience is ever applied. See Knox, "Notes on Authority in the Church," 102–3.

systematic connections that Knox gathered following on from his biblical-theological work. Thus, his ecclesiological interlocutors are enigmatic, as they are largely undisclosed, fading into the background of biblical inquiry.

The starting point for Knox's ecclesiology was the text of the Bible, both the Old and New Testaments. Knox observed how *ekklēsia* is understood across the canon of Scripture as a gathering. He identified the precedent for the New Testament gathering in the Old Testament gathering of the people of Israel at Sinai. This gathering is of the nation that God has called out, and is gathered before the presence of the Lord. In the New Testament, Jesus is gathering in his presence the people he has called out. Knox identifies the presence of Christ as the great promise of the *ekklēsia*. As he looks on in the New Testament, Christ is risen and he is gathering believers to himself in heaven. We may question whether Knox has taken anomalous positions regarding the few foundational passages of his ecclesiology. Does his exegesis of Matthew 16 fit reasonably into the scope of legitimate hermeneutical options? In particular, is his observation of the grammatical nuance of *epi* with the dative (or locative) rationally persuasive?

After establishing the basic notion of the church as a gathering around Christ, Knox addressed issues of time and place. If Christ is no longer on earth, and yet he is building his church, where and when is the church to be found? Knox identified in the New Testament the present heavenly presence that all Christians enjoy. Thus, all Christians are being gathered, spiritually, to Christ in the heavens. As such, church is to be thought of primarily as a heavenly reality. The foundation for Knox's conclusion that the church is primarily a heavenly reality is found in his exegesis of Matthew 18 and Hebrews 12. Again, we might well ask whether Knox has overemphasized nuance in a few passages to build his ecclesiology. Does Matthew 18 emphasize the presence of Christ as the constituent element of the church, or is it more a passage on confidence in settling disputes? Is the verbal nuance of the perfect tense in Hebrews 12 speaking of a present reality believers experience?

Knox explored the relationship of the heavenly and earthly church, or what has classically been called the invisible and visible church. He believed the heavenly gives physical expression of its spiritual reality in the local assembly, which is a full representation thereof and is gathered by the Holy Spirit. There is reciprocity: in heaven, believers are spiritually present with Christ's physical presence; on earth, believers are physically present with Christ's spiritual presence. As the church is understood as a present heavenly reality with earthly expression, it is seen that questions of creedal qualities are to be understood in terms of confessional realities. The heavenly church is *the* "one, holy, catholic, and apostolic" church. Therefore, efforts for ecumenism or building any "ecclesial" institution beyond the local church are pointless, as *the* church on earth is the local church. Knox stressed that the local church is full expression of the heavenly. But if this is so, how is the heavenly *the* church in which the creedal attributes are to be found? Should not these creedal attributes also be manifested in the local assembly, if it is indeed the full expression? Also, how does the eschatological tension of already/not-yet fit within this understanding?

Furthermore, one of the more pressing questions asked about Knox's understanding of the relationship of the visible and invisible church is whether or not it is, in essence, platonic. We saw that a similar charge was leveled at Robinson. If it is, then is this representative of a biblical philosophy, or is this an example of the external, alien influence of classical philosophy? Even if Knox's idea was *not* platonic, it may have possessed some resonance with Platonism. This philosophy asserts that the material is a pale and corrupt copy of the supreme spiritual reality—the domain of the Forms. Knox believed that the heavenly is the primary and ultimate reality finding expression in the earthly. However, he believed that the earthly was the *full* representation of the heavenly. Therefore, the church on earth is not a shadow of the heavenly, but *the* physical manifestation of the heavenly. Questions that linger concern the exact connection of these two realities, and how they are best to be understood in light of time.

After establishing the time and place of the church, Knox detailed the purpose of the church as fellowship, as it gathers to encounter Christ. This encounter is spiritual, as believers encounter the Spirit of Christ in each other. Fellowship occurs as the people gathered participate in the Word of God; the Word is the substance of the fellowship. Worship is a product of what the church does, but it is not the primary or unique function, as worship extends beyond the gathering in the lives of individuals. Fellowship, too, extends beyond the gathering both amongst individual and congregational relationships. Natural patterns form in this fellowship of churches, making denominations. These denominations are service structures for the church, but are not the church itself. Thus, denominations have no ultimate authority over the local church. Rather, the Word of God is authoritative over the local church. Knox's emphasis on the purpose of fellowship—a fellowship achieved through Word activities—raises questions about why fellowship is the purpose of the church when it occurs beyond the local church. If God is constantly present in believers' lives by his Spirit, is fellowship with the Trinity not experienced constantly in the Christian's life? If fellowship is for encountering the Holy Spirit in the lives of others, why move beyond a family gathering into a larger "local assembly?" Is there some kind of "deficiency" in the smaller gathering? If not, is there a further quality to the uniqueness of the local assembly that needs to be identified? And, with regard to authority, if institutions arise naturally to aid in fellowship, to what extent are congregations free to submit themselves to denominational regulation?

We will find the distinction between the qualitative and the quantitative constituency of the church of particular importance. How much of the apparent incongruence between the earthly church and heavenly church may be explained in stating the qualitative properties of the *ekklēsia*? Are the qualities the same for both the heavenly and earthly? Is there fair distinction because of realms, and can the two be the same if they are in different realms with different properties? Again, how does time and the experience of time factor into this inquiry?

It is to these questions and others that we now turn our attention as we evaluate Knox's ecclesiology.

8

Evaluation of Knox's Ecclesiology

HAVING DESCRIBED AND ANALYZED D. Broughton Knox's ecclesiology, we turn now to evaluation. This evaluation will seek to ask questions of the ecclesiology's biblical, logical and traditional value.[1] We will engage the key propositions of his theology of the church in turn. These propositions are as follows:[2]

1. *Ekklēsia*. The church is the gathering of believers around Christ.

2. *The Heavenly Gathering*. Church is primarily a heavenly reality, gathered around Christ where he is.

3. *The Local Gathering*. The heavenly gives physical expression of its spiritual reality in the local assembly, which is a full representation thereof and is gathered by the Holy Spirit.

4. *Presence*. There is a reciprocal relationship of presence in the earthly and heavenly gatherings. Believers are present spiritually in the heavenly places where Christ is present physically, and believers are present physically in the earthly gatherings where Christ is present spiritually.

---

1. As noted in our evaluation of Robinson, these categories are broad and undefined. This is intentional, wishing to highlight the general nature of the questions to be raised. It is important for my evaluation to be an engagement of Knox's theology on his own terms.

2. These propositions are the product of the description of Knox's ecclesiology in the previous chapter. These are my summaries of the key points he makes concerning the nature of the church. These are presented in an order I have chosen as the best logical sequencing. These propositions are mutually dependent.

5. *Purpose: Fellowship.* The local assembly gathers for the purpose of fellowship as it gathers to meet with Christ. This encounter is spiritual as believers encounter the Spirit of Christ in each other.

6. *Activity: The Word of God.* The distinguishing mark of Christian fellowship is the Word of God. The Word gives shape and substance to the gathering.

7. *Authority.* The Word of God has authority over the congregation. As the congregation is the only legitimate church on earth, there is no institutional authority naturally set over the local church, though the church may willing choose to fellowship with other churches in an institution.

EVALUATION

Anticipating what we will say in our conclusion, there is obviously overlap here between what was said about Robinson and what must be said here about his senior colleague. We begin our evaluation by commenting on Knox's theological method, before moving to consider the propositions of his ecclesiology. The strength of Knox's theological method was his construction of theological propositions from biblical-theological investigation. He did not merely parrot the ecclesiology of others throughout history. Instead, he sought a first principles approach drawn from the text of Scripture. However, he was not ignorant of his own Anglican tradition, or of broader reformed Protestantism. Where appropriate he commented on the nature of the church from within his Anglican framework. However, his primary agenda was to demonstrate what the Bible said about the church, rather than history, and to do that theologically.

It is this preoccupation with the teaching of Scripture that explains what is for many readers the leading weakness of Knox's approach. In seeking to demonstrate what the Bible teaches about the church, he seldom acknowledged his interlocutors. Even when, in an honest effort to understand the Bible's teaching on the church, he *did* engage other contemporary and historical voices, he seldom recognized their contribution to the development of his thought. Nevertheless, although he did not make much use of academic apparatus, at least as the conventions of his discipline demand today, we should not dismiss Knox's work as lacking rigor or as an unhelpful contribution to the field of ecclesiology. We must remember that he did not seek to write for the academy, except in a few instances.³ Profound claims, steeped in the text of the Bible, can be made in simple form. We recall that Knox primarily understood his audience to be theological students in training for local church ministry, not the academic guild.

As we have attempted in this book to set forth Knox's ecclesiology in a clear and coherent manner, for academic engagement, we have observed that his theology provides stimulating conclusions of a caliber beyond their popular presentation. We now seek to evaluate the theological quality and integrity of the key propositions of Knox's ecclesiology.

1. *Ekklēsia*

The church is the gathering of believers around Christ.

Knox, like Robinson, concluded that *ekklēsia* should be rendered "gathering." In fact, he concluded more firmly than Robinson that this was the *only* appropriate rendering of the terms as it is used in the Bible.⁴ As we speculated earlier, it is likely that Knox's understanding of *ekklēsia* was derived from the work of Robinson. This is probable since there was a noticeable shift in Knox's understanding sometime during the 1950s. His earlier studies still employed etymological studies for an understanding of meaning. This method was common amongst theologians at the time.⁵ However, later he spent more time examining the usage of words in context. This shift may have come from his interaction with Robinson, who was developing the biblical-theological method that would later become characteristic of Moore College.⁶ The shift also indicates recognition of the sort of critique James Barr later made famous, though Barr's *Semantics of Biblical Language* was not published until 1961.

Moving from the foundational lexical conclusions that he shared with Donald Robinson, Knox demonstrated how *ekklēsia* was understood conceptually throughout the Bible. His anchor was the proto-*ekklēsia* at Sinai (Exod 19; Deut 4). He believed that this gathering was the type that anticipated the Christian gathering that Jesus would establish. Knox found direct New Testament correlates in Matthew 16 and Hebrews 12, identifying unity and development of the concept of *ekklēsia* in the Bible. His observations

---

3. For example, Knox, *Doctrine of Faith*.
4. Knox, "De-Mythologizing the Church," 30.
5. For instance, Torrance, "Israel of God."
6. This method is epitomized in the work of Graeme Goldsworthy, who identifies Robinson as *the* formative influence on his method. See Goldsworthy, *Christ-Centered Biblical Theology*, 13–15.

of Hebrews 12 were grounded in the direct citation of the Sinai gathering (Heb 12:20; Exod 19:12, 13). His conclusions about Matthew 16 were based on conceptual similarities with Sinai, built upon lexical and grammatical similitude with the Greek of the LXX.

On a macro level Knox's conclusions are profound conceptual observations of intertextuality. Matthew 16 has long been a source of tension for Roman Catholic, Orthodox, and Protestant ecclesiological dialogue. However, Knox did not move to simply identify the "building on the Rock" as building on Peter's *confession* of Jesus as the Christ, as many Protestant scholars have done.[7] Instead, he looked to the Old Testament precedent for the difficult text. His evidence-based connection is compelling and on a macro level is a legitimate identification of an indirect intertextual reference. However, on the micro level of exegesis, Knox's conclusions are not quite as convincing.

Knox made two exegetical observations in Matt 16:18 do much work. First, he believed that there had been a long-standing misinterpretation of *epi*, rendering the word as if it governed a word in the accusative case (e.g., "on"; "upon"), rather than governing the dative case as it stands in the text (e.g., "at"; "before"). Though Knox did not speak with direct reference to how he understands the dative case being used in this instance, we may assume he believed *epi* to be functioning in a locative sense.[8] The difficulty with Knox's proposition is that there is a greater semantic range than he gives account to in his analysis. Rendering *epi* as "on" or "upon" *is* a legitimate translation of the dative use of the preposition.[9] However, this is not to say that Knox's conclusion is inaccurate, as his rendering is *also* a legitimate translation of the dative/locative use as well. Knox's nuancing is a helpful insight supplying a different, and perhaps more accurate, translation of Matt 16:18.

Second, Knox moves from identifying a varied translation of the preposition *epi* to an examination of the object of the preposition—*petra*. He argued that though *Petros* and *petra* feature in close proximity in Matt 16:18 and are similar words, they should not be understood to refer to the same

7. Details of this argument are offered in Caragounis, *Peter and the Rock*.

8. The number of cases in Koine Greek has been debated. In older grammars, scholars often advocated an eight case system in which the dative form could be understood in either an instrumental, locative or dative sense. Newer grammars promote a five case system, with the dative form able to be employed in a broader sense that encompasses the locative and instrumental uses. Knox's understanding of *tautē tē petra*, the phrase which *epi* governs, would therefore be categorized as follows: older system—locative case; newer system—dative of place or dative of sphere. For a detailed conversation of the five and eight case systems see Wallace, *Greek Grammar*, 139–40.

9. See ibid., 376.

thing. *Petra* means a rock, whereas *petros* means a stone, implying a fragment of a rock. Peter's confession was a confession of Jesus as the Christ, and in affirming Simon's confession Jesus gives him a name (*Petros*) that identifies the veracity of his confession and refers to his divine identity (*petra*). We noted earlier that though the lexical nuance of Knox's claim may be called into question, several standard and reputable lexicons supported his suggestion. Advocates of Roman Catholic ecclesiology, who understand the terms to be synonymous, would question the differentiation in the meaning of each form of the words. However, this differentiation can be justified based on the lexical evidence. The challenge for Knox's comments on *petra* lies in the connection Knox draws to the Old Testament understanding of the word. Is *petra* primarily associated with God in the Hebrew canon, and if so can we assume that Jesus is here disclosing his divine identity?

Earlier in Knox's writing he identified *petra* in Matt 16:18 with Mt. Sinai itself (the rock of Horeb). In that line of argument Knox drew on the identification of Jesus as "the rock" in 1 Cor 10:4. The trouble is that the identification of the rock in 1 Cor 10:4 is of the rock that travelled with the Israelites in the desert, not specifically the mountain. We should note that the identification of Christ with the rock that followed and with Sinai/Horeb are not mutually exclusive.[10] Both at the mountain, and in the following rock, God was present with his people, but the rock served different purposes in each instance. Knox is careful to say that Matt 16:18 speaks of Jesus drawing believers before/at himself, "the rock," following the type of the Mt. Sinai gathering where Israel gathered to listen to YHWH. However, identifying Jesus as the rock that followed the Israelites is not representative of the same sort of gathering. The rock that followed signified God's presence, but it did not serve as the focus of Israelite attention as at the Sinai gathering. Instead of being drawn before the rock at Sinai, the rock that followed seems to have pursued the people.

It is worth noting that Knox sought to be comprehensive in his examination of the details in Matthew 16. Where he dismissed Peter as the Rock, he did not dismiss Peter altogether. Knox sought to identify the Old Testament type of which Peter was the antitype. He concluded that Peter was Moses, but in better form.[11] Moses stood as the representative of the Israelites, but failed in faith. Peter, on the other hand, stood as a representa-

---

10. We should take care to note here that God was not the mountain. But the presence of God settled upon the mountain, and therefore the mountain became representative of the presence of God. Nor was the rock that followed the Israelites in the wilderness actually Christ, but it is representative of the provision and presence of Christ, spiritually, to the people in the wilderness.

11. Textual support for this identification may have come from Acts 7:37–38.

tive of the church and succeeded in faith. The confession of Peter about the identity of Christ was the representative faith claim of all who would follow in the fellowship of the church.

Most commentators do not support Knox's identification of Jesus as the rock. A straightforward reading of the verse understands Peter is the rock, with the difference in words between the naming of Peter and the designation of the rock being a matter of gender rather than identity. So, David Turner writes, "Another argument is that Peter is not the foundation of the church because πέτρα [*petra*] means bedrock and Πέτρος [*Petros*] means an individual stone. But this extremely subtle distinction would make metaphorical speech impossible. Jesus is speaking of Peter in 16:18 just as clearly as Peter is speaking of Jesus in 16:16."[12] Likewise, R. T. France comments,

> The Greek reader would therefore see here a difference in form but not in meaning, since *petros* was not now (if it ever had been) the term for a "stone." If Jesus was speaking in Aramaic, there would be no difference at all, with *kēph*à occurring in both places. The reason for the different Greek form is simply that Peter, as a man, needs a masculine name, and so the form *Petros* has been coined. But the flow of the sentence makes clear that the wordplay is intended to identify Peter as the rock.[13]

How likely is Knox's interpretation then? Some scholars—most notably another Australian, Leon Morris of Melbourne—have acknowledged that the identification of Jesus as the rock is a credible interpretation, although they themselves did not take this position.[14] Knox's position had a biblical-theological rationale, but it also had support from careful linguistic analysis: Jesus used the relative pronoun "this" over and against the personal pronoun of "you." If Peter were intended as the rock, why didn't Jesus say, "upon *you* I will build my church?"[15]

Knox's argument may raise some exegetical questions, but it finds conceptual support in his examination of Hebrews 12. The text there draws a direct correlation between the Sinai gathering and the new gathering of God's people—the heavenly church. This new gathering exceeds the old as a spiritual, rather than physical, gathering. In both the Sinai proto-*ekklēsia* and the Hebrews *ekklēsia* the constitutive element is the presence of God. Therefore, the connection of Jesus with the Rock in Matthew 16, the focal

---

12. Turner, *Matthew*, 406.

13. France, *Gospel of Matthew*, 621.

14. For example, Green, *Message of the Church*, 86–90. Also Morris, *Gospel according to Matthew*, 422–25.

15. See Morris, *Matthew*, 422–25.

point of the gathering as at Sinai, is a legitimate connection on the basis of Hebrews 12. Though this interpretation fails to find favor with most commentators, it remains a viable interpretation of the text, especially given its consistency with the conceptual development of the *ekklēsia* in the Bible.

2. Heavenly

Church is primarily a heavenly reality, gathered around Christ where he is.

Within Knox's examination of Hebrews 12 he concluded that the church is primarily a heavenly reality. This is based both on his textual observation (e.g., Heb 12:22–24) and logical deduction. Textually, Knox observed that the enrollment of Christians is present and in heaven, as *proselēlythate* is the 2nd person plural perfect active indicative form of the verb *proserchomai*. As a perfect verb in the indicative mood, the word carries a sense of a completed action with present implications.[16] Therefore, those under the new covenant have been gathered to a better place than Sinai, to the heavenly places. This is not something that is anticipated, but something actual.

As we remarked earlier, Knox's emphasis on the current participation of believers in the heavenly church has been criticized as platonic.[17] This accusation comes from the seeming dualistic understanding of the church. How can there be both a heavenly and an earthly reality to the church, let alone simultaneously? Some might argue this concept of a dual nature of the church is simply a way to account for the membership of the church, with the true believers belonging to the heavenly congregation and many believing and non-believing members to the earthly. It is easy to move from this line of argument to assuming that Knox believed that the heavenly represents the pure form, of which the earthly is but a shadow.

Of particular interest is the question of time. How does the believer simultaneously experience the heavenly and earthly? Knox did not explain the means by which the reality of the church's dual nature held together, but rather recognized it as a reality taught in Scripture. The reality of the heavenly has present implications for the believer. Many scholars have sought to

---

16. Wallace says, "The force of the perfect tense is simply that it describes an event that, completed in the past (we are speaking of the perfect indicative here), has results existing in the present time (i.e., in relation to the time of the speaker)." Wallace, *Beyond the Basics*, 573. The issue of what is signified by this verbal tense is currently disputed. But even in verbal aspect theory, this reading would be reinforced. See Campbell, *Verbal Aspect*, 161–211.

17. See Giles, *What on Earth*, 14, also 190–95. For an understanding of what is meant here by Platonism, see Plato's *Republic*, 7.513–20, 220–27.

explain the issue of time and experience in this passage. We noted O'Brien and Peterson, amongst others, in our evaluation of Robinson.[18] Kevin Giles explained this issue as follows:

> We have here the common Jewish apocalyptic idea that what lies in the future already exists above. In this present time, the author of Hebrews is affirming, Christians can think of themselves through faith as already one with all those gathered around the throne of God in heaven as they will be on the last day. In other words, this passage speaks of the end-time existence as present possibility for the believer.[19]

One means, then, of reconciling the temporal problem of the simultaneous heavenly and earthly church experience of the believer is to understand the heavenly as simply a future reality that can be recognized by faith presently.

But Knox was not content with seeing the heavenly church experience as an allusion to a future reality. He believed this reduced the earthly church to a lesser reality than the heavenly form. While the heavenly certainly expresses eschatological hope of a realized physical presence, there is a present consequence of a spiritual presence that Christians currently know. Again, this conclusion was based on Knox's exegetical and logical conclusions. Exegetically, Knox was convinced that the text spoke of something enjoyed by believers in the present ("we *have* come"). Logically, Knox recognized that because the constitutive element of the church is the presence of Christ, and Christ is building his church where he is (in heaven), then the presence that Christians experience in heaven must have some consequence on earth. Clearly this presence cannot be physical, as living believers are material and temporal. Therefore, the heavenly experience of the believer must be spiritual. The decisive difference between Knox's ecclesiology and Platonism is that Knox believes that the ontological constitution of the heavenly church, the presence of Christ, is extended to the earthly church via the Holy Spirit.[20] Christ *is* present in the earthly church by his Spirit. Therefore, the church on earth *really is* the church, not just a "shadow." We will explore further the implications of presence in Knox's thought in another section below.

Finally, Knox's position regarding the heavenly church was that the heavenly is the only expression of the universal church. There is no universal church on earth. Giles, again, took issue with Knox on this matter. He wrote,

18. See pp. 109–10 above.
19. Giles, *What on Earth*, 156.
20. For a discussion of ontological dependency of objects, see Kraut, "Introduction to the Study of Plato," 10–12, esp. 12.

> The thought that the Christian community on earth in some way can see itself as part of the worshipping community on earth in heaven is an inspiring vision, but on the basis of the use of the word *ekklēsia* in this passage [Heb 12:18–24] some have argued that we have here one sure-proof text that this word, when not geographically circumscribed, refers exclusively to a heavenly gathering. However, this claim does not bear scrutiny. Even if it was agreed that the second group among those gathered in heaven, "the assembly of the first born," included believers both living and dead, it does not follow that the word *ekklēsia* without geographical qualifier refers exclusively to a heavenly gathering. Rather, it speaks of the church on earth, the Christian community, and the church in heaven, seen as two aspects of one reality.[21]

Giles and Knox agreed that the Hebrews text speaks of two aspects of one reality. However, their positions differ in how they understand relationships of these two aspects. Again, the difference is temporal and spatial. Knox believed that the heavenly and the earthly are simultaneous realities, while Giles believed that one was a present reality and the other a future reality. Giles is concerned that this passage is made to do too much work elsewhere in the New Testament when authors refer to a more "universal" understanding of church. But this text is not an anomaly in the New Testament as there are other passages that speak to the same reality. O'Brien argues that Paul in Ephesians (e.g., 1:22–23; 2:6) references the *same* reality, there providing a geographical qualifier. However, differing slightly from Knox, O'Brien believes the reference to heaven in Ephesians is metaphorical. O'Brien writes, "It is a figurative manner of speaking about Christians being personally related to Christ as they are related to one another."[22] Foundational to the differences between Knox (and O'Brien) and Giles is their rendering of *ekklēsia*. The church is only ever a gathering; therefore, it cannot be a more general entity or identity on earth as Giles suggests. So, when there is no geographical referent in the text, and the universal church is implied, Knox (and O'Brien) understand this universal gathering to be the heavenly church as this is the reality depicted as *the* universal church in the New Testament.

---

21. Giles, *What on Earth*, 156.
22. O'Brien, *Letter to the Ephesians*, 147. See also O'Brien, *Colossians, Philemon*, 60.

3. Local

The heavenly gives physical expression of its spiritual reality in the local assembly, which is a full representation thereof and is gathered by the Holy Spirit.

Knox believed that as the universal church is only ever heavenly, so the earthly church is only ever local. This local church is the full expression of the heavenly gathering. Indeed, the local church is necessary for giving expression to the heavenly reality.

As we saw in Robinson, Knox's comments on the binary locale of the church (local, heavenly) are a shift away from the historic Protestant understanding of the threefold locale of the church (local, general, heavenly).[23] With Knox, as with Robinson, the binary locale is demanded by the essential definition of *ekklēsia* as a gathering. There cannot be a greater ecclesial reality on earth beyond the local church, as nothing greater actually gathers. But this binary locale does not imply two separate churches. Rather, there is one church that can be experienced in two realms—in heaven and on earth.

The challenge is how the church in each realm correlates. Knox believed that the earthly church was a full expression of the heavenly church, the earthly being physical and the heavenly spiritual. But a tension arises here. Surely there must be some restriction to the spiritual finding its *full* expression in the physical. The underlying issues are twofold, one of time and the other of space. Again, we shall see that the challenge comes from the difficulties posed by each realm.

Temporally, we note that the earthly church is an intermittent activity, whereas the heavenly is a continuous gathering. This poses a potential problem when considering how one remains while the other does not. As we discussed earlier, Knox understood the spiritual reality to be a matter of position in Christ. Therefore, the spiritual is not a temporal expression, but rather constancy must be thought of eternally, that is, beyond the scope of time. The believer's position in Christ is a reality that exceeds time. Some may ask at this point whether time is experienced in heaven. Unfortunately, Knox did not explore how time comes to bear on the matter of the heavenly church experience. We have seen that those who followed him, such as P. T. O'Brien, attempted to locate the heavenly reality of the *ekklēsia* temporally in the eschaton. O'Brien believed that the heavenly church would only be realized at the end of time. However, this represents a departure from Knox's position, as he constantly stressed the present reality—the positional reality—of the heavenly experience.

---

23. See discussion in Cole, "Doctrine of the Church," 3–4.

Spatially, presence seems to imply material properties. The relationship between the heavenly and the earthly requires clarity about what is meant by presence. If presence were limited to physical space (demanded by the bodily resurrection and ascension of Jesus), then it would seem impossible for the two locales to coexist simultaneously. But if presence can be experienced apart from a physical presence, as it must in Knox's theology, then the earthly and the heavenly can by experienced at the same time. The theology of God's omnipresence negates any real spatial challenge, and therefore presence can be known apart from a physical experience.

The temporal and spatial challenges of Knox's ecclesiology hang on what is meant by heaven and earth. If these are both physical and temporal places, then we must seek an account of how they correlate. Perhaps they may be conceived of as different realms, as we have suggested. If this is true, it still does not remove the fact that time and space must be accounted for in each realm. It would seem that heaven would demand time and space as Christ remains corporeal. But again, if this is true, answers should be sought as to how Christ's temporality and spatiality in the heavenly places comes to bear on the earthly churches existence.

Knox's answer to all of these issues of time and space was the third Person of the Trinity. It is by the Holy Spirit that Christians are present in the heavenly places with Christ, and by whom Christ is present with Christians in the earthly gatherings. We will explore further the notion of presence in our next section. Before moving to this section, we should examine how Knox found continuity between his theology and Christian tradition.

Knox believed that the two realms (the binary locale) of the church have historically been confessed in the Apostles' Creed. The heavenly church is represented in the confessed "holy catholic church," and the earthly is represented in the confessed "communion of saints." This conclusion is not dissimilar from that of Martin Luther, that the *communio sanctorum* is primarily the church (e.g., gathering, assembly), though Luther also extended the notion to Christendom.[24] This position is the classic Christian position, though it came to be understood otherwise in the Roman Catholic Church.[25] Knox was not original, then, in identifying the binary locale of the church in the Apostles' Creed. The difference in his thought is that he identified the "communion of saints" to the local church, rather than extending it to a global church / Christendom (Luther), or to a church in purgatory (Roman Catholicism).[26]

---

24. Luther, *Large Catechism*.
25. McBrien, *Church*, 284–85.
26. Knox, *Thirty-Nine Articles*, 142.

Knox believed that the Nicene Creed's four properties of the church—One, Holy, Catholic, and Apostolic—belonged to the heavenly gathering. The heavenly gathering, along with its properties, remains an object of faith—something to be confessed.[27] But how is it that the local is the full expression of the heavenly church, especially in view of the confessional properties that seem to belong to the heavenly church alone? Is there a limit to the potential of the material/temporal church that can only be true of the heavenly/eschatological church? We recall that Knox believed that the earthly and the heavenly church were not two churches, but one. Therefore, we must view his understanding of the church in light of his perspective about each of the realms in which the church is experienced.[28] The creedal properties belong to the heavenly church because this is the realm in which these properties are experienced and true. This makes sense of how Knox understood the church, but it does not fully resolve the tension identified by those who see Knox's ecclesiology as platonic. The distinctive realms of experience, one being seemingly *fuller* in its expression of the reality, seem to lend credence to the accusation. We can only make sense of Knox's position in view of his understanding of presence in correlation to time and space.

Before moving beyond Knox's theology of the local church, we conclude with comments about what he believed fundamentally about the constitution of the local church. Knox's ecclesiology never viewed the constitution of the church in terms of quantity (except in minimum—"two or three"), but rather in terms of quality—the presence of Christ. A quorum of two or more believers is the only quantitative matter of concern. This understanding of quality over quantity is of great significance when faced with the issue of ecclesial unity. Ecclesial unity is demonstrated where Christ is present. The heavenly church *is* one. The local church *is* one. There is no other ecclesial unity to be sought because there is no other church.

4. Presence

There is a reciprocal relationship of presence in the earthly and heavenly gatherings. Believers are present spiritually in the heavenly places where Christ is

---

27. So too, Calvin on the unity of the church as an object of faith: Calvin, *Institutes of the Christian Religion*, 4.1.3.

28. Miroslav Volf has a detailed discussion of the fullness of the local church as a proleptic experience of the eschatological community of the people of God. This position, like O'Brien's temporal location of the heavenly gathering at the eschaton, may be a helpful complement to Knox's position. Volf, *After Our Likeness*, 137–45. Also, O'Brien, "Church as a Heavenly and Eschatological Reality," 88–119.

present physically, and believers are present physically in the earthly gatherings where Christ is present spiritually.

Knox believed that the unequivocal constitutive element of the church is the presence of Christ. Christ is physically present in the heavenly places, where he has ascended to reign at the right hand of his Father, and believers are present spiritually there with Christ. On earth, Christ is present spiritually wherever believers gather physically. Thus, there is a reciprocal relationship of presence between the earthly and heavenly gatherings. The Holy Spirit maintains the relationship, since it is by the Spirit that the presence of Christ is experienced.

Historically the presence of Christ and the presence of the Holy Spirit have been claimed as *the* constitutive presence for the church. Veli-Matti Kärkäinen has made too much of the difference between Ignatius claiming Christ's presence constitutes the church, and Irenaeus claiming the Spirit's presence does.[29] But there is no good reason to believe that either of the Fathers saw this as a mutually exclusive decision. In fact, Kärkäinen correctly remarks, "Christology and Pneumatology must be seen as simultaneous rather than exclusive."[30] Nevertheless, such a statement requires careful nuancing. The presence of Christ is known through the Holy Spirit, but there is distinction between the presence of Christ known by the Spirit in the gathering and the continuous presence of the Spirit in the Christian life. It is probable that this is why Knox drew upon Ignatius rather than Irenaeus for theological support. Ignatius understood that the church—the catholic church—is where Christ is.[31] Irenaeus, on the other hand, believed that wherever the Spirit is, there is the church.[32] While Irenaeus' claim is certainly true, Knox intended to stress the special promise of Christ's presence by the Spirit when believers gather, over and against the continual presence of the Spirit in the lives of believers.

For Knox, the believer's experience of the presence of Christ was related to the believer's positional reality. That is, the believer finds his or her spiritual being in Christ. It is an ontological reality. While not being divine—since only Christ is consubstantial with God—the believer is brought into the life of the Triune Godhead by means of the work of Christ made effectual by the Holy Spirit. So it is by the Spirit that the believer is present with Christ in heaven. The challenge of time and space in Knox's theology, which he himself left largely unexplored, is answered when we

---

29. Kärkäinen, *Introduction to Ecclesiology*, 23.
30. Ibid.
31. Ignatius, *Letter to the Smyrneans*, 8.2 (p. 90).
32. Irenaeus, *Adversus Haereses*, 3.24.1 (p. 458).

recognize that the Holy Spirit bridges the heavenly and earthly realms for believers. Calvin hinted at this when he wrote, "As if it were not in God's power somehow to come down to us, in order to be near us, yet without changing place or confining us to earthly means; but rather by these to bear us up as if in chariots to his heavenly glory, a glory that fills all things with its immeasurableness and even surpasses the heavens in height."[33] In the Holy Spirit, Christians experience the positional reality that they have in Christ, being seated with him in the heavenly places. Likewise, it is by the Holy Spirit that Christ's presence is known amongst believers in the *ekklēsia*.

5. Purpose: Fellowship

The local assembly gathers for the purpose of fellowship as it gathers to encounter Christ. This encounter is spiritual as we each encounter the Spirit of Christ in each other.

Knox believed that fellowship is a larger category than ecclesiology; in other words, ecclesiology is a subset. Fellowship belongs to the system of theology proper, as the definition of fellowship is revealed in the relationship between the three Persons of the Triune Godhead. Fellowship in the *Christian life*, then, comes at the intersection of theology proper, soteriology, ecclesiology, anthropology and pneumatology.[34] When considering fellowship in the church we ask, how is it that the fellowship that God enjoys in himself is communicated and experienced in humanity? The answer, for Knox, is that humans enjoy fellowship with God in the company of other Christians, gathered in Christ by the Holy Spirit around the Word of God.

Continuing on from his beliefs about presence, Knox believed that the purpose for which Christians come together is fellowship. This fellowship is with other believers by the Spirit and in the Spirit. The common bond that believers possess is the indwelling Holy Spirit. So, believers gather to meet with one another and to meet with God. Knox made clear reference to 1 John 1:3 speaking of the fellowship that believers share with the Father and the Son. However, while Knox hinted at how believers experience fellowship with the Triune God—gathered together and by the Holy Spirit—he could have elaborated more about how this occurs, especially in view of 1 John 4:7–16.

---

33. Calvin, *Institutes*, 4.1.5.

34. Volf argues that "the correspondences between the church and the Trinity can be demonstrated only *after* the development of anthropology, soteriology, and ecclesiology." Volf, *After Our Likeness*, 200.

The fellowship of believers with the Triune God is experienced in the face of one another. Christians, who mutually possess the Spirit of God, meet God in the face of one another. As Christians gather to love one another according to the truth of God's word, God reveals himself to believers as he abides by his Spirit. This is explicit in 1 John 4:7–17, especially in v. 12, "No one has ever seen God; if we love one another, God abides in us and his love is perfected in us." This passage is reminiscent of John 1:18, which reads, "No one has ever seen God; the only God, who is at the Father's side, he has made him known."[35] So the progression of revelation and experience of God is as follows: Christ came to reveal the Father and make a way for believers to access the Father. After Christ ascended he sent his Spirit. Now the revelation of God comes spiritually as each believer loves one another in the fellowship of the Spirit. Knox's position would have been all the more compelling had he articulated this biblical-theological point more clearly, as this was his concern in his reflections on Hebrews 12. However, he stopped short of explaining that the fellowship with believers and with God can happen in one and the same activity.

We are not advocating here inter-Trinitarian fellowship as the social program for the church.[36] There remains an otherness to the fellowship that God shares in and amongst himself. Yet God allows human beings, by the atoning work of Christ on the cross, to commune with him. This communion has both vertical and horizontal implications. Vertically, redeemed humans are permitted fellowship with God. Horizontally, humans are permitted fellowship with one another. The commonality between the vertical and the horizontal is the possession of the Holy Spirit. As Knox identified in his theology, fellowship is sharing of a common possession, and in the instance of those who believe in Christ, they possess the Spirit of God.

As fellowship is a broader category than ecclesiology, Knox believed that fellowship occurs across congregations, but not in a manner that constitutes a greater ecclesial entity. The denomination functions as a service structure for local churches. Knox believed that this fellowship with other congregations is a necessary expression of interdependence. But it remains unseen how these entities can be extra-ecclesial, and yet required for proper ecclesiality. Perhaps Knox has in mind the occasions in Scripture in which members from various congregations gather (e.g., Acts 15) or collaborate for mission (e.g., Rom 15). But these expressions, while being collaborative endeavors for kingdom work, do not necessarily express *interdependence*.

---

35. This notion is expanded in John 14.

36. For example, Volf, "Trinity Is Our Social Program," 403–23. Also see the response from Husbands, "Trinity Is *Not* Our Social Program," 120–41.

Critics could easily attribute the Jerusalem council in Acts 15 to the apostolic foundation of the church. Even the missionary cooperation of Romans 15 might be seen as an optional opportunity for a generous gesture.

We recall that Knox's beliefs about inter-congregational fellowship were grounded in his view of the singular heavenly church. But this grounding was not expressed clearly in his theology, as he contended for this fellowship based on pragmatic reasons (e.g., mission collaboration, theological education, etc.). As prudent as these pragmatic reasons may be, Knox's position would be more persuasive if he provided a more explicit theological rationale for cooperation. For example, he could have taken the position of Volf in viewing the church as the confessing community. Volf argues that churches—where two or more gather to confess Christ—are independent because Christ is fully present in each local church. Nevertheless, he believes that there is commonality in the confession of Christ between local churches. No matter their affiliation, there is a relationship between each congregation. He writes, "The same presence of Christ through the Spirit that makes each local church 'independent' of the other churches simultaneously connects them with one another."[37] The connection of these churches, in Volf's theology, is one that comes in view of eschatological people of God gathered in singular confession. He continues, "Openness to all other churches is the *interecclesial minimum* of the concrete ecclesial proleptic experience of the eschatological gathering of the whole people of God."[38] This is similar to Knox's theology, especially in the view of the plurality of earthly gatherings and singularity of the heavenly gathering. Volf offers a firm commitment to the independence of local congregations, which appears to be consistent with Knox's theology (though Knox was reluctant to commit fully to this congregationalism), but maintains a healthy balance of their connection in light of the eschatological community to which all believing congregants belong. The regard for other churches is, therefore, more a regard for other Christians than for other congregations. This agrees with what Knox believed about fellowship being a greater category than ecclesiology, and again demonstrates how fellowship is a discussion at the intersection of many systems of doctrine.

6. Activity: The Word of God

The distinguishing mark of Christian fellowship is the Word of God. The Word gives shape and substance to the gathering.

37. Volf, *After Our Likeness*, 155.
38. Ibid., 157.

If fellowship is the purpose of the church, how is this purpose achieved? Knox believed that the fellowship that Christians enjoy with one Triune God and with one another happens around the Word of God. He stressed that hearing the Word is a personal activity, for to hear the Word is to hear God himself. Therefore, since fellowship is by possession of the Holy Spirit, the substance of this fellowship comes from God's Word. This emphasis on fellowship was intended to guard against a static understanding of coming to church merely to receive something. Christians do not gather to receive; they gather to relate. Likewise, church is more than just worship, since worship is the totality of the Christian life. Worship is fueled in the congregation, as worship is the appropriate relational response to encountering God.

Knox found support for the centrality of the Word in the congregation in Article XIX of the Thirty-Nine Articles. He believed that the Word was central because the church is composed of believing persons. To believe, he argued, implies having received the Word—"faith comes from hearing, and hearing through the word of Christ" (Rom 10:17). The ministry of the Word, in both preaching and participating in the sacraments, is the ministry of mutual encouragement. As believers gather around the Word faith increases, as faith springs from hearing the Word.

The exclusivity of fellowship as the purpose of the church, with the Word as its central activity, may be construed as a deficient or narrow position. Is there not more to the church than fellowship around the Word of God? Does an emphasis on the Word come at the neglect of other ecclesial activities? Not necessarily. Knox hinted at how he understood many other activities such as worship and prayer within the life of the church and the life of the Christian. However, he did not offer a full pragmatic model for readers to engage. What Knox believed at a base level was that the distinction between the ecclesial gathering and individual Christian living is the fellowship enjoyed in the assembly. Worship, reading the Word, hearing the Word, praying, and other Christian activities happen both in the gathering and throughout everyday living in the Christian life, but fellowship is a unique *corporate* activity. This is not to say that the other activities are not part of the fellowship, but that fellowship is the umbrella under which these other activities sit in the corporate Christian experience.

One further area for development is the relationship between the Spirit and truth. If the Holy Spirit is a common possession of believers, how does the gathering in and by the Spirit necessitate the Word (John 4:23–24)? Apart from simple exegetical evidence, there is room to develop the notion that fellowship around the Word guarantees the confession of Christ in the congregation, aiding in the prevention of ulterior purposes for gathering. A good starting point for this development would be an investigation to the purpose of the Word in the body in Eph 4–5, particularly with a view towards the relationship of Eph 4:11–16 and Eph 5:15–20 (cf. Col 3:16).

7. Authority

The Word of God has authority over the congregation. As the congregation is the only legitimate church on earth, there is no institutional authority naturally set over the local church, though the church may willingly choose to fellowship with other churches in an institution.

Knox built upon his understanding of the church as a gathering for the purpose of fellowship to articulate his position regarding authority in the congregation and beyond. Knox believed that within the congregation the Word of God had ultimate authority. Outside of the congregation there is no authority over the local church, especially not in any denominational form. Therefore, in view of Knox's position on the denomination having no responsibility in the life of the congregation, or authority over the congregation, we can conclude that Knox believed the local church is autonomous.[39] However, this autonomy does not necessitate independence, but rather is understood with regards to authority. But there are several questions that follow Knox's position regarding authority, especially in view of his Anglicanism.

First, if the church has no authority over it in any denominational form, how then should churches interact with denominational structures? Within Anglican polity, it would seem that the traditional expectation of the subservience of rectors to the bishop would be upset. Knox believed that denominations and/or any other extra-ecclesial institutions had no right to sanctions in the congregation. These institutions are simply designed to bolster local church ministry. Although Knox offered helpful suggestions of the kinds of help the institution could add to the congregations (and the restrictions to their exercise of authority!), he did not explain explicitly how his theology coincided with Anglican polity. We might suggest that his polity would be more akin to an inverse pyramid than a traditional upright pyramid of the episcopal hierarchy. Yet in this system there still needs to be specification of how the denomination and churches interact. For instance, it should be determined when, if ever, the denomination is permitted to interfere with the life of the local church and its ministry. Perhaps the usefulness of denominations, as declared by Knox, permits local churches to enter

---

39. Knox, "Notes on Authority," 101–2.

into a voluntary submission to the institution and its officers. But even then, there would need to be an arrangement, of sorts, to define the boundaries of authority. Otherwise, the relinquishing of authority might call to question the authenticity of the local congregation. Of course, the resourcing of local churches by dioceses clouds all of these matters, as the dioceses often own land that local churches congregate on.

In view of Knox's ecclesiology, what seems to be required of an Anglican polity is a clear establishment of the primacy of the local church within the ecclesial infrastructure. Building on Knox's ecclesiology, Mark Thompson writes of the purpose of the denomination: "It provides encouragement to remain faithful to the gospel, resources to those in need, and support in a common mission to honour God by proclaiming Christ to the world."[40] He continues,

> The tension between local fellowship and larger institutional structure need not be destructive and is present even within the pages of the New Testament itself. Nevertheless, it has tended to become destructive in the face of the claims of larger organisational entities . . . in too many parts of the world compulsion is used by institutional bodies and office bearers against those congregations and individuals who protest in the name of biblical truth against their "official and agreed" innovations.[41]

Thompson highlights the significant purpose that institutional organizations can serve in aiding local church ministry. But he also cautions against prizing the institution over the local congregations it serves. This balance represents Knox's position well and further stresses the need for clear guidelines for the relationships of the congregations and the institution so as to uphold the primacy of the local church.

Second, if the preached Word is central to the life of the church, does this imply that a preacher is essential? If so, who is qualified/permitted to preach? Knox argued that pastors have authority in and over the church so long as they preach the Word of God. But the issue of whether or not a preacher is required for a *bona fide* church becomes important in view of Article XIX of the Thirty-Nine Articles, which defines the church as a "congregation of faithful men where *the Word of God is preached*" (emphasis mine). Pressing the issue further, this matter becomes pertinent when the church is not defined quantitatively. If the church only requires a quorum of two people (Matt 18:20), being defined qualitatively by Christ's presence, and a preacher is required, then one of the two must preach. Alongside this

---

40. Thompson, "Church of God," 238–39.
41. Ibid., 241.

matter rises the issue of qualifications of such a preacher. In fact, the issue of pastoral rule comes to bear. Knox did not address these issues in detail, though his ecclesiology demands these matters be explored further.

Volf offers helpful answers to the matters of ministers and the church based on similar conclusions to Knox. He writes,

> The presence of Christ is not attested merely by the institution of office, but rather through the multidimensional confession of the entire assembly. In whatever way "office" may indeed be desirable for church life, either in apostolic succession or not, it is *not necessary for ecclesiality*. Ordained office belongs not to the *esse*, but rather to the *bene esse* of the church. This claim does not constitute any devaluation of the particular service of proclaiming God's word, but rather suggests that proclamation should be understood as a dimension of pluriform, communal confession of faith.[42]

So, what constitutes the church is not the presence of a minister, but rather believers gathered in the presence of Christ. Pastors are helpful for growing the local church through ministry of the Word, but this ministry does not hang on the minister. It is a ministry shared by every believer in every congregation. Knox would no doubt agree with Volf's position, especially in that the essence of the church is the presence of Christ in believers gathered in his name.

The strength of Knox's position on authority was his consistency in application. Believing the church to only be a gathering, he extended that conclusion to its logical end: there can be no external institutional authority over the local church, as there is no greater ecclesial entity on earth. Even where his conclusions seemingly conflicted with his Anglicanism, he did not shy away. What is desirable is a more developed polity based upon his conclusions on the nature of the church. There must be a reconciliation of his understanding of the church's nature and the Anglican understanding of an institutional (national) church. We refrain from exploring these matters here as this is beyond the scope of our study of the nature of the church, but suggest (as we have in the paragraphs above) that a possible agreement between Knox's theology and denominationalism is a *willing* partnership, even submission, of local churches to the institution. This sort of relationship must only ever be voluntary and not coercive, as the primacy of the local church must be maintained.

---

42. Volf, *After Our Likeness*, 152.

CONCLUSION

We set out in this evaluation to appraise the biblical, logical and traditional value of D. Broughton Knox's ecclesiology. Having examined the seven core propositions of his theology of the nature of the church, we can draw the following conclusions.

First, Knox sought fidelity to the biblical text and built his conclusions upon exegetical evidence. On a macro level, he drew together many helpful conceptual threads, demonstrating knowledge of how the Bible worked together as a whole. The challenge to his biblical work, however, is that his conclusions are open for dispute on a micro exegetical level. At times he made minor details do too much work. This is not to say that anything Knox argued falls outside of the realm of legitimate interpretation, but at points his conclusions are exegetically indeterminate and against the consensus of scholarship. This being said, his conclusions were strengthened by the biblical-theological connections he made concerning the development of concepts in the canon. These conclusions may offer helpful insight into the interpretive conversation, especially with regard to the identity of "this rock" in Matthew 16.

Second, logically Knox worked outwards from the foundation of the church as a gathering. In his understanding of the church as gathering, Knox began with God and Trinitarian fellowship, and then situated the church within the plans and purposes of God to draw a people unto himself. It is primarily in the gathering that the redeemed community enjoys the fellowship restored by the atoning work of Christ. Central to the vertical and horizontal experience of fellowship is the presence of the Holy Spirit in the lives of believers. Knox's theology did not waver from his foundational propositions. He sought to push through these propositions to their logical (and biblical) ends. At points, Knox may be accused of coloring his reading of the biblical text according to primary theses, especially difficult texts like Matthew 16. But from another vantage point we might see Knox employing consistency in his hermeneutic; when in doubt about a difficult text he sought understanding from biblical theology. This practice demonstrates his consonance with the practice enjoined by Thomas Cranmer, Article XX of the Thirty-Nine Articles, and the First of the Homilies. This meant that he often arrived at places that stood against traditional views of the church, such as a universal church on earth or authority beyond the local congregation.

Third, Knox understood his theological heritage as thoroughly Anglican, but as a biblical first-principles thinker he did not feel bound to his ecclesiastical heritage. In fact, at several places his conclusions put him at odds with historic Anglican teaching and practice, especially with regard to authority. However, he left much to the imagination in terms of the praxis of his doctrine, which in some ways avoided the details of how his ecclesiology conflicted with traditional Anglican practice. But Knox's conclusions were not maverick, even in spite of the lack of explicit engagement with interlocutors in his work. He believed that the doctrine he was identifying fitted well within the history of the Christian church, especially the creeds, even if he did not always show how. If anything, Knox offered a different approach, albeit a historical approach, to the theology represented in the creeds. The historicity of this theology would have been better served had he demonstrated more clearly the points at which his conclusions found congruence with other historical Christian voices.

Knox's doctrine of the church reads as a fresh contribution to the field of ecclesiology because he did not seek to merely replicate received ecclesiology. Instead, he made bold conclusions based on what he saw in the text of the Bible. However, where his ecclesiology appears most profound—particularly regarding the realms of experience of the church and the notion of presence in the constitution of the church—his conclusions would be more convincing if he had provided more explicit exegetical grounding and historical-theological engagement in the unfolding of his arguments. Knox possessed a great mind, but it was not always a detailed mind, as he saw the big picture and sometimes squeezed the details to fit. This evaluation has sought to address some of the loose ends and points of clarity required for Knox's ecclesiology to gain greater and lasting influence.

SECTION IV

Conclusion

9

Conclusion

HAVING DESCRIBED, ANALYZED, AND evaluated the ecclesiologies of Donald Robinson and D. Broughton Knox, we now move to conclude our study. We have intended for the evaluative chapters to serve the purpose of much of the conclusive work of this book, though those chapters were integrated with description and analysis. Here, we wish to draw threads together, particularly in discerning a model and suggesting how we might appraise that model. We will begin by offering a synthesis that will briefly display congruence and then detail difference between the two ecclesiologies, with an end product of a "model." Afterwards, we will offer an appraisal of the "model" including constructive comments for how the ecclesiology might advance.

SYNTHESIS

Symmetry is not required for a synthesis. The ecclesiologies of Robinson and Knox possess great symmetry at many foundational points, as we will explore further. But there are also several incongruences that need to be reconciled if there is to be an agreeable "Knox-Robinson view" presented. Nevertheless, these differences are not mutually exclusive or contradictory, at least not on a macro (and thus prohibitive) level. We will argue here that there is indeed good reason to hold to a model, taking the two ecclesiologies as complementary. Each man brings a recognizably distinct contribution to bear on the subject, despite substantial overlap and large tracks of agreement.

As we have seen in our description and analysis of both ecclesiologies, there is great agreement between Robinson and Knox.[1] The funda-

---

1. We shall hereafter refer to the respective ecclesiologies by the scholars' names.

mental proposition in both ecclesiologies is that the church is a gathering; all other propositions follow from this thesis. This conclusion is built upon the linguistic analysis of *ekklēsia*. Donald Robinson carried out most of this analysis, and it is likely that Knox called upon this work for his own conclusions. It is because Robinson supplied and developed this foundational proposition, and not just the simple fact that he wrote more extensively on the subject and earlier, that we have featured Robinson's ecclesiology first in this study. It may be proposed, therefore, that the commonly called "Knox-Robinson view" may be more appropriately named the "Robinson-Knox view" of the church.[2]

Building upon the primary premise of the church as a gathering, Robinson and Knox also agreed that the church is only ever local or heavenly; there is no third category of the universal church on earth. Both scholars agreed that the church is only one—the earthly is an expression of the heavenly reality. Unity is a present reality. The heavenly takes precedent, because that is where Christ is presently. However, the earthly is no less real or complete. The reality and fullness of each church is grounded in the constitutive element of the church—the presence of Christ.

Both Robinson and Knox also addressed how the church occurs in heaven and on earth. Robinson focused on the categories of place, form, and time. These categories exposed the different experiences of the earthly and heavenly church more than the similarities. Knox also examined the distinctive properties of each experience, but gave particular focus to the presence of Christ in each realm. This focal point was not in contrast to Robinson's distinctions but aided in reconciling the differences between the heavenly and the earthly. The bridge between the two realms, for Knox, was the Holy Spirit.

Robinson and Knox agreed that the Word has authority over the gathering. Questions were raised (gently) about institutional authority in the form of a denomination. Both argued that there was no external authority over the local church, because the church is only a gathering; however, neither dismissed the significance of the denomination. Fellowship with other Christians and churches through organized institutions provided great opportunities for cooperative ministry.

---

2. We may speculate that the name "Knox-Robinson view" places Knox first because of his charisma. Also, Knox's style was looser than Robinson's more careful approach, making Knox seem edgier to his students. In the development of ideas, this would have made the original propositions attractive. It also may have been due to the fact that Knox was the senior partner—he was older, he was the principal, he had earned his doctorate, etc. One way or another, Knox was identified as the primary source. The reality, at least in our understanding of their thought, is that Robinson did the preliminary legwork for the ecclesiology that developed.

But for all of the great similarities between Robinson and Knox, there were several key differences. Of the minor differences, the most obvious are their style and approach. Robinson was an exegete who paid great attention to detail, while Knox was a theologian who thought more about the big picture. Each of them raised questions just as much as they provided answers because of the method they adopted and its limitations. Robinson neglected some significant theological questions that arose from his exegetical work because he did not always think in broader systematic categories. Likewise, Knox asked good questions as a theologian, but at points did not attend to exegetical detail. This obvious difference in style and method is one reason why Robinson and Knox complement each other. They both agreed on the truth and trustworthiness of the Bible and wanted to anchor their ecclesiology in the Word. Robinson aided in going deeper into the text and detecting details carefully. Knox helped to move beyond the details and draw threads. Together, they had good attention to detail and the right theological finishing required for establishing defensible doctrinal convictions.

There were also several more substantial differences between the thought of Robinson and Knox. First, they emphasized different matters in the relationship between the heavenly and earthly churches. Robinson demonstrated the place, form, and time of the heavenly and earthly churches, exposing the differences between them. At the conclusion of this study, while confessing the oneness of the church across the realms, Robinson's findings left the reader questioning how the earthly and heavenly could be the same church in the face of such differences.

Knox, on the other hand, focused less on the properties of the gathering and more on the presence of Christ within those gatherings. Knox stressed that the presence of Christ constitutes the church. Robinson would have certainly agreed. But what Knox did differently was to ask *how* Christ is present in each congregation. Knox was convinced that believers participate in the heavenly church in the present, rather than just at the eschaton. He articulated a reciprocal relationship of presence between the two realms, with the key to Christ's participation in both realms being the Person of the Holy Spirit.

The second major difference—regarding the purpose for the gathering—followed on from the first. Knox carried forward his thesis that the church is where Christ is present. He concluded from this that the church's purpose is fellowship, both with God and with other Christians. Robinson was not necessarily averse to this purpose, though he was cautious to not make this *the* purpose of the church.[3] But for Knox, fellowship was *the* pur-

---

3. Robinson, "'Church' Revisited," 269.

pose of the church, especially in view of the constitution of the church. If the church is defined by the presence of Christ amongst believers, then the purpose correlates to that defining quality: believers have a unique opportunity to meet with Christ when they meet with others in his name. Christ is present in and amongst believers by his Holy Spirit.

The final major difference was Robinson's inquiry into the relationship of Israel to the church. His concern throughout his study in ecclesiology was to better understand salvation history. He recognized a preservation of both Jewish and Gentile identities within the church, with the new redeemed community being part of a "new man." Knox did not include much in his study about the relationship of Israel to the church—only one article on "The Church and the People of God in the Old Testament." His silence on the matter is somewhat surprising considering so much of his theology was built upon biblical-theological development of God meeting with his people. At points Knox drew attention to the contrast between Israel gathered at Sinai and the church gathered at Mt. Zion (heaven). One would think he would have been more concerned about the "who" of the church, and the "how" of soteriology since "salvation is from the Jews" (John 4:22). We have no evidence that he disagreed with Robinson about Jew and Gentile relationships. We do know that both Robinson and Knox agreed that the church is not an identity, as if a synonym for the people of God; rather the church is an activity of the people of God.

In accordance with the research we have presented, we propose that the ecclesiologies of Robinson and Knox are best considered together as a model. This is not to say that the ecclesiologies are not distinctive, but that they are strongest when paired. Robinson's thoughts can stand alone, but they are underdeveloped without the theological refinement that Knox provided. Similarly, but to a lesser extent, Knox's theology can stand on its own. Even so, the theological propositions that Knox developed need Robinson's exegetical support and biblical-theological developments in order to gain traction as a viable biblical ecclesiology. Therefore, it is important to recognize the distinctive approach of each scholar, particularly their own methods of theological inquiry, as these distinctions contribute to a more comprehensive ecclesiology. Robinson has given us a detailed biblical theology of the church, grounded in careful semantic work. Knox built upon the conclusions of Robinson's biblical-theological conclusions and developed them more systematically and brought larger theological categories such as "fellowship" to bear. Therefore, we cannot go so far as to say that the two ecclesiologies are mutually dependent, but we can say that they greatly complement one another.

We have seen the complementary nature of Robinson and Knox's ecclesiologies, especially highlighted in the points of contrast. The contrasts are not mutually exclusive. Instead, the main distinctions are in emphases—usually one expounded an area that was undeveloped by the other. It appears that the greatest of these distinctions is Knox's emphasis on the presence of Christ (and subsequently the purpose of fellowship), which answers the tension left in Robinson's description of the location, form, and time of the church. Together, Robinson and Knox combine biblical and systematic theology to provide an ecclesiology that is attentive to both exegetical detail and systematic issues.

APPRAISAL

The ecclesiology of Robinson and Knox developed in the face of several challenges, especially the rise of the ecumenical movement and the push for a new constitution for Australian Anglicans. Robinson and Knox did not think in a vacuum. In fact, their studies in ecclesiology, though not specifically directed by the movements of their day, engaged these movements head-on. Their questions came from the demands of their context, but their answers to these questions were not so much reactionary as they were genuine attempts to expound the Bible in this context. The fruit of their work was an ecclesiological model that challenged and engaged the major ecclesiological voices of their day and offered alternative ecclesiology.

It is likely that the greatest contribution from the Robinson-Knox ecclesiology is the removal of the "third category"—a universal church on earth. This was a shift away from thinking of the church as an identity, to thinking of the church as an activity; from thinking institutionally to thinking in terms of concrete relationships and genuine propinquity. This kept the church in perspective, as many things are ascribed to the people of God that do not necessarily belong to the church (e.g., evangelism). But also, because the church is only ever a gathering, the church is already united and efforts of pursuing institutional ecclesial unity are superfluous. It appears that this major thesis—that the church is only ever a gathering, never an identity—is agreeable based on textual evidence, and demands further attention in the ecclesiological conversation.

The primary work that remains outstanding with regard to this ecclesiology is an examination of the many images of the church in the New Testament for community. There needs to be a fresh exploration of these images, with the aim of discerning abstract versus concrete realities. Which of these metaphors apply to the church and which to the people of God?

Paul Minear has done a great work in identifying the many metaphors in his *Images of the Church in the New Testament*; however, this work needs revisiting on the basis of the Robinson-Knox thesis. The strength of the Robinson-Knox position over and against Minear's is that its search for the nature of the church came before an investigation into the church as a category. In contrast it appears that Minear, like Giles, begins with the assumption that all notions of community/corporate identity automatically belong to the church.

Another significant contribution from the Robinson-Knox theology is the emphasis on presence in the gathering. Knox especially took great care to draw out the pneumatological implications of this proposition. Christ is present amongst the church on earth by his Spirit. Jesus, by his Spirit, is present in and through *other* believers. That is, other believers have the Spirit indwelling them, and as believers gather they encounter the Spirit of Christ in one another. This is an idea that needs further development in light of Knox's (and Robinson's) work. The gathering is not just vertical—towards God—but also simultaneously horizontal—towards one another. This connection of the vertical in the horizontal adds much more weight to why Christians need to gather with other believers regularly—when they gather, *they meet God* in fellowship with one another. Without this fellowship, the believer is deprived of an opportunity to fellowship with God. It also is worth noting that both Robinson and Knox heavily stressed the importance of fellowship around the Word of God; the Word providing shape and substance to the gathering, all with the help of the Spirit present amongst it.

Finally, the Robinson-Knox model has supplied readers with a biblical-theological "first-principles" approach to ecclesiology. More specifically, it has developed a helpful foundation on the nature of the church. However, this foundation, as useful as it is for our understanding, does not answer many questions of practice. There is much work to be done in exploring how the nature of the church bears on praxis. In particular, there must be discerned a clear way forward for the interaction between the local church and the denomination. Neither Robinson nor Knox sought to develop a robust polity. In fact, they almost consciously avoided it, at least for Robinson's case until he became archbishop. It would appear that the refrain from developing a theology of governance was in an attempt to not let the nature of the church be clouded by these matters. Nevertheless, what they *have* contributed are plausible principles upon which a polity can be constructed. How, if the church is only local on earth, should an Anglican think about their involvement within a denomination? How should a local church respond to institutional authority? How can congregations maintain autonomy and yet interdependence and cooperation?

Miroslav Volf has identified a phenomenon of an increase in churches embracing a congregational understanding of the nature of the church. He writes,

> Today's global developments seem to imply that Protestant Christendom of the future will exhibit largely a Free Christian form. Although the episcopal churches will probably not surrender their own hierarchical structures, they, too, will increasingly have to integrate these Free Church elements into the mainstream of their own lives both theologically and practically. Although restorative efforts will slow the appropriation of these elements, they will be unable to obstruct them entirely. It seems to me that we are standing in the middle of a clear and irreversible "process of congregationalization" of all Christianity.[4]

The interesting dynamic of Volf's contribution is the inclusion of the social analysis and observable ecclesiological trends. These trends and social facets did not factor in the work of Robinson and Knox, but when considered with their detailed theological investigation, their model appears to meet the social needs and to fit within the ecclesiological trends. Perhaps the Robinson-Knox ecclesiology is exactly what is necessary for episcopal churches to "integrate these Free Church elements" theologically and practically. If their ecclesiology is persuasive as a biblical-theological model, why shouldn't it find relevance in the contemporary ecclesial scene? Should we assume that this trend is simply a sociological phenomenon and not the work of God blessing what he has ordained? Perhaps Robinson and Knox have developed an ecclesiology that will last beyond their time and find great usefulness amongst many denominations in the contemporary conversation on what the church is and how it should function in this world. There are numerous indications that this is the case.

---

4. Volf, *After Our Likeness*, 13. Volf draws on others who agree with this hypothesis, including Joseph Cardinal Ratzinger and Russell Chandler. See ibid., 12–13.

Bibliography

Adams, Edward. "The Cosmology of Hebrews." In *The Epistle to the Hebrews and Christian Theology*, edited by Richard Bauckham et al., 122–39. Cambridge: Eerdmans, 2009.
Anglican Church of Australia. "Constitution." http://www.anglican.org.au/governance/pages/constitution.aspx.
Ashford, Bruce Riley, ed. *Theology and Practice of Mission: God, the Church, and the Nations*. Nashville: B&H Academic, 2011.
Augustine. *Writings in Connection with the Donatist Controversy*. Edited by J. R. King. Edinburgh: T. & T. Clark, 1872.
Barr, James. *The Semantics of Biblical Language*. Oxford: Oxford University Press, 1961.
Barth, Karl. "The Living Congregation of the Living Lord Jesus Christ." In *Man's Disorder and God's Design*, edited by Willem A. Visser 'T Hooft, vol. 1, *The Universal Church in God's Design: An Ecumenical Study Prepared under the Auspices of the World Council of Churches*, 67–76. London: SCM, 1948.
Bauer, Walter. *A Greek-English Lexicon of the New Testament and Other Early Christian Literature (BDAG)*. Revised and edited by Fredrick W. Danker. 3rd ed. Chicago: University of Chicago Press, 2000.
Bicknell, E. J. *A Theological Introduction to the Thirty-Nine Articles of the Church of England*. 2nd ed. London: Longmans, Green, 1925.
Bolt, Peter G., and Mark D. Thompson, eds. *Donald Robinson: Selected Works*. Vol. 1, *Assembling God's People*. Vol. 3, *Appreciation*. Camperdown, NSW: Australian Church Record, 2008.
Bray, Gerald. *The Faith We Confess: An Exposition of the Thirty-Nine Articles*. London: Latimer, 2009.
Breward, Ian. *A History of the Australian Churches*. St Leonards, NSW: Allen & Unwin, 1993.
Bultmann, Rudolph. *Jesus Christ and Mythology*. London: SCM, 1960.
———. *Kerygma and Myth: A Theological Debate*. London: SPCK, 1962.
Cable, K. J. "T. C. Hammond." In *Australian Dictionary of Biography*, Vol. 14, *1940–1980*, edited by John Ritchie, 367–68. Carlton South, Victoria: Melbourne University Press, 1996.

Calvin, John. *Institutes of the Christian Religion*. 1559. Edited by John T. McNeill. Translated by Ford Lewis Battles. Louisville: Westminster John Knox, 1960.
Cameron, Donald. "Donald William Bradley Robinson: An Appreciation." In *In the Fullness of Time: Biblical Studies in Honour of Archbishop Donald Robinson*, edited by David Peterson and John Pryor, xi–xvi. Homebush, NSW: Lancer, 1992.
Cameron, Marcia. *An Enigmatic Life: David Broughton Knox, Father of Contemporary Sydney Anglicanism*. Brunswick East, Victoria: Acorn, 2006.
———. "Moore College under Nathaniel Jones, 1897–1911." In *The "Furtherance of Religious Beliefs": Essays on the History of Theological Education in Australia*, edited by G. R. Treloar, 96–123. Sydney: Centre for the Study of Australian Christianity for the Evangelical History Association of Australia, 1997.
Campbell, Constantine. *Verbal Aspect, the Indicative Mood, and Narrative: Soundings in the Greek New Testament*. New York: Lang, 2007.
Campbell, J. Y. "The Origin and Meaning of the Christian Use of the Word ΕΚΚΛΗΣΙΑ." *Journal of Theological Studies* 49 (1948) 130–42. Reprinted in J. Y. Campbell, *Three New Testament Studies*, 41–54. Leiden: Brill, 1965.
Caragounis, Chrys C. *Peter and the Rock*. New York: de Gruyter, 1990.
Cole, Alan. *The Body of Christ: A New Testament Image of the Church*. London: Hodder & Stoughton, 1964.
———. *The New Temple: A Study in the Origins of Catechetical "Form" of the Church in the New Testament*. London: Tyndale, 1950.
Cole, Graham. "The Doctrine of the Church: Towards Conceptual Clarification." In Webb, *Explorations 2*, 3–17.
Davis, John. *Australian Anglicans and their Constitutions*. Canberra: Acorn, 1993.
DeYoung, Kevin, and Gregory Gilbert. *What Is the Mission of the Church? Making Sense of Social Justice, Shalom, and the Great Commission*. Wheaton, IL: Crossway, 2011.
Dibelius, Otto. *Das Jahrhundert der Kirche*. 2nd ed. Berlin: Furche, 1927.
Dickey, Brian. "Jones, Nathaniel." In *The Australian Dictionary of Evangelical Biography*, edited by Brian Dickey, 191–92. Sydney: Evangelical History Association, 1994.
Driscoll, Mark, and Gerry Breshears. *Vintage Church: Timeless Truths and Timely Methods*. Wheaton, IL: Crossway, 2008.
Dulles, Avery. "A Half Century of Ecclesiology." *Theological Studies* 50 (1989) 419–42.
Dumbrell, William. "The Meaning and Use of EKKLESIA in the New Testament with Special Reference to Its Old Testament Background." MTh thesis, University of London, 1966.
Flew, R. Newton. *Jesus and His Church: A Study of the Idea of the Church in the New Testament*. London: Epworth, 1938.
Foord, Martin. "We Meet Again! In Heaven or on Earth? Donald Robinson's Ecclesiology." In Bolt and Thompson, *Appreciation*, 225–34.
Foulkes, Francis. "The Church and Evangelism: A Rejoinder." *Interchange* 17 (1975) 26–33.
France, R. T. *The Gospel of Matthew*. NICNT. Grand Rapids: Eerdmans, 2007.
Galbraith, D. "Just Enough Religion to Make Us Hate: An Historio-Legal Study of the Red Book Case." PhD thesis, University of New South Wales, 1998.
Giles, Kevin. *What on Earth Is the Church? An Exploration in New Testament Theology*. Eugene, OR: Wipf & Stock, 1995.
Goldsworthy, Graeme. *According to Plan: The Unfolding Revelation of God in the Bible*. Leicester: InterVarsity, 1991.

———. *Christ-Centered Biblical Theology: Hermeneutical Foundations and Principles.* Downers Grove: InterVarsity, 2012.

———. *Gospel and Kingdom: A Christian Interpretation of the Old Testament.* Exeter, UK: Paternoster, 1981.

Green, Chris. *The Message of the Church: Assemble the People Before Me.* Nottingham, UK: InterVarsity, 2013.

Griffith Thomas, W. H. *The Principles of Theology: An Introduction to the Thirty-Nine Articles.* London: Longmans, Green, 1930. 6th ed., London: Vine, 1978.

Hammond, T. C. "Article XIX." Unpublished. Archives, Moore College Library, Moore Theological College, Sydney.

———. "The Church." Radio address on 2CH, April 10, 1960.

———. *In Understanding Be Men: A Synopsis of Christian Doctrine for Non-Theological Students.* London: Inter-Varsity Fellowship, 1936. 6th ed., edited by David Wright, London: IVP, 1968.

———. *The One Hundred Texts of the Society for Irish Church Missions: A Manual of Theology.* 6th ed. London: Society for Irish Church Missions, and Marshall, Morgan & Scott, 1962.

———. "One View on the Draft: Case for the Constitution." Edited by D. B. Knox. *ACR* (28 Feb 1957) 12.

———. *Perfect Freedom: An Introduction to Christian Ethics.* London: Inter-Varsity Fellowship, 1938.

———. *Reasoning Faith: An Introduction to Christian Apologetics.* London: Inter-Varsity Fellowship, 1943.

———. "The Synod and the Constitution." *ACR* (11 Aug 1949) 8.

———. *Verbatim Notes from Moore Theological College Th.L. Doctrine II Lectures.* Transcribed by G. W. Christopher. Unpublished, 1943. Archives, Moore College Library, Moore Theological College, Sydney.

Hill, Graham. *Salt, Light, and a City: Introducing Missional Ecclesiology.* Eugene, OR: Wipf & Stock, 2012.

Hirsch, Alan. *The Forgotten Ways: Reactivating the Missional Church.* Grand Rapids: Brazos, 2006.

"An Homily of the Right Use of the Church or Temple of God, and of the Reverence Due unto the Same." In the Second Tome of Homilies. London: SPCK, 1938.

Hooker, Richard. *Of the Laws of Ecclesiastical Polity.* 2 vols. London: Dent, 1907.

Hort, Fenton John Anthony. *The Christian Ecclesia: A Course of Lectures on the Early History and Early Conceptions of the Ecclesia and Four Sermons.* London: Macmillan, 1897.

Husbands, Mark. "The Trinity Is Not Our Social Program." In *Trinitarian Theology for the Church: Scripture, Community, Worship,* edited by Daniel J. Treier and David Lauber, 120–41. Downers Grove: InterVarsity, 2009.

Ignatius. *Letter to the Smyrneans.* In *Anti-Nicene Fathers,* edited by Alexander Roberts and James Donaldson, revised by A. Cleveland Coxe, vol. 1, *The Apostolic Fathers, Justin Martyr, Irenaeus,* 86–92. Peabody: Hendrickson, 1994.

Irenaeus. *Against Heresies.* In *Anti-Nicene Fathers,* edited by Alexander Roberts and James Donaldson, revised by A. Cleveland Coxe, vol. 1, *The Apostolic Fathers, Justin Martyr, Irenaeus,* 315–567. Peabody: Hendrickson, 1994.

Jensen, Michael. *Sydney Anglicanism: An Apology.* Eugene, OR: Wipf & Stock, 2012.

———. "Sydney Anglicanism: A Response." *St Mark's Review* 226 (2013) 112–26.

Jensen, Peter. "Broughton Knox on Training for the Ministry: The First Lecture Given in the New Building." In *Broughton Knox: Principal of Moore College, 1959–1985*, by Marcus Loane and Peter Jensen. Newtown, NSW: Moore Theological College, 1994. Reprinted as "Broughton Knox on Training for the Ministry." In *D. Broughton Knox: Selected Works*, vol. 1, *The Doctrine of God*, edited by Tony Payne, 21–36. Kingsford, NSW: Matthias, 2000.

Joint Commission on Church Union. *The Church: Its Nature, Function and Ordering and Proposed Basis for Union*. Melbourne: Christian Unity Committee and the Board of Christian Education, 1964.

———. *The Faith of the Church*. Melbourne: Joint Board of Graded Lessons of Australia and New Zealand, 1959.

Jones, Grace. "Grace Jones' Account of Nathaniel Jones." Unpublished. Archives, Moore College Library, Moore Theological College, Sydney.

Jones, Nathaniel. *A Handful of Corn upon the Top of the Mountains: Bible Readings and Addresses*. Sydney: Madgwick, 1905.

———. *Resurrection Life: A Prayer Book Study for Easter Tide*. London: Stock, 1909.

———. *The Teaching of the Articles: A Plain Exposition of the Doctrines of the Articles of the Church of England, with Their Scripture Proofs*. Sydney: Church Missionary Society, 1944.

Judd, Stephen, and Kenneth Cable. *Sydney Anglicans: A History of the Diocese*. Sydney: Anglican Information Office, 1987.

Judge, Edwin A. "Contemporary Political Models for the Interrelations of the New Testament Churches." *RTR* 23 (1963) 65–76.

Kärkäinen, Veli-Matti. *An Introduction to Ecclesiology: Ecumenical, Historical & Global Perspectives*. Downers Grove: IVP Academic, 2002.

Käsemann, Ernst. *New Testament Questions of Today*. Philadelphia: Fortress, 1969.

Kaye, Bruce. "Foundations and Methods in Ecclesiology." In *"Wonderful and Confessedly Strange": Australian Essays in Anglican Ecclesiology*, edited by Bruce Kaye, 5–20. Adelaide: ATF, 2006.

Kinnamon, Michael, and Brian E. Cope, eds. *The Ecumenical Movement: An Anthology of Key Texts and Voices*. Geneva: World Council of Churches, 1997.

Knox, D. Broughton. "Acts 2:42." In *Church and Ministry*, 49–55.

———. "The Biblical Concept of Fellowship." In Webb, *Explorations 2*, 59–82. Reprinted in *Church and Ministry*, 57–84.

———. "The Body of Christ." In Birkett, *Church and Ministry*, 37–41.

———. *The Christian Life*. Vol. 3 of *D. Broughton Knox: Selected Works*. Edited by Tony Payne and Karen Beilharz. Kingsford, NSW: Matthias, 2006.

———. "Christian Unity." Protestant Faith radio broadcast 26 June 1977. Published in *Church and Ministry*, 35–36.

———. "The Church." Protestant Faith radio broadcast 22 March 1970. Published in *Church and Ministry*, 19–22.

———. *Church and Ministry*. Vol. 2 of, *D. Broughton Knox: Selected Works*. Edited by Kirsten Birkett. Kingsford, NSW: Matthias, 2003.

———. "The Church and the People of God in the Old Testament." *RTR* 10 (1950) 12–20. Reprinted in *Church and Ministry*, 9–17.

———. "The Church, the Churches and the Denominations of the Churches." *RTR* 48 (1989) 15–25. Reprinted in *Church and Ministry*, 85–98.

———. "The Constitution." *ACR* (11 Aug 1949) 8–9.

———. "Constitutions New and Old." *ACR* (28 Jul 1949) 8.
———. "De-mythologizing the Church." *RTR* 32 (1973) 48–55. Reprinted in *Church and Ministry*, 23–32.
———. "The Diocese of Sydney and the Draft Constitution." *ACR* (31 Jan 1957) 6.
———. *The Doctrine of Faith in the Reign of Henry VIII*. London: Clarke, 1961.
———. *The Doctrine of God*. Vol. 1 of *D. Broughton Knox: Selected Works*. Edited by Tony Payne. Kingsford, NSW: Matthias, 2000.
———. "The Draft Constitution Analysed." *ACR* (18 Aug 1955) 3.
———. *The Everlasting God*. Kingsford, NSW: Matthias, 2009.
———. "Evils of the Proposed Constitution." *ACR* (29 Sep 1955) 7.
———. "Four Fatal Flaws in the Draft Constitution." *ACR* (14 Feb 1957) 8.
———. "Government by Consent, Not Coercion." *ACR* (18 Aug 1955) 2.
———. "Heaven Is People." In *Church and Ministry*, 247–52.
———. "Impressions of Lund." *ACR* (18 Sep 1952) 3.
———. "Look Before You Leap! A Vital Defect in the Proposed Constitution." *ACR* (14 Jul 1949) 8–9.
———. "The Need for Unanimity Before Going to Parliament for a New Constitution." *ACR* (28 Feb 1957) 2.
———. "The New Constitution." *ACR* (11 Mar 1948) 3–4.
———. "The New Constitution." *ACR* (13 May 1954) 4–5.
———. *Not by Bread Alone: God's Word on Present Issues*. Edinburgh: Banner of Truth, 1989.
———. "Notes on Authority in the Church." In *Church and Ministry*, 101–3.
———. "The People of God in the Old Testament." *RTR* 10 (1950) 12–20. Reprinted in *Church and Ministry*, 9–18.
———. "The Priority of Preaching: Prepare and Preach Properly or Perish." In *Church and Ministry*, 239–42.
———. "Profit and Loss in the Constitution." *ACR* (13 Oct 1955) 3.
———. "Retain the Ancient Catholic Principle." *ACR* (21 Jul 1955) 2.
———. "Safeguard Not Adequate." *ACR* (22 Dec 1955) 7.
———. *Sent by Jesus: Some Aspects of Christian Ministry Today*. Edinburgh: Banner of Truth, 1992.
———. "Sermon Notes." In *Church and Ministry*, 99.
———. "The Spirit, the Church and the Denomination." Protestant Faith radio broadcast 7 March 1976. Published in *D. Broughton Knox: Selected Works*. Edited by Kirsten Birkett. Vol. II, Church and Ministry, 33–34. Kingsford, NSW: Matthias, 2003.
———. "Sydney Accepts Constitution." *ACR* (28 Mar 1957) 1, 15.
———. "Sydney's Eight Amendments to the Constitution." *ACR* (8 Sep 1949) 2.
———. *Thirty-Nine Articles*. Sydney: Anglican Information Office, 1976. Reprinted in *Church and Ministry*, 107–98. Kingsford, NSW: Matthias, 2003.
———. "Undefined Comprehensiveness Will Destroy the Church." *ACR* (3 Feb 1955) 2.
———. "What the Church Is." Unpublished paper, April 1988. Box 16, Folder 1, D. B. Knox Archives, Moore College Library, Moore Theological College, Sydney.
Knox, D. B., and D. Robinson. "The Need to Examine the Draft Constitution Now." *ACR* (21 Jun 1956) 2–3.

Knox, D. J. *What Is "The Red Book"? An Account of the Bathurst Case*. Sydney: Church Publican Society, 1946.

Kraut, Richard. "Introduction to the Study of Plato." In *The Cambridge Companion to Plato*, edited by Richard Kraut, 1–50. Cambridge: Cambridge University Press, 1992.

Latourette, Kenneth Scott. "Ecumenical Bearings of the Missionary Movement and the International Missionary Council." In *A History of the Ecumenical Movement*, vol. 1, *1517–1948*, edited by Ruth Rouse and Stephen Charles Neill, 353–402. 3rd ed. Geneva: World Council of Churches, 1986.

Lawton, William. "The Better Time to Be: The Kingdom of God and Social Reform Anglicans and the Diocese of Sydney 1885–1914." PhD thesis, University of New South Wales, 1985.

———. *The Better Time to Be: Utopian Attitudes to Society among Sydney Anglicans 1885–1914*. Kensington, NSW: New South Wales University Press, 1990.

———. "Nathaniel Jones." In O'Brien and Peterson, *God Who Is Rich in Mercy*, 361–76.

Loane, Ed. "The Church." *St Mark's Review* 226 (2013) 48–58.

Loane, Marcus. Review of *Better Time to Be*, by William Lawton. *Lucas: An Evangelical History Review* 11 (1991) 41–42.

———. *A Centenary History of Moore Theological College*. Sydney: Angus & Robertson, 1955.

———. "David Broughton Knox." In *Broughton Knox: Principal of Moore College, 1959–1985*, 1–12. Newtown: Moore Theological College, 1994.

———. *Mark These Men: A Brief Account of Some Evangelical Clergy in the Diocese of Sydney who were Associated with Archbishop Mowll*. Canberra: Acorn, 1985.

———. *Men to Remember*. Canberra: Acorn, 1967.

Luther, Martin. The Large Catechism. Part Second: Of the Creed, Article III. Book of Concord. http://bookofconcord.org/lc-4-creed.php.

McBrien, Richard P. *The Church: The Evolution of Catholicism*. New York: HarperOne, 2008.

McIntosh, John. "Anglican Evangelicalism in Sydney 1897–1953: The Thought and Influence of Three Moore College Principals—Nathaniel Jones, D J Davies and T C Hammond." PhD Thesis, University of New South Wales, 2014.

Minear, Paul. *Images of the Church in the New Testament*. Louisville: Westminster John Knox, 2004.

Morris, Leon. *The Gospel according to Matthew*. PNTC. Grand Rapids: Eerdmans, 1992.

Neill, Stephen. *Men of Unity*. London: SCM, 1960.

Nelson, Warren. "T. C. Hammond." In *The Australian Dictionary of Evangelical Biography*, edited by Brian Dickey, 150–53. Sydney: Evangelical History Association, 1994.

———. *T. C. Hammond: Irish Christian: His Life and Legacy in Ireland and Australia*. Edinburgh: Banner of Truth, 1994.

O'Brien, Peter T. "The Church as a Heavenly and Eschatological Reality." In *The Church in the Bible and the World: An International Study*, edited by D. A. Carson, 88–119. Grand Rapids: Baker, 1987.

———. *Colossians, Philemon*. WBC 44. Waco: Word, 1982.

———. *The Letter to the Ephesians*. PNTC. Grand Rapids: Eerdmans, 1999.

———. *The Letter to the Hebrews*. PNTC. Grand Rapids: Eerdmans, 2010.

O'Brien, Peter T., and David G. Peterson, eds. *God Who Is Rich in Mercy: Essays Presented to Dr. D. B. Knox*. Homebush, NSW: Lancer, 1986.

Peterson, David. *Hebrews and Perfection: An Examination of the Concept of Perfection in the "Epistle to the Hebrews."* Cambridge: Cambridge University Press, 1982.

Peterson, David, and John Pryor, eds. *In the Fullness of Time: Biblical Studies in Honour of Archbishop Donald Robinson*. Homebush, NSW: Lancer, 1992.

Piggin, Stuart. *Spirit of a Nation: The Story of Australia's Christian Heritage*. Sydney: Strand, 2004.

Plato. *The Republic*. Edited by G. R. F. Ferrari. Translated by Tom Griffith. Cambridge: Cambridge University Press, 2000.

Porter, Muriel. *Sydney Anglicans and the Threat to World Anglicanism: The Sydney Experiment*. Farnham: Ashgate, 2011.

Robinson, Donald. "The 'Authority of the Church.'" *RTR* 21 (1962) 33–45. Reprinted in *Selected Works*, 1:298–311.

———. "The Biblical Doctrine of the Church." In *Selected Works*, 1:205–11.

———. "Church." In *New Bible Dictionary*, edited by J. D. Douglas et al. London: IVP, 1962. Reprinted in *Selected Works*, 1:222–29.

———. "The Church in the New Testament." *St Mark's Review* 17 (1959) 4–14. Reprinted in *Selected Works*, 1:212–21.

———. *The Church of God: Its Form and Unity*. Punchbowl: Jordan, 1965. Reprinted as "The Church of God: Its Form and Unity," in *Selected Works*, 1:230–53.

———. "'The Church' Revisited: An Autobiographical Fragment." *RTR* 48 (1989) 4–14. Reprinted in *Selected Works*, 1:259–71.

———. "The Church Universal and Its Earthly Form." *ACR* (2 Feb 1956) 3.

———. "The Church Universal and Its Earthly Form: 2—The Church in the New Testament." *ACR* (16 Feb 1956) 9.

———. "David Broughton Knox: An Appreciation." In O'Brien and Peterson, *God Who Is Rich in Mercy*, xi–xiii.

———. "David Broughton Knox: What We Owe Him." Anglican Church League. http://acl.asn.au/?s=David+Broughton+Knox.

———. "The Diocese of Sydney and Its Purpose." In *Selected Works*, 1:312–17.

———. "The Distinction between Jewish and Gentile Believers in Galatians." *ABR* 13 (1965) 29–48. Reprinted in *Selected Works*, 1:130–51.

———. "The Doctrine of the Church and Its Implications for Evangelism." *Interchange* 15 (1974) 156–62. Reprinted in *Selected Works*, 2:103–13.

———. *Donald Robinson: Selected Works*. Edited by Peter G. Bolt and Mark D. Thompson. Vol. 1, *Assembling God's People*. Vol. 2, *Preaching God's Word*. Vol. 3, *Appreciation*. Camperdown, NSW: Australian Church Record, 2008.

———. "Letter to the Editor." *Interchange* 21 (1977) 62–63. Reprinted as "The Church and Evangelism," in *Selected Works*, 2:114–16.

———. "Liturgical Patterns of Worship." In *Christ Calls Us to a New Obedience*. NEAC Papers 1971. Sydney: Information and Public Relations Office of the Diocese of Sydney, 1971. Reprinted in *Selected Works*, 1:318–36.

———. "Origins and Unresolved Tensions." In *Explorations 11: Interpreting God's Plan: Biblical Theology and the Pastor*, edited by R. J. Gibson, 1–17. Carlisle: Paternoster, 1998.

———. "The Present Constitution When Adopted and Why." *ACR* (17 Jan 1957) 6.

———. "The Unity of the Spirit in the Bond of Peace." *ACR* (2 Feb 1956) 2.

———. "W.C.C." *ACR* (22 Jul 1954) 4.
Robinson, D. W. B., and D. B. Knox. "Contradictory Principles in the New Constitution." *ACR* (3 Mar 1955) 2.
Schmidt, K. L. "ἐκκλησία." In *TDNT*, vol. 3, *Q–K*, edited by Gerhard Kittel, translated and edited by Geoffrey Bromiley, 501–36. Grand Rapids: Eerdmans, 1965.
Stanley, Brian. "Edinburgh 1910 and the Oikoumenē." In *Ecumenism and History: Studies in Honour of John H. Y. Briggs*, edited by Anthony R. Cross, 89–105. Milton Keynes: Paternoster, 2002.
Stibbs, Alan. *The Church Universal and Local: Being Mainly a Survey of Bible Teaching, with Some Application to the Present Day*. London: Church Book Room, 1948.
———. *God's Church: A Study in the Biblical Doctrine of the People of God*. London: Inter-Varsity Fellowship, 1959.
———. "New Testament Teaching Concerning the Church (1950)." *Inter-Varsity Magazine* (summer term 1950). Reprinted in *Such a Great Salvation: The Collected Essays of Alan M. Stibbs*, edited by Andrew Atherstone, 231–35. Fearn, Ross-Shire, Scotland: Mentor, 2008.
Teulon, J. S. *The History and Teaching of Plymouth Brethren*. London: SPCK, 1883.
Thompson, Mark D. "The Church of God and the Anglican Church of Australia." In *"Wonderful and Confessedly Strange": Australian Essays in Anglican Ecclesiology*, edited by Bruce Kaye, 223–43. Adelaide: ATF, 2006.
———. "Donald William Bradley Robinson." In Robinson, *Selected Works*, 3:3–8.
———. "Hammond, Thomas Chatterton." In *The SPCK Handbook of Anglican Theologians*, edited by Alistair McGrath, 135–38. London: SPCK, 1998.
———. "Knox, David Broughton." In *The SPCK Handbook of Anglican Theologians*, edited by Alistair McGrath, 158–60. London: SPCK, 1998.
Torrance, T. F. "Israel of God: Israel and the Incarnation." *Interpretation* 10 (1956) 305–20.
Turner. David L. *Matthew*. BECNT. Grand Rapids: Baker Academic, 2008.
Van der Bent, Ans Joachim. *Historical Dictionary of Ecumenical Christianity*. London: Scarecrow, 1994.
Visser 't Hooft, W. A. *The Genesis and Formation of the World Council of Churches*. Geneva: World Council of Churches, 1987.
Vlach, Michael. *Has the Church Replaced Israel? A Theological Evaluation*. Nashville: Broadman & Holman, 2010.
Volf, Miroslav. *After Our Likeness: The Church as the Image of the Trinity*. Grand Rapids: Eerdmans, 1998.
———. "The Trinity Is Our Social Program." *Modern Theology* 14 (1998) 403–23.
Wallace, Daniel B. *Greek Grammar Beyond the Basics: An Exegetical Syntax of the New Testament*. Grand Rapids: Zondervan, 1996.
Webb, B. G. *Explorations 2: Church, Worship and the Local Congregation*. Homebush, NSW: Lancer, 1987.

Names Index

Adams, Edward, 109
Anderson, John, 17n12
Archdall, Mervyn, 10n25
Augustine, 66, 155n69, 173n116

Barnett, Paul, 123
Barr, James, 56n27, 99–101, 102, 103n15, 184
Barth, Karl, 33n7, 58–59
Begbie, H. S., 3n1, 11
Bellarmine, Robert, 19–20
Bicknell, E. J., 20n20, 21, 26n48, 136
Bidwell, J., 3n1, 11
Boyce, F. B., 16
Bray, Gerald, 85n107
Bultmann, Rudolph, 151n55

Cable, Kenneth, xiii, 17–18, 147
Calvin, John, 193n27, 195
Campbell, J. Y., 50, 54, 66
Cameron, Marcia, 5, 39, 138
Carey, William, 31
Cashel, Frederick, 4
Chambers, G. A., 3n1, 11
Cole, Alan, 60, 133
Cole, Graham, 80, 99n3, 102–3, 104, 106n24, 113, 116
Cole, R. A., 132n4
Cranmer, Thomas, 202

Davies, David John, 16

Denman, S. H., 3n1, 11
Dibelius, Otto, xiiin1
Dodd, C. H., 50, 57
Dulles, Avery, xiiin1
Dumbrell, William, 52n9

Fisher, Geoffrey, 42
Flew, R. Newton, 50, 54, 57
Foulkes, Francis, 123
France, R. T., 187

Gilbert, T. W., 132
Giles, Kevin, 56n27, 68n64, 101–2, 107, 111, 112, 189–190, 212
Goldsworthy, Graeme, 57, 184n6
Griffith Thomas, H. G., 16, 21, 106n24

Hammond, T. C., 14–29
    Australian Church Constitution, 43, 44
    ecclesiology, 22–29
    historical and ecclesial context, 15–18
    influence, 29
    and Robinson, 50
    theological method, 18–21, 136
Hebert, Gabriel, 57–58
Henderson, Grace *see* Jones, Grace
Hooker, Richard, 21
Hort, F. J. A., 53, 65
Howe, H. G. J., 3n1, 11

NAMES INDEX

Ignatius of Antioch, 21, 148, 150, 159–60, 194
Irenaeus, 194

Jensen, Michael, 104–5
Jensen, Peter, 136, 137
Johnstone, J. R. L., 45
Jones, Grace, 4, 5
Jones, Nathaniel, xvi, 3–13, 16
Judd, Stephen, xiii, 17–18, 147
Judge, Edwin, 55–56

Kärkäinen, Veli-Matti, xiii, 32, 194
Käsemann, Ernst, 33
Kirkby, S. J., 3n1, 11
Kittel, Gerhard, 56n27
Knox, David Broughton
    Australian Church Constitution, 43–44, 45, 46
    on authority, 175–78
    ecumenical movement, 39–40
    on *ekklēsia*, 140–46
    on fellowship, 162–70
    historical context, 132–39
    on the locus of the church, 146–62
    methodology, 135–39, 209
    relationship with Robinson, 61, 139, 141, 184
    on the task of the church, 170–75
    World Council of Churches, 36–37
Knox, David James, 3, 8–9, 11, 132

Langford Smith, S. E., 3n1, 11
Lawton, William, 3–4, 7, 8–12
Loane, Sir Marcus, 11, 15, 16, 19, 51, 132, 137, 138
Luther, Martin, 192

McIntosh, John, 12n32
MacKinnon, Donald, 33n7
Minear, Paul, 113, 212
Morris, Leon, 187
Mott, John, 31
Moule, C. F. D., 50
Mowll, Howard West Kilvington, 16, 17, 36–37, 43, 50, 134

Neill, Stephen, xiiin1, 30
Nelson, Warren, 20–21

Nygren, Anders, 33n7

O'Brien, P. T., 108, 109, 110, 135n12, 189, 190, 191, 193n28
Oldham, J. H., 34
Origen, 142n32

Packer, J. I., 58, 59
Peterson, David, 109–10, 189

Ramsey, Michael, 33n7
Robinson, Donald
    Australian Church Constitution, 43–44, 45, 46
    on authority, 90–93
    ecumenical movement, 39–40
    on *ekklēsia*, 63–66
    historical and ecclesial context, 49–52
    influences and interlocutors, 52–62
    on Jew–Gentile relationship, 78–83
    on Knox, 133, 134
    on the locus of the church, 66–72
    method, 62–63, 209
    on the task of the church, 83–90
    on unity, 72–78
    World Council of Churches, 37–38
Robinson, Richard Bradley, 3, 11, 49–50

Schlink, Edmund, 33n7
Schmidt, K. L., 54n15, 56
Shelley, K. N., 45
Shipp, P. G., 50, 52–53
Smith, Saumarez, 16
Söderblom, Nathan, 34
Stanley, Brian, 31n3
Stibbs, Alan, 60–61, 69n67

Thompson, Mark, 200
Torrance, T. F., 33n7
Turner, David, 187

Visser 't Hooft, W. A., 35–36
Volf, Miroslav, 193n28, 195n34, 197, 201, 213

Wade, A. L., 3n1, 11
Wallce, Daniel, 188n16
Wright, John Charles, 16
Wylde, A. L., 17

Subject Index

Anglican Church (of Australia)
   and Hammond, 21
   and Knox, 137–38, 173, 183, 199–200, 201, 202–3
   and Robinson, 127
   see also Australian Church Constitution; "Sydney Anglicanism"
Anglo-Catholicism, 15–16, 41–45
apostles, 87–88, 91
apostolic succession, 28
Article VI, 127n64
Article XIX, xv
   evaluation of Knox, 200
   evaluation of Robinson, 116–17
   Jones's commentary, 6–8
   Knox's commentary, 156, 173
   Hammond's commentary, 22
   Robinson's commentary, 84–85, 86, 122
Article XX, 28n56, 116–17, 125, 202
Article XXI, 125
Article XXIII, 116–17
Article XXIV, 116–17
Article XXVI, 8, 117, 156
Article XXVII, 156
Article XXXIII, 118
Article XXXIV, 118, 125
Article XXXV, 117
Article XXXVI, 118
Article XXXVII, 118
Australian Church Constitution, 17–18, 41–46, 51–52, 74, 133–34
An Australian Prayer Book, 45, 127; *see also* Book of Common Prayer
authority, in the church
   Australian Church Constitution, 43
   evaluation of Knox, 197–200
   evaluation of Robinson, 125–26
   Hammond's commentary, 27–29
   Knox's commentary, 46, 175–81, 183
   Robinson's commentary, 46, 90–93, 98
autonomy, of churches, 46, 199

biblical theology
   evaluation of Robinson, 126–27
   Knox's method, 137
   Robinson's method, xvi, 56–58, 62–63, 120, 122, 137
   see also "promise and fulfillment" theology
"body of Christ" metaphor, 72, 111, 112, 162
Book of Common Prayer, 15, 17, 41–43; *see also An Australian Prayer Book*
Brethrenism, 4, 7, 9–11

SUBJECT INDEX

catholicity, 148–49, 150, 159–61
Christ
    constitution of the church, 90, 179, 193–95, 208, 209
    and fellowship, 165, 175, 180
    heavenly and earthly gatherings, 114, 71
    locus of the church, 68–69, 97, 107, 110, 146, 147, 152–53
    perfection of the church, 109–10
    presence, 68–69, 71, 86, 98, 106–7, 111, 147, 150, 152–53, 160, 165, 175, 179, 182, 189, 192, 193–95, 197, 201, 208, 209–10, 212
    as the "rock" (Matt 16:16–18), 144–45, 186–87
    unity of the church, 23, 27, 35, 72–73, 78, 114, 148, 160, 208
the church
    as activity, 64–65, 80–81, 86, 94, 95, 97, 98, 102, 104, 122, 157, 210
    authority, 27–29, 43, 46, 90–93, 98, 125–26, 175–81, 183, 197–200
    continuity, 71–72, 98, 112–14
    form, 69–71, 98, 110–11
    locus (place, time and space), 66–69, 97, 114–15, 120–21, 146–70, 179, 191–92
    metaphors, 60, 72–73, 105, 111, 112–13, 162, 211–12
    perfection, 66, 109–10
    task, 83–90, 98, 122–25, 170–75
    unity, 23, 24, 25–27, 33, 72–78, 98, 114–20, 148, 157–63, 193, 208
    see also ekklēsia; gathering; local church; visible and invisible church
Church of England in Australia, see Anglican Church (of Australia)
"communion of saints", 150
congregation, see local church
covenant, 51, 59, 120–22, 145, 167; see also new covenant; old covenant
creeds
    Robinson's commentary, 73–74, 115
    Knox's commentary, 150, 157–58, 179–80, 192–93

dēmos, 65, 105
denominations
    and authority, 90–91, 125–26, 176–78, 199–200, 201, 208
    and fellowship, 157, 167–70, 180, 196
    and unity, 78, 115, 119
Diocese of Sydney, 9, 12, 29, 92–93, 119–20; see also "Sydney Anglicanism"
Dispensationalism, 57

earthly gatherings, see heavenly and earthly gatherings
ecumenical movement, xiii, 30–40
    and Knox, 161
    and Robinson, 51–52, 72, 76–77, 114–15
    see also unity, of the church
ēdâh, 53, 101–2
ekklēsia
    continuity of the church, 112–13
    evaluation of Knox, 184–88, 190
    evaluation of Robinson, 98–105, 110–11
    form of the church, 69–71
    Giles's commentary, 101–3
    Jew-Gentile relationship, 83
    Jones's commentary, 6
    Knox's commentary, 140–46, 179, 182, 191
    locus of the church, 74, 75, 191
    Robinson's commentary, 53–54, 63–66, 97
    soteriology, 79
    task of the church, 84, 85
Episcopal Church, 90
eschatology/the eschaton
    evaluation of Knox, 189, 191, 197
    evaluation of Robinson, 108–9, 110
    Robinson's commentary, 114
    Knox's commentary, 166–67, 175,
Evangelicalism, 29, 41–45; see also "Sydney Anglicanism"
evangelism/evangelists, 85, 87–90, 122, 123–25

SUBJECT INDEX

Faith and Order Commission, 37, 133
fellowship
    evaluation of Knox, 195–97
    Knox's commentary, 157, 162–70, 180, 183, 209–10, 212
    New Delhi Council statement, 35
    Robinson's commentary, 212
    task of the church, 85

gathering
    evaluation of Knox, 167, 184–88, 190, 191, 201, 202, 211, 212
    evaluation of Robinson, 98–99, 103, 105, 106, 107, 110–11, 114–15, 121, 122, 211, 212
    Hort's commentary, 53
    Knox's commentary, 140, 141–44, 146, 171, 179, 208
    Robinson's commentary, 53, 62, 64–65, 68–71, 75, 82, 85, 94, 95–96, 208
    see also heavenly and earthly gatherings
General Synod, 42, 44, 45, 133
Gentiles, *see* Jew–Gentile relationship
George Whitefield College (GWC), 132–33
God
    character and glory, 170–72
    presence, 164, 167, 174, 179, 186, 187, 192
    soteriological purposes, 62–63, 78–80, 82, 87, 94, 120
    see also Trinity
gospel, 87, 89–90

heavenly and earthly gatherings, 147–62, 179, 182, 188–90
    see also the church, locus; visible and invisible church
Heilsgeschichte, 57n28
Holy Spirit
    and faith, 145
    and fellowship, 157, 163–64, 171, 172, 180, 195–96

heavenly and earthly gatherings, 111, 149, 150, 189, 192, 194–95, 208
    and mission, 89
    presence, 162, 202
    unity of the church, 38, 76, 114, 115, 161–62

identity
    of Anglicanism, 16, 42
    of believers, 71–72, 76, 81, 104, 107, 112–14
    of the church, 6, 65, 71–72, 95, 106, 157, 210, 211
    ekklēsia, 94, 101
    of Israel, 54, 82, 120
"illegitimate identify transfer", 102, 112
"illegitimate totality transfer", 100–101, 103
individualism, 111, 112, 125
International Missionary Conference (1910), 31, 34
invisible church, *see* visible and invisible church
Israel
    Campbell's commentary, 54–55
    Giles's commentary, 101
    Flew's commentary, 54
    Hort's commentary, 53
    Robinson's commentary, 82–83, 121–22
    see also Jew–Gentile relationship

Jesus, *see* Christ
Jew–Gentile relationship, 78–83, 98, 120–22, 210
Joint Commission on Church Union, 38

Katoomba Convention, 5
"Knox-Robinson view" of the church
    ascription and definition, xiv, 9, 135, 139
    evaluation, 210–11
    influence, xvii
    as misnomer, 61, 202

linguistic analysis
  Knox's method, 140–41
  evaluation of Robinson, 98–105, 126
  Robinson's method, xvi, 50, 52–56, 208
"Little Flock" theology, 4, 9–10
local church
  evaluation of Knox, 190–95
  evaluation of Robinson, 110–11
  Judge's commentary, 56
  Knox's commentary, 147, 149–51, 166–71, 182
  Robinson's commentary, 56, 69, 74, 75, 91, 106, 114
LXX (Septuagint), 143n34, 145n40

metaphors, for the church
  Cole's method, 60
  concrete and abstract realities, 112–13
  evaluation of Knox, 211–12
  evaluation of Robinson, 105, 211–12
  form of the church, 111
  unity of the church, 72–73, 162
mission, 39, 87–90, 122, 123–25, 127
Moore Theological College, xvi
  under Davies, 16
  under Hammond, 14, 15–17, 19
  under Jones, 3, 5
  under Knox, 51, 132
  and Robinson, 50–51, 132
Moses, 145, 186–87
Mount Sinai, 143–44, 184–85, 186

new covenant, 120–22, 145, 154, 188
New Delhi Council (1961), 34–35
"new man" theology, 78, 79, 120, 122

old covenant, 82, 120–21, 154
ontology
  of the church, 73, 98, 104, 107, 109, 110, 114, 189
  of fellowship, 165

Pentecost, 114, 161n81, 164
"people of God"
  ekklēsia, 54–55, 64–65, 94, 97, 142, 146, 154
  eschatology, 110, 197
  evaluation of Robinson, 95–96, 102, 104, 112–13, 123–24, 127
  evangelism, 85, 122, 211
  Jew–Gentile relationship, 78–82, 98, 120–21
  metaphors, 112–13, 211
  relationship to "the church", 64–65, 71, 80–81, 157, 210
  soteriology, 122
  task of the church, 84, 85, 98
Peter (apostle), 144–45, 185–87
Platonism, 107, 109, 180, 188
Plymouth Brethrenism, *see* Brethrenism
polity, xv, 21, 27, 120, 199–200, 212
Prayer Book, *see An Australian Prayer Book*; Book of Common Prayer
preaching, 173n116, 200–201; *see also* Word of God
premillenialism, 11
Presbyterian Church, 90
presence
  of believers, 154, 160, 161, 171, 179, 182, 189, 192, 193–95
  of Christ, 68–69, 71, 86, 98, 106–7, 111, 147, 150, 152–53, 160, 165, 175, 179, 182, 189, 192, 193–95, 197, 201, 208, 209–10, 212
  of God, 164, 167, 174, 179, 186, 187, 192
  of the Holy Spirit, 162, 202
"promise and fulfillment" theology, 50, 51, 56, 59, 62, 83, 120; *see also* biblical theology

qāhāl, 53, 55, 101–2

"Red Book Case", 17–18, 42
the "rock" (Matt 16:16–18), 143–45, 185–88, 202

SUBJECT INDEX 229

Roman Catholicism
   "communion of saints", 192
   ecumenical movement, 33
   and Hammond, 15, 17, 19, 22, 23, 26, 27, 29
   the "rock" (Matt 16:16–18), 144, 186
   visible and invisible church, 23
root analysis, 141
sacraments, 28, 43, 173, 198
Scripture
   and church authority, 27–28
   Knox's method, 136, 137, 183–84, 202
   World Council of Churches, 39–40
   see also Word of God
Septuagint (LXX), 143n34, 145n40
soteriology
   biblical theology, 62–63
   fellowship, 164
   Jew–Gentile relationship, 78–83, 120
   purposes of God, 62–63, 78–80, 82, 87, 94, 120
   task of the church, 170
Student Christian Movement, 31
supersessionism, 54
"Sydney Anglicanism", 16, 36–40, 147
synagōgē, 53, 101
systematic theology, xvi, 62–63, 136, 178–79

Thirty-Nine Articles of Religion, xv
   Australian Church Constitution, 42–43, 44
   evaluation of Robinson, 116–19
   Hammond's commentary, 18–19, 23, 29
   Jones's commentary, 6–8
   Knox's method, 136, 155–56
   see also Article . . . Trinity, 162, 165–66, 171–72, 178, 194, 195–96

unbelievers, 24, 124, 156
Uniting Church, 38
unity, of the church
   evaluation of Robinson, 114–17
   definitional issues, 33
   Hammond's commentary, 23, 24, 25–27
   Knox's commentary, 147, 157–63, 193, 208
   Robinson's commentary, 72–78, 98, 208
   see also ecumenical movement

Vatican II, 158n75
visible and invisible church
   evaluation of Robinson, 105–6
   Hammond's commentary, 20, 22–26, 27
   Jones's commentary, 6–7
   Knox's commentary, 153
   Robinson's commentary, 66–67

Westminster Confession of Faith, 23
Westminster Larger Catechism, 7n18
witness, 88
   see also evangelism; mission
Word of God
   authority, 91–92, 125, 175–76, 180, 183, 197–99, 208
   and evangelism, 90
   and fellowship, 166, 172–73, 180, 183, 212
   and the task of the church, 122
   and worship, 86
   see also Scripture
World Council of Churches, xiii, 30–40
   and Knox, 133, 134, 158–59, 161
   and Robinson, 75–76, 114
worship, 86, 173–74, 180

Young Men's Christian Associations (YMCA), 31

Scripture Index

GENESIS

12:3	83

EXODUS

19	95, 184
19:4–5	142
19:12–13	185
19:17	86
34:6	172

DEUTERONOMY

4	184
4:10	143

PSALMS

18:31	144

ISAIAH

42:6	82
49:6	82

JOEL

2:28–32	76

MATTHEW

7	143
16	179, 184, 185, 202
16:16–18	144
16:16—18:20	78
16:18	83, 100, 142, 143, 147, 160, 185–88
18	179
18:17	100
18:20	65, 68, 69, 81, 86, 106, 147, 149, 151, 165, 200
22:31	172
28:20	111

LUKE

2:30–32	82

JOHN

1:18	196
4:22	210
6:28–29	164
10:16	142
10:30	76
14	196n35
14:23	164
17	32, 75–76, 114
17:11	76
17:17	76
17:21	76, 164
17:22	76

ACTS

1	114
2	76, 114, 124
2:39	142
2:47	142
7	142
7:37–38	186n11
7:38	64
8:1	70, 81, 121
9:31	70, 106
11:22	81
11:26	81
12	81
13	81
13:47	82
14:23	81
15	196–97
15:16	81
19:32	142
19:39	64, 142
20:28	75

ROMANS

6	63
11	83, 122
12:1	174
15	196
15:27	91

1 CORINTHIANS

1:2	73, 108
10:4	144
10:32	78
11:22	78
12:27	75
13:12	151
14	124
14:23	124n60
15:1–3	91

2 CORINTHIANS

2:5–10	91
3:16–18	166

GALATIANS

3:7	82
3:27	63
4:21–31	81
6:16	82

EPHESIANS

1:3	68
1:20	68
1:22–23	72, 190
2	110, 114
2:4–7	72
2:6	24, 27, 146, 152, 190
2:14–16	72
3:1–12	63
3:4–6	72
3:8	170
3:10	170
3:10	68
4	114, 115
4:1–7	32, 38
4:3	72n75, 115
4:4–6	72
4:11	124

4:11–16	72
5:8	115
5:19	173
5:23	72
5:25	147
5:30	72
6:12	68

PHILIPPIANS

3:3	82
4:15	89

COLOSSIANS

3:1–4	71, 72, 146
3:4	159
3:16	173
4:15–16	91

1 THESSALONIANS

4:10	91

2 THESSALONIANS

2:1	159

HEBREWS

2:10–13	86
2:12	65, 68, 70–71, 81
12:18–24	155
4:1–11	110
10:25	149, 150, 171, 173
12	110, 153, 184–85, 187–88, 196
12:18–24	146, 190
12:20	185
12:22–23	170
12:22–24	70–71, 86, 110, 188
13:14	110

1 PETER

2:1–10	82
2:11	64, 81

1 JOHN

1:3	166, 195
1:3–4	172
3:2	151, 158
4:7–16	195
4:7–17	196

3 JOHN

5–10	89

JUDE

17–23	115
19	115

REVELATION

4	86
5	86
14:1–3	170
21:3	166, 167
21:14	158

www.ingramcontent.com/pod-product-compliance
Lightning Source LLC
Chambersburg PA
CBHW051635230426
43669CB00013B/2316